REEDUCATING
THE EDUCATOR

SUNY series, Teacher Preparation and Development

REEDUCATING THE EDUCATOR

Global Perspectives on Community Building

Helen Christiansen and S. Ramadevi, editors

With a Foreword by Sigrun Gudmundsdottir

State University of New York Press

Published by
State University of New York Press, Albany

For information, address State University of New York Press,
90 State Street, Suite 700, Albany, N.Y., 12207

Production by Kelli Williams
Marketing by Anne M. Valentine

Library of Congress Cataloging-in-Publication Data

Reeducating the educator : global perspectives on community
building / Helen Christiansen and S. Ramadevi, editors ; with a
foreword by Sigrun Gudmundsdottir.
    p.   cm. — (SUNY series, teacher preparation and development)
    Includes bibliographical references and index.
    ISBN 0-7914-5121-6 (alk. paper) — ISBN 0-7914-5122-4 (pbk. : alk.
paper)
    1. Teachers—Training of. 2. Community and school. I. Christiansen,
Helen, 1940- II. Ramadevi, S. (Seshagiri), 1947-2001 III. SUNY series in
teacher preparation and development.

LB1707 .R435 2001
370'.71'1—dc21
                                                              2001020147

10 9 8 7 6 5 4 3 2 1

For Rama
Your community will miss you.

Contents

Foreword
    Sigrun Gudmundsdottir   ix
Acknowledgments   xiii
Introduction   xv

Part I: Opening the Conversation

1   Community and Community Building in Teacher Education   3
    Helen Christiansen and S. Ramadevi
2   Finding New Words for Old Songs: Creating
    Relationships and Community in Teacher Education   17
    Mary Beattie
3   Enhancing First-Time Teaching at the Postsecondary Level:
    A Story of Collaborative Mentorship   39
    Katie Flockhart and Vera E. Woloshyn

Part II: Focus on Paradigms

4   The Posttraditional Community:
    A New Concept for a New Era   55
    Lorraine M. Ling, Eva Burman, and Maxine Cooper

5   From "Common Grounds" to the "Rough Ground" of Teacher
    Education: Experiencing Teacher Education as a Collaborative
    Practice   71
        Hans Smits and David Friesen
6   Situating Ourselves within Narrative:
    Reeducating the Educator   91
        Florence Samson, Bev Brewer, Angela Chan, Maureen Dunne,
        and Vicki Fenton
7   The Postmodern Challenge: Using Arts-Based Inquiry to
    Build a Community of Teacher Collaborators and Selves   107
        Carol A. Mullen and C. T. Patrick Diamond

Part III: Focus on Programs

8   Creating Community in Online (Electronic) Environments   127
        Ann I. Nevin, Antonette W. Hood, and Mary E. McNeil
9   Building Communities in Teacher Education:
    The M.Teach Experience   151
        Robyn Ann Ewing and David Langley Smith
10 Project Partnerships: An Account of Partnership-Based
    Teacher Education at Victoria University   169
        Brenda Cherednichenko, Jan Gay, Neil Hooley, Tony Kruger,
        Rose Mulraney, and Maureen Ryan
11 Creating a Community of Teacher Educators   185
        Miriam Ben-Peretz and Moshe Silberstein

Part IV: Closing the Conversation

12 Gathering the Threads   201
        Helen Christiansen and S. Ramadevi

Epilogue   207
References   209
About the Contributors   229
Index   235

Foreword

Everyone who has contributed to this volume is an accomplished writer and established scholar in the field of teacher education. In the book the authors open up an unexamined part of the teacher education enterprise; the teacher educators themselves and the graduate programs that socialize them into what they are and how they think. We have previously studied teachers, teaching, learning, curriculum, and student teachers. Here the focus for our research endeavor is now on us, teacher educators, and our work in building the kind of communities that enable young people to grow and prosper. We have for years studied "down," conducting research on student teachers, teachers, and other practitioners. With this book we are actually starting to look "sideways." At last we, as teacher educators, are concerned with ourselves, our communities, and our pedagogical activities.

What we read in this book are exceptional communities, with structures that allow for people to organize themselves in order to do a better job. There is no "one-size-fits-all" type of solution that is imposed from above or as a special add-on phenomenon. Instead, it has evolved naturally and is kind of "owned" by the participants, some of whom happen to be authors of chapters. It is clear that the authors have not only benefited from their communities; their colleagues must have also, since they are an integral part of the sociocultural context. They share the sociocultural space, so to speak, interacting with the authors, providing models, and anti-models such as "I don't want to be like X so I won't do that." The most powerful mentors are, however, usually positive models. Sometimes they stay with us throughout our professional life, talking to us inside our heads, guiding us in critical situations. Even when they are not physically present, we continue to hear the echo of their voices, sometimes years later. The best gift any community can give its offspring is a positive role model. The art of caring and empowerment cannot be taught. It can only be learned by participation in sociocultural settings that are characterized by these qualities.

The communities seem to be involved in a continuous process, a kind of moving and ever-shifting target. Once you think you have arrived, the target has moved on to new heights. If there is an end in sight it is only an illusion. It is the process that is the target. The process is told in narratives that unfold and fade away, only to reappear again, reinforced, enriching the readers' understanding and convincingly demonstrating how the authors and their colleagues have emerged as stronger and more mature human beings.

The well-crafted chapters in this volume show that the solutions have to be culture specific if they are to work. We read about different kinds of mentoring, brown-bag lunches and seminars, all aiming to facilitate dialogue and create the kind of sociocultural context that nourishes professional growth. A good teacher education community and a good teacher educator have much in common with a good school, a good class, and a good teacher. Be it young adults or children, it is basically all about empowerment and caring attitudes. It means helping people to grow and find their identity as professionals and claim a distinct voice of their own from the heteroglossia of voices that surround them in teacher education and graduate school.

These words are not meant to be understood as if there is a uniformity in the narrative descriptions of the processes. There is a great diversity across the chapters inasmuch as several countries are represented. And even where there is more than one institution described from each country, the approaches are as varied as from one country to another. The culture of each institution overrides any cross-country differences. The communities described in the book are not about application of generalizable, reliable, and proven techniques. There is no more a single best method or technique of teacher education than there is one best method of teaching first grade multiplication. Yet, some approaches are better than others. Here such an approach has to lead to empowerment and professional growth. And empowerment is also a process, a moving target.

What is so exciting about this book is that it is the women who are doing most of the talking. They talk about their own socialization and the communities they are part of. We get to see the communities through the eyes of the women authors. The characteristic of that discourse is the merging of private and professional lives. In academia, such a merger is dangerous and "anti intellectual" according to a masculine paradigm. But this is the reality for many teacher educators, both men and women. This private/professional aspect of their lives has been silenced, until now. In a profession where language and naming are power, silence is oppression. Some of the teacher education communities described in the book are thoroughly "feminized" through their emphasis on voice, empowerment, and caring. Of the thirty-odd chapter authors, only seven are men, all of whom join the discourse on the women's terms. What is also wonderful about this book is that all but one chapter are multivoiced through multiple authorship. The one chapter with a single author, has only one voice because it is a very personal account of the author's development as a teacher educator and scholar.

With the publication of *Reeducating the Educator: Global Perspectives on Community Building* the different local solutions to a common problem are now in circulation. The different solutions now have the opportunity to become a common property, like language. They no longer belong to the authors. They now belong to anyone who wants to "borrow" them and make them their own. They now belong to the teacher educators of the world who want to reeducate themselves. The different solutions belong to a global teacher education community as we begin the twenty-first century.

SIGRUN GUDMUNDSDOTTIR

Acknowledgments

What began as a project became a book largely because of a lot of work "behind the scenes." We want to thank colleagues and friends at both of our institutions for supporting us throughout. We thank the administration at the Central Institute of English and Foreign Languages (India) and the Faculty of Education, University of Regina (Canada) for making it possible for Rama to come to Canada at a critical moment in the book project.

In India, a special thank you to Meena, Lalitha, Rama, Iype, Tanja, and Ranjan. Our community is where the personal and professional happily merge. In Canada, a special thank you to Janice Hawkey, our electronic wizard, for compiling a single manuscript from many different sources. In that regard we would be remiss if we did not mention Christopher Taylor, who also provided valuable technical support. Critical readers contributed their expertise. Here we must thank colleagues Carol Schick, Bernard Laplante, and Douglas Stewart. We gratefully acknowledge the "crash course" in computer searches as well as the comments and suggestions offered by Marianne Thauberger, Reference Librarian, and Bill Sgrazutti, Head of the Education/Fine Arts Library. We need to acknowledge the moral and financial support of Meredith Cherland, Associate Dean of the Faculty of Education, and Nancy Fraser Child, Director of French Education.

Early in the life of the book project—before it was even a project—a very special person, whom the editors met in India at the English Language Teaching Seminar, convinced both of us that compiling a book on a global scale would be a very worthwhile experience. How right you were, Jean McNiff! Thank you. Thank you as well to Sigrun Gudmundsdottir, who agreed to write the Foreword early in the life of the project, and who understood what we were trying to do.

We want to acknowledge the people at SUNY Press and the reviewers whose insightful comments resulted in a more coherent manuscript. We are also grateful for the support of the series editor, Alan Tom.

Finally, we would like to acknowledge the influence in our lives of Amma, Raja, Bruno Sahut, and the rest of our families, whose support and faith in us never waivers.

Introduction

What This Book Is About

The idea for editing and contributing to a book on community building in teacher education grew out of long discussions between the two editors when Helen was among the resource persons invited to participate in an International Seminar on English Language Teaching, at the Central Institute of English and Foreign Languages (Rama's institution) in Hyderabad, India. After several false starts over a two-year period, we discussed a possible outline for the book and contacted potential contributors when Rama spent a semester in the Faculty of Education at the University of Regina, Canada (Helen's institution).

Community building among partners in teacher education is not a new idea. Indeed, the teacher education literature over the past decade or so contains many stories of successful and not so successful partnerships (See for instance, Christiansen, Goulet, Krentz, and Maeers 1997; Clandinin and Connelly 1995; Johnston 1997). There is not much in the literature, however, about partnerships between and among faculty in teacher education programs. What are we doing in our faculties to build community among ourselves? What are some of the daily challenges we face as professional faculties within the academy? What does collaboration mean to who we are, and to what we do as teacher educators and as persons?

Key questions and issues with regard to community building in faculties of education or teacher training institutions vary from one country to another, and even from one faculty to another. Wherever we are, our cultures and histories have shaped, and continue to shape us. Yet the fact that we are all involved in teacher education, and as such are part of a university culture, means we have issues in common. The differences among us, on the other hand, provide us with opportunities for greater understandings of the process of educating teachers as we continue to educate ourselves.

The book is divided into four parts or sections, all of which explore some aspect of community building and collaboration among teacher educators. Each chapter was written by colleagues who work, or have worked in the same institution for a short or longer time. Some continue to be close colleagues (i.e., work in the same physical environment), others are like the editors, meeting virtually (through e-mail), at conferences, and in one another's institutions whenever possible, sometimes even co-teaching a course or part of a course.

People, paradigms, and programs form an integral part of any scholarly discussion about community building in teacher education. Some would argue that opening a book with a section focused on paradigms would have provided readers with a theoretical framework right from the beginning. The editors, however, believe that community begins with each individual, and so chose to focus on people as community builders first, then to focus on paradigms for community building, and finally to return to a focus on people within programs. A "strong" theme throughout the book is community as lived experience. These are stories of individuals interacting with one another in communities.

Part One, in which individuals reflect on their efforts at community building, begins with a chapter co-authored by the editors. The purpose of chapter 1 is to open the conversation by pondering possible definitions for community, a concept understood by all, but not necessarily in the same way or ways. To give the discussion a context we also share our stories of community as lived in our institutions—a midsized university on the Canadian prairies, and a nationally recognized postgraduate training institute in South Central India. In chapter 2, Mary Beattie reminds us that a practice of community starts with each of us, and with the question: Who am I in community with others? For Beattie, community takes place within responsible, reciprocal relationships. In chapter 3, Katie Flockhart and Vera Woloshyn discuss such relationships as they tell their story of mutual mentoring when teaching two sections of the same course.

In Part Two, contributors use different paradigmatic lenses to share their stories of community building. In chapter 4, Lorraine Ling,

Eva Burman, and Maxine Cooper argue that the meaning of the word *community* has probably changed, suggesting that in the postmodern era one has a sense of belonging to multiple communities. In chapter 5, Hans Smits and David Friesen link community and identity, using hermeneutics as a theoretical tool in order to reflect on their experience of planning and teaching a generic course in teacher education at their university. Sometimes a paradigm can be a powerful force in creating community by bringing together likeminded persons. This is at the heart of the discussion in chapter 6. In it, Florence Samson and her colleagues at the University of Toronto explore ways in which the community at the Centre for Teacher Development shapes and is being shaped by narrative inquiry. The community story these educators tell is one that is still emerging out of the shared physical and intellectual space at the Centre. Sometimes a community can reach inside itself and toward others at the same time. This is the story Carol Mullen and Patrick Diamond tell about arts-based inquiry in collaborative communities in the final chapter in this section, chapter 7. These educators suggest that communities can be thought of as entities "stitched together" in a kind of patchwork quilt or montage.

Part Three focuses on links between community building and program development in the United States, Australia, and Israel. Chapter 8 breaks new ground as it discusses the process of creating communities online. This raises an interesting question: Do people need to have face to face contact (F2F) in order to build community? In chapter 9, Robyn Ewing and David Smith describe the new Master of Teaching Degree program at the University of Sydney. Here there is a lot of "F2F" as education students and faculty, teachers and administrators work together in school and university classrooms. What about partnerships? How do these enrich the lives of teacher educators? This is an underlying question in chapter 10, which explores the different kinds of partnerships initiated by the Victoria University of Technology.

The final chapter in Part Three focuses on community building within the framework of a professional specialization program at the MOFET Institute in Israel. In chapter 11, Miriam Ben-Peretz and Moshe Silberstein provide a theoretical framework for their study of community building as they explore the implications of two polar opposites: *Gemeinschaft* (community) and *Gesellschaft* (society). Thomas Sergiovanni suggests that schools "possess characteristics of both" and that "as *gesellschaft strengthens, gemeinschaft* weakens" leading to "a loss of community with all of its negative consequences" (1994, 13, author's emphasis). This leads us to ponder the implications of Sergiovanni's suggestion for faculties of education. Are the latter more like a university (which may or may not be more like an organization) or more like a school? It could be argued that more than most of the other university units, a faculty of education's principal mandate is to serve the public through educating its future teachers. And so, both teachers and teacher educators are part of the same educational community. Unlike teachers in schools, however, an important part of the communities teacher educators serve are outside of the actual physical space in which they work. Their offices and classrooms are in the university, but a large part of a teacher educator's other responsibilities pertain to supervision and co-ordination of student teaching practica in schools. More often than not, a significant part of teacher education research also takes part in schools. And so, teacher educators are typically involved in creating communities of inquiry with teachers and administrators.

Like teachers, teacher educators work across communities. Like teachers, an important part of their community building is not with peers. Like their colleagues in schools, teacher educators work at building community with their students. With the increasing enrollments of "mature" students in university classes, and especially in graduate level courses, it is even possible for a teacher educator to teach with a former student as happened with Flockhart and Woloshyn. Moreover, teacher educators often encounter former education students in the schools now in the role of mentors or cooperating teachers.

Part Four contains a single chapter written by the editors. Contributors' stories provide evidence to suggest there are a lot of similarities from one teacher education faculty to another—from one country to another. There are common threads because all the contributors are engaged in some way or another, in the practice of teacher education. The purpose of chapter 12 is to pull together these threads. The book closes with an Epilogue.

Part I

OPENING THE CONVERSATION

Part One, as its title indicates, opens the conversation. To a large extent this part of the book is about individual efforts to build community, although the first chapter is slightly different because the editors thought it was important to place a few ideas "on the table" right at the beginning. And so chapter 1 focuses on the changing role of the university at the beginning of the new millennium, on community as defined in the literature, and on ways in which change within community comes about. In the latter part of the chapter, each editor has authored her own story of "community as lived" in our respective institutions.

In chapter 2, Mary Beattie takes readers on a journey of professional development as she reflects on her first seven years as a teacher educator. She describes her attempts at community building with her students and colleagues in her own institution and elsewhere. She explores the development of trusting relationships and reciprocal learning in "authentic communities of inquiry."

Katie Flockhart and Vera Woloshyn began their relationship as student and teacher. They continued that relationship as friends, and as colleagues when they taught two sections of the same course at Woloshyn's institution. In chapter 3, the final chapter in this section, Flockhart and Woloshyn reflect on that team teaching experience and discuss the role of mentoring in community building at the postsecondary level.

1 Community and Community Building in Teacher Education

Helen Christiansen and S. Ramadevi

> To learn to be human is to develop through the give-and-take of communication an effective sense of being an individually distinctive member of a community; one who understands and appreciates its beliefs, desires, and methods, and who contributes to a further conversion of organic powers into human resources and values.
>
> —John Dewey

The intention of this chapter is to open the conversation about community and community building in teacher education. Here we play two roles as members of the book "community." First, as editors we discuss, albeit briefly, the three interconnected "c's" of climate, community, and change. Second, we author our own stories of community as lived in each of our institutions. We begin with a brief examination of the broader context or climate in which many postsecondary institutions find themselves at the beginning of the new millennium.

THE CHANGING CLIMATE IN POSTSECONDARY INSTITUTIONS

Those of us who have been in and around postsecondary institutions for more than a decade cannot help but notice that the educational climate has changed. For one thing, students have changed. In Canada, Barnard, Cosgrave, and Welsh (1998) argue that the members of what they have labeled the "Nexus generation,"[1] born in the 60s and late 70s, are a generation shaped by the effects of computerization (chips) and popular media culture (pop). Members of Nexus, who form the majority of postsecondary students, grew up with change, expect change, and adjust to it quite well. According to Barnard and his colleagues, the Nexus generation may not have much faith in institutions such as the university, or as they put it, "Nexus has some significant doubts as to the abilities of existing institutions to 'fix' what is broken" (6).

At the Central Institute of English and Foreign Languages (CIEFL), the most important language institute in India, as its name suggests, the clout it still wields among its teacher trainees remains enormous. As far as its funding organization, the University Grants Commission (UGC) is concerned, however, there has been a steady erosion in the credibility of its courses for college (undergraduate level) and university (graduate level) teachers. This is evident in the dilution of the institute's rigorous teacher education programs brought about by the following moves of the UGC: the introduction of three week refresher courses for college teachers, two of which have been equated to the CIEFL's nine-month Diploma; allowing several universities which may not be specialist institutes of the same type as CIEFL to offer such courses; the creation of English Language Teaching (ELT) departments in various universities in the country, which instead of working together with CIEFL have become alienated from and are now sometimes in competition with CIEFL. And so CIEFL's expertise and status of a deemed university have been neutralized and undermined. Added to this, a financial crunch at the level of higher education has seen the urgent need for fundraising programs by universities including CIEFL to meet any expenses beyond basic requirements. Many at the institute find this drive to raise extra revenue coloring all our programs without discrimination as "outrageous", considering the service oriented nature of teacher education and the institute's culture of helping underprivileged educational institutions improve the quality of teaching and learning of English.

Until fairly recently, in North America at least, it could well be that the biggest change in teacher education practice was the move from normal schools to faculties of education housed in the universities. In the eyes of its proponents, moving teacher education to the universities would make teaching and the preparation of future teachers more professional, thus giving a higher profile to education and educators. One of the results of this move may have been to create a second-class group of academics, professors of education who, according to Alan Tom (1997) have "never been granted legitimacy by arts and sciences faculty because they are not perceived as having successfully established a claim on a subject matter" (57). It may also have created a group of professionals who are not at all certain how to live out their careers in the academy. Hans Smits and David Friesen write about teacher educators being caught up in an "ambiguous space" as they try to meet the demands of the university to conduct research and publish while, at the same time, trying to meet the demands of the profession to educate tomorrow's teachers.

In North America and elsewhere, the past decade has witnessed the growth of professional development schools in close partnership with faculties of education. Indeed, the professional literature is filled with stories of the more and less successful collaborative arrangements between faculties of education and schools (See for instance, Christiansen, Goulet, Krentz, and Maeers 1997; Darling-Hammond 1994; Deer and Williams 1995; Johnston 1997; Levine and Trachtman 1997; Lieberman and Miller 1990; Petrie 1995; Sirotnik and Goodlad 1988). Within the new professional context, different kinds of educational communities are emerging.

COMMUNITY AS DEFINED: A BRIEF OVERVIEW OF SOME OF THE LITERATURE

As a discussion of community and community building is the underlying theme of all of the chapters in this book, this section is intended as a brief overview only. Its purpose is to provide a few initial definitions of community by highlighting some of the writings of key researchers.

Two researchers often cited in the literature about community are Thomas Sergiovanni and Etienne Wenger. Sergiovanni (1994) believes that communities are "collections of individuals who are bonded together by natural will and who are together binded to a set of shared ideals and ideas" (xvi). For Sergiovanni, successful community building depends on each institution creating its own practice of community. This idea is developed further by Ben-Peretz and Silberstein (this volume). Wenger (1998) defines community as "a way of talking about the social configurations in which our enterprises are defined as worth pursuing and our participation is recognizable as competence" (5). He argues that "placing the focus on participation" can have "broad implications for what it takes to understand and support learning" (7). Wenger believes we need to "value the work of community building" and ensure that "participants have access to the resources necessary to learn what they need to learn in order to take actions and make decisions that fully engage their knowledgeability" (10).

Wenger is probably best identified with the expression "communities of practice," coined with Jean Lave in earlier research on sociocultural perspectives of learning (Lave and Wenger 1991), and developed by him in later writing (1997, 1998). For Lave and Wenger (1991) a community of practice is "a set of relations among persons, activity, and world, over time and in relation with other tangential and overlapping communities of practice." Furthermore, it is the social structure of this practice that "define(s) possibilities for learning." For these two researchers, "a community of practice is an intrinsic condition for the existence of knowledge" (98). In more recent work, Wenger argues that what makes a community of practice is the sharing of practice, adding "the concept of practice connotes doing. . . . in a historical and social context [and it is that which] gives structure and meaning to what we do" (1997, 38).

Wenger (1998) believes that in some way or another "we all belong to communities of practice" (6); they are "an integral part of our daily lives" (7). In fact, for him, we belong to multiple communities, most of which "do not have a name and do not issue membership cards" (7). Finally, Wenger suggests that "we can probably distinguish a few communities of practice in which we are core members from a larger number . . . in which we have a more peripheral kind of membership" (7).

How do communities of practice function in education? In their research on "teachers' professional knowledge landscapes" (Clandinin and Connelly 1995), Jean Clandinin and Michael Connelly write about "knowledge communities," which they define as "relational places dotted on the professional knowledge landscape, safe places found outside the line of authority in schools and often outside of schools themselves" (141). For these educators, a "significant feature of knowledge communities is that they are places where educators are vibrantly present, where their voices are unconditionally heard, where their relationships are authentic and secure" (141–142). Belonging to a knowledge community is voluntary, for such communities cannot be "imposed or mandated" (142). They "emerge and grow as teachers come together in their professional knowledge landscapes" and "they involve people from different places in the matrix of relationships on the landscape" (142).

Much of the education literature uses the terms *learning community, community of inquiry,* and even *professional development community* in discussions of communities of practice involving teacher educators, teachers, and often students in education or in school classrooms (see for instance, Minnes Brandes and Erickson 1998; Oakes and Quartz 1995; Short 1992). Sometimes learning communities are formal arrangements such as in the Learning Community program at the University of Wisconsin, which brings together teacher educators, cooperating teachers, and education students (Ford 1994). Whether communities are formal or informal, all seem to involve teacher educators and at least one other group of educational stakeholders in a wide variety of collaborative arrangements. In the United States, such communities have been created in response to the recommendations of the Holmes Group (1986), especially with regard to working more closely with the schools.

> If university faculties are to become more expert educators of teachers, they must make better use of expert teachers in the education of other teachers, and in research on teaching. In addition, schools must become places where both teachers and university faculty can systematically inquire into practice and improve it. (Tomorrow's Teachers: A Report of the Holmes Group 1986, 4)

In India, the situation may be quite different. Authors of a review of Indian research in teacher education argue that although "by its very nature the teacher education system must maintain a symbiotic relationship with the school system. . . . this appears to be incompatible with what [they] see taking place" (Govinda and Buch 1990, 141). Furthermore, much of the research in education is "done by individual scholars working on academic degrees" (157) who often use statistical research methods, and "fail to present . . . findings in any form that is translatable to action" (156). These educators recommend that "interdisciplinary team work be encouraged in (Indian) teacher education," adding that it is "urgent that professionals concerned with teacher education . . . come together to inject an element of dynamism into the field through effective institutional-level research projects" (157).

Against this background, there have been a few significant projects in the area of English language teacher education in the country initiated by CIEFL, and located within a paradigm of collaboration and reflective self (teacher) development. A recent research project undertaken by CIEFL, and funded by the UGC to develop a resource book to teach English at the postsecondary level, adopted a research methodology which incorporated principles of collaborative action research (Mathew 1997). The three and a half year project involved thirty-five college teachers across the country in the role of "insider" collaborative researchers and a five member team of CIEFL researchers as "outsider" collaborative researchers engaging in self-observation and reflection related to the nature and number of initiatives taken by teachers toward curriculum renewal. This culminated in individual action research projects undertaken by the collaborating teachers.

Yet another major study on curriculum implementation conducted by CIEFL in collaboration with two other organizations, the Central Board of Secondary Education (CBSE), and the British Council (1993–97), adopted a stakeholder model of curriculum evaluation in which the stress was on multiperspective description and triangulation of different data sources. All the stakeholders were seen as important in constructing the curriculum collaboratively, and translating the curriculum-as-intention into classroom realities. It involved "insiders" especially teachers, in the evaluation of the curriculum, since a major premise of the study was that any curriculum renewal effort becomes meaningful and sustainable only when teachers are actively involved as researchers in the process of change. The action research approach to curriculum evaluation, where the teachers themselves are seen as the major stakeholders, formed one of the major thrusts of the study. The study was also significant because of the collaboration of several groups of ELT professionals, including individuals and organizations such as non CBSE teachers, academic researchers and teacher trainers from other ELT institutions in the country.

Apart from these institution-based innovative efforts in the area of teacher education, one grassroots teacher development movement located in Bangalore is worth mentioning. This is the English Language Teaching Community (ELTC), a voluntary teacher development group comprised of college teachers in Bangalore. The ELTC has thirty members and is committed to staying small and manageable. Based on the principles of decentralisation and rotating leadership, the ELTC has been meeting regularly in plenary and special interest group sessions for over twelve years. Teachers share ideas and report on progress of action research projects carried out individually and collaboratively, and engage in the process of reflection and self-development. The ELTC has also been active through publications and participation in seminars across the globe.

CHANGE WITHIN COMMUNITY

> We can take it as a given that there will always be pressure for educational change in pluralistic societies. These pressures increase as society becomes more complex.

—M. Fullan

Given this new emphasis on community, it would seem there is a case to be made for the reeducation of the educator; for a change related to how teaching is viewed and done; and for a change in attitudes toward and perceptions of teacher education. What is under discussion here is planned change brought about by deliberate human action. It is the fact of planned human intervention that makes change complicated.

A North American educator associated with the change literature is Michael Fullan (e.g., 1991, 1993, 1999). For Fullan (1991), the "crux of change is how individuals come to grips" with it (30). We need therefore to think about "what change really means as we are experiencing it at the personal level" and "what it means for others around us who may be in change situations" (30). Fullan warns educators about the dangers of "false clarity," which "occurs when people *think* that they have changed but (in fact) have only assimilated the superficial trappings of the new practice" (35, emphasis in the original). Educational change, moreover, "is a process of coming to grips with the *multiple* realities of people, who are the main participants in change" (95, emphasis in the original). In other words, members of an educational community may not all see things the same way, or may think they are changing when, in fact, they are in a situation of "false clarity." This phenomenon is expressed rather succinctly in the French expression, "Plus ça change; plus c'est la même chose" (the more things change, the more they stay the same).

COMMUNITY AS LIVED: A TALE OF TWO INSTITUTIONS

If, as Wenger (1998) suggests, "we all belong to communities of practice" (6), the way in which those communities are lived can vary considerably. One of us (Helen) lives and works in the capital of the province of Saskatchewan (Canada), considered as a "have not" province (i.e., struggling economically) in a highly developed country. The other

(Rama) lives and works in what was once (and still is, to some extent) the premier institution for English language teaching in India, a developing country fraught with problems of the most basic kind (i.e., feeding and sheltering its people). In this final part of the chapter, the editors share their stories of community as lived, anticipating that some aspects will resonate with colleagues elsewhere.

Helen's story The University of Regina is a midsized institution in a small city (168,000) in a thinly populated (slightly over one million), primarily agricultural province on the Canadian Prairies. I joined the Faculty of Education in 1989. Much of my career in the faculty has unfolded during a period of transition. Indeed, there have been many changes over the years. For one thing, of the present fifty-five members of faculty, only nineteen were there when I began. There have been three deans (two of them "outsiders") and associate deans (all from faculty ranks). Founding members of the faculty, the "old guard," who had been hired in the sixties, and who had built a teacher education program inspired by teaching effectiveness models, and constructed around a professional development cycle of lecture, microteaching laboratories, in-school practice, reflective seminar, would nearly all retire during the first five years I was in the faculty. The significant personnel changes posed a serious challenge to any efforts at community building. What is more significant, perhaps, is that all of these changes occurred during a period of severe budget restraint. And so people who retired or took positions elsewhere (in my program, I am the only one left of six who were there when I began) were not always replaced by tenure track professors. A number of our courses continue to be taught by clinical professors (seconded teachers) and sessional instructors, who contribute their practical knowledge of the school classroom but at the same time will never have a real stake in the future of the faculty, and have neither obligation nor commitment to research and publication. This makes it challenging to define shared goals—an important aspect of community building.

　　Furthermore, it may be that as a faculty we are not even sure as to who "we" are. A significant teacher in my life as a second language educator, Caleb Gattegno,[2] liked to tell the following story about the effect of experience on memory. He said that experience was like an old reliable bicycle with which we cannot bear to part. We buy it new and ride it for a while. As time goes by we replace the tires, the seat, the handlebars, and whatever else needs to be changed. Eventually nearly every part of the original bicycle has been replaced, except the frame itself. Yet, we continue to refer to it as that "good old bike." This story comes to mind as our faculty engages in a process of appreciative inquiry (Hammond and Royal 1998) in order to "envision a shared future that builds upon our strengths as a Faculty" (Cherland and Friesen 1999). The numbers tell me that in our faculty which may be typical of many, the education "community" has been almost completely replaced over the years. How has that affected who "we" are now? What does this mean to "our" community of teacher educators? To our "common" goals? Is the mission of teacher education still the basic "frame"?

There have been other changes as well. When I began in the faculty, I assumed my career path would be much like those who came before me; if I worked hard in the program I would be rewarded with tenure and promotion as a matter of course. Furthermore, when I looked around me, this assumption did not appear to be unreasonable. And so, my colleagues and I were shocked when my application for tenure was denied five years later, on the grounds that I was not *an academic.* That decision was later reversed, but the events surrounding it marked a watershed in the faculty. Since that time, new faculty members have been made very aware of the need to conduct research and publish, and further encouraged with a nonteaching semester a year before they have to apply for tenure (in our university, the fourth or fifth year of a probationary appointment). Having to pay close attention to one's record of research and publication has meant that faculty members are often torn between their two major roles of teacher educators and university scholars, all the while continuing to believe (or at least continuing to affirm) that our teacher education practice must be grounded in the field.

Rama's story   The Central Institute of English was established by the Indian Government (with the blessings of the prime minister of the day, Pandit Jawaharlal Nehru) across from Osmania University in Hyderabad, a large city (population of about nine million) in Central India. The initial objectives of the center were the training of teachers, the production of teaching materials, and "helping to improve the standards of teaching English in the country as a whole" (Krishnaswamy and Spiraman 1994, 64). The scope of the institute's activities was expanded in 1972 when it was renamed the Central Institute of English and Foreign Languages (CIEFL) to include the teaching of major foreign languages in its programs. CIEFL is a national institution of higher education, deemed to be a university. It offers programs leading to the Master of Philosophy degree, or M.Phil. (prerequisite to doctoral studies in India), and to the Doctor of Philosophy (Ph.D.). In the academic year 1999–2000 there were 230 students taking a postgraduate diploma in

English teaching, seventeen registered in the M.Phil. and twenty in the Ph.D. programs. Since CIEFL is a specialist institute we train only English (and foreign language) teachers both for secondary and post-secondary levels. Our research programs are in three areas: linguistics, literature, and language teaching. The institute also offers an average of twelve to fifteen short-term training programs for primary, secondary, and postsecondary levels each year. Each of these programs has a minimum enrollment of forty.

In addition to conducting the training programs, institute faculty are engaged in textbook and resource production for teaching languages in the entire country, and there are also several national-level research and training projects on hand. One of the recent additions to the training programs has been a three-month training program for English teachers from Krygzstan and Kazakhstan, as well as a three-month English proficiency program for foreign nationals (professionals such as doctors, engineers, and diplomats from different countries such as Burma, Cambodia, Vietnam, Iraq, and Yemen). Professors and students are provided with on-campus accommodations. The fact that we all live on campus and that many faculty members are raising families means we are a very special academic community whose members see one another all of the time, and under many different circumstances.

I have been at CIEFL for more than twenty years. As a matter of fact, I did my doctoral work at CIEFL (the only institution in India where one could get a Ph.D. in English Language Teaching at the time), and took a position in the Materials Production Department even before I had completed my thesis. I identify myself as a teacher educator and collaborative researcher but mainly as an English Language Teaching (ELT) person. ELT is an important term in my life.

There is a small group of us, mostly women, within the large number of ELT academics at the institute, who share views on a particular paradigm for ELT, and who share an educational ideology. We should form a community, yet each of us seems to be working in isolation within the institute. For a while we get together, and then we split, and often we seem to be just sitting around by ourselves, each in her own office with her own problems.

There have been a lot of changes during the time I have been at the institute. There was an element of simplicity in the old days. Changes in the context of teacher education have occurred quite dramatically especially in the last ten years or so. Everyone seems to recognize that the original mandate of the institute has to be modified, drastically changed at some points, and most definitely added to substantially. On the other hand, faculty are not equally sure or even broadly agreed as to what exactly those changes should be.

There is a lot of criticism within the institute about a drop in student enrollment, yet if one looks carefully, what can be seen is that students are no longer registering for the same courses. Our total numbers have not really gone down. When I began at the institute there were eighty or ninety teacher-students enrolled at the post graduate diploma level. The research courses were fairly new, and there were no more than six to eight scholars enrolled for these. Recently, the exact opposite has been the case. There has been a significant increase in the number of students taking research degrees.

Our courses used to be filled with experienced teachers; nowadays we get more "freshers" (i.e., students fresh from the university with Master's degrees in English literature). These students are not at all sure what kind of career they want to pursue. And so the diploma course has become a "stop gap" arrangement for them while they "shop around" for more lucrative job and study options. Others opt for courses in the program that enable them to choose careers which will keep them out of the classroom as much as possible. And yet the major thrust of the institute is language teacher education. It would seem then that the students' goals do not match the goals of the program. In the end these conflicting interests have not done much good to either the programs, the faculty teaching them, or the students themselves.

One noticeable feature in our attempts to bring about changes in CIEFL's programs has been the immense resistance on the part of many faculty. In other words, "Let's not give up on what we have; these are time tested methods and material. Everything old is not bad!" In the end, most of what is old is retained.

We don't make the mistake of saying, "Everything old is gold!" but that in effect is the mood of the faculty. Change, even as a remote possibility, is thought of only in cosmetic terms. And yet being more relevant to society has become an important topic for discussion at the institute. That relevance is interpreted in different ways—catering to the market economy for some; being socially relevant to the disadvantaged by others. Professionalism is seen as commitment to the profession by some, whereas for others that professionalism is market driven.

Over the years I have noticed a lot of antagonism between colleagues in linguistics and those in ELT—a lot of polarization. There is conflict between what is valid as theory in English Language Teaching, and conflict about the kinds of texts that should form the core of the subject area. There is also conflict between theorizing and about what could be valid theory in ELT. So we get into arguments about psy-cholinguistic and applied linguistic approaches within a positivist framework on the one hand, and conceptualizations leaning more to-ward situating educational theory within qualitative paradigms (e.g., phenomenological, hermeneutical, collaborative action research). This division among faculty and students about what constitutes ELT and teacher education has contributed substantially to the confusion sur-rounding the kinds of changes in programs that should be initiated.

COMMONALITIES AND CONNECTIONS

Our stories of community as lived demonstrate the interconnectedness of the three "c's" of climate, community, and change. At the University of Regina as at CIEFL, times have changed and that change is continu-ing. If at CIEFL "everything old" may no longer be "gold," at the University of Regina, although we may not choose to "throw out the baby with the bath water," we may have to make some decisions about the future of the "baby" as its "parents" are no longer around. In both of our institutions, faculty members have to come to grips with the com-plexities of a new era, in which the role of the university and that of its professors is in transition.

For Helen, a central issue in our faculty may well be linked to a be-lief that teacher education must be grounded in the field (i.e., in the daily lives of teachers and children). Although few will dispute that, the question may need to be reexamined as: What does this mean in terms of who we are and how we work within the framework of a university? We may not be able to spend as much time in school classrooms as we have in the past; that may not even be desirable. Research and publica-tion may be important, not only to our academic careers, but also to a contribution to knowledge of what it means to educate a teacher. For Rama, a central issue at the institute may well be linked to resolving the tension between individual needs and those of the community. Faculty members who have grown accustomed to being *the* "consultants" in English language teacher education in India may have to reexamine the role of the Institute in the face of changing needs of its students. In both our institutions there appear to be tensions between the needs of indi-viduals and those of the institution and society as a whole. This is linked to our first theme of changing climate.

What are the links between our stories and the second theme of communities of practice? For Helen, it would seem that the Faculty of Education community is redefining itself and its goals, trying to keep what has worked well for it in the past, and at the same time trying to accommodate the needs of new faculty and a new era in teacher education. For Rama, uncertainty about the relevance of some programs and territorial struggles linked to that uncertainty mean that CIEFL must also redefine itself, at a time of severe budget restraint and multiple demands of a society that continues to struggle at the most basic level in a global economy. In both our institutions, previously held beliefs and practices are being challenged.

Is the university itself more like an organization than a community? That may depend on how one conceives the role of the university—a role that is changing as universities are being held more "accountable" in the preparation of future members of the "work force." Peter Drucker argues that "community and society are defined by the bonds that hold their members together . . . [whereas] an organization is defined by its task" (1992, 100, cited in Sergiovanni 1994, 13). Drucker concludes that "society, community and family are all conserving institutions. . . . But the modern organization is a destabilizer . . . it must be organized for constant change" (op cit., 14). Certainly change is a part of the life of all institutions at the beginning of the new millennium—part of the new climate in postsecondary institutions.

Change occurs at the interface between the individual and the collective. Each of our stories tells of a search for our places in the community, of ways in which we tried to come to terms with changing contexts. For Rama and her colleagues, funding cuts brought with them the need to be more relevant to the needs of the "market place." For Helen and her colleagues, changes in funding could mean that faculty need to pay more attention to research and publication. Finally, like all of the other contributors to this book, we continue to shape and be shaped by the contexts in which we live and work—in our individual and collective processes of reeducating the educator.

Notes

1. "Nexus" means link or bridge. The authors chose it because they believe this generation is uniquely positioned to play "some key bridging roles in society" (2), first of all because "it is sandwiched" between the Baby Boomers and their children, and secondly because "it sits right in the middle of society's shift from the . . . Industrial Age . . . to the Information Age" (2). Barnard, R.; Cosgrave, D.; and Walsh, J. 1998. *Chips and pop: Decoding the nexus generation.* Toronto: Malcolm Lester Books.

2. Caleb Gattegno developed the "Silent Way," a learner-centered approach to second language teaching. This approach was based on five key ideas: (1) Teaching should be subordinated to learning; (2) Learning is not primarily imitation or drill; (3) In learning the mind "equips itself" by its own working; (4) As it works, the mind draws on everything it has already acquired; and, (5) If the teacher's activity is to be subordinate to that of the learner, then the teacher must stop interfering with and sidetracking that activity. (See H. D. Brown, *Principles of language learning and teaching.* [Englewood Cliffs, N.J.: Prentice Hall Regents, 1994]; C. Gattegno, *The common sense of teaching foreign languages* [New York: Educational Solutions Inc., 1976]; E. W. Stevick, *Memory, meaning, and method.* [Rowley, Mass.: Newbury House, 1976]).

2 *Finding New Words for Old Songs*

Creating Relationships and Community in Teacher Education

Mary Beattie

Own only what you can always carry with you;
know languages, know countries, know people.
Let memory be your travel bag. Use your memory!
It is those bitter seeds alone which might sprout and
grow someday.

—Solzhenitsyn

Solzhenitsyn's advice serves to introduce an account of one teacher educator's efforts to research her own practice and professional development over time, and to focus on the role that relationships and community have played in that development. The journey described here is a reflective one whose purpose it is to give an account of my professional development during my first seven years as a teacher educator/researcher, an account that is a temporal one and will always be a work-in-progress. In an effort to look at the ways in which I was trying to shape a community that was simultaneously shaping me, I have drawn on the writing done in a professional journal kept during this time, on some of my published writing, and on the writing of students that inspired me and influenced my practice during that time. It is hoped that this self-study will make a contribution to the research on teacher thinking, faculty development, and professional knowledge, to the nature and art of teaching in higher education, when teaching is understood in the context of relationship and of community, and to the ways in which teaching, research, and the creation of community can be connected. In the words of Maxine Greene (1990):

> [W]e are in a new country as we education professors try to recreate our purposes and find new words for old songs. We will be outside the law until we find a language for compassion; and then we will write our new maps and keep exploring; gorge after untapped gorge. And there will be norms we can agree on, principles we can freely make our own in a sphere of compassion, a sphere of care. . . . (16)

I begin by describing the context for this inquiry and my conception of faculty development as a process of recognizing and valuing one's own voice, hearing and responding to the voices of others, and of balancing the voices through the creation of shared values and community. This view of professional learning is based on Dewey's notion of growth as the reconstruction of experience, on a conception of learning as the re-forming of understandings, and on educational reform as "the polyphonic re-forming and re-construction of understandings by all parties involved . . . [rather than] the monologic imposition of ideas, beliefs and values by one person or group on another" (Beattie 1995, 146).

THE CONTEXT FOR INQUIRY AND PROFESSIONAL DEVELOPMENT

This self-study is located in the context of the initial teacher education of prospective secondary school teachers. The intention of the self-study is to make a contribution to the growing number of university teachers researching the experience of teacher educator/researchers who seek to model inquiry and the creation of community for students (Clandinin and Connelly 1992; Conle 1996; Diamond 1993; Knowles and Cole 1994; Oberg and Underwood 1989; Yeager 1996). It seeks also to contribute to the research that highlights the development of teacher educators' and teachers' voices as a significant aspect of professional development (e.g., Beattie 1995, 1997; Bullough and Gitlin 1995; Diamond 1993; Knowles and Cole with Presswood 1994). Many educational researchers consider the development of the prospective teacher's voice as a critical aspect of becoming a reflective, reflexive, meaning-making practitioner, who has the ability to articulate beliefs and under-standings, and acquire new perspectives as central aspects of the construction, reconstruction, and transformation of knowledge (Aiken and Mildon 1991; Bullough 1991; Bullough and Gitlin 1995; Clandinin 1989; Knowles and Cole with Presswood 1994; Knowles and Holt-Reynolds 1991; Nias 1989). It is also hoped this self-study will con-tribute to the research that testifies to the interconnectedness of the personal and the professional in teachers' lives, as it has been docu-mented and is ongoing in the work of Butt, Raymond, McCue, and Yamagushi (1992); Connelly and Clandinin (1990); Elbaz (1991); Goodson (1992).

Addressing both teacher educators and public school teachers, Belenky, Clinchy, Goldberger, and Tarule (1986) call for educators and educational settings that enable students "to develop their own authen-tic voices" by emphasizing "connection over separation, understanding and acceptance over assessment, and collaboration over debate" (229). They call for the kinds of educational programs that accord "respect to and allow time for the knowledge that emerges from firsthand experi-ence" and for educators to replace the imposition of "their own expec-tations and arbitrary requirements, [in order to] encourage students to evolve their own patterns of work, based on the problems they are pur-suing" (229). In addition to developing their own authentic voices, prospective teachers must develop the capacity to hear the voices of others (Beattie 2001). Many researchers in the field of initial teacher ed-ucation have pointed out that the wealth of knowledge about teaching and learning student teachers bring to professional education settings is knowledge gained from their experiences as students. This knowledge shapes their perceptions of teaching and their developing practice (e.g., Calderhead 1991; Elbaz 1983; Leinhardt 1988; Nias 1989; Zeichner, Tabachnick, and Densmore 1987), and as these researchers point out, much of this knowledge is unarticulated, and needs to be adapted in the context of learning, to the role of teacher rather than that of student. Calderhead (1991) and others point out that student teachers try to enact their personal images and theories of teaching and learning in their practical settings, in spite of the situational and contextual realities with which they are dealing. In order to learn to teach in ways other than those in which they themselves were taught, prospective teachers need to experience learning situations in which they are encouraged to articulate their held knowledge about teaching and learning, to exam-ine it, and reconstruct it within the context of becoming a teacher. Before they can adapt what they know to a new situation, prospective teachers have to understand what it is that they do know, to understand its origins and consider other possible ways of envisioning classrooms and learning situations. Thus, self-exploration, self-expression, and the ability to hear, understand, and incorporate the ideas and perspectives of others into one's own understandings, are necessary and critical aspects of professional education and ongoing professional development. Teacher educators who will create these kinds of settings and experiences for their students will of necessity be able and willing to model and explicate the processes of inquiry and the creation of shared values and community building in their classroom practices and professional lives.

This study focuses on one teacher educator's attempt to enact a pedagogy focused on educating reflective practitioners through the "development of sustaining relationships, the nurturing of ideas [and] the fostering of creativity" (Beattie 1995, 19). Drawing from the theoretical foundations provided by constructivist theories of teaching and learning, the theories of experiential philosophers (e.g., Carr 1986; Dewey 1916, 1934; MacIntyre 1981; Schwab 1983), feminist theory, and the concepts developed by educational researchers such as Connelly and Clandinin (1988), Eisner (1985), and Hunt (1987), I have worked to create what I call a "Holistic and Narrative Pedagogy." In such a pedagogy, practices are focused on enabling prospective teachers to find their voices in relation to the theory and practice of teaching, to use them to articulate their questions and concerns, and take ownership and responsibility for their own learning. These practices are democratic, cooperative, and concerned with connected and relational approaches to learning. Here, professional education is understood as taking place in the context of an individual's whole life. Thus, the cognitive, emotional, social, spiritual, moral, and aesthetic dimensions of the individual's knowledge are interconnected in the process of becoming a teacher. Through the experience of a collaborative community where individuals are supported in their individual and collective inquiries, prospective teachers come to new understandings of themselves as professionals, of the students they teach and of the classrooms, schools, and educational communities in which they live and work. I have written about this elsewhere (Beattie 1997) and about the important role played by students' own writing and constructive feedback from the teacher in this context. In this self-study, it is my own writing and inquiry, and the feedback I get from students and others that is the focus and the source of insights and understandings.

The creation of a community of inquiry in the professional classroom involves the sharing of insights, understandings, dilemmas, contradictions, and the difficulties of teaching on the part of the teacher educator, as well as by those she teaches. It requires pedagogical practices that are creative, inclusive, and democratic, and allow the teacher educator, in Heaney's (1995) words, to be a "hunter and gatherer of values, [whose] very solitudes and distresses are credible, insofar as they too, are in earnest of [our] veritable human being(s)" (29). In sharing aspects of our inquiries with those we teach, we expose some of the questions, contradictions, and dilemmas we are dealing with in our lives as teachers, and the ways in which we are trying to deal with them. In so doing, we enact and model a reconceptualized role of the teacher; a role that positions us as co-learners in the classroom whose main purpose it is to create a learning community for collaborative meaning making.

BALANCING INTERNAL VALUES AND EXTERNAL EXPECTATIONS: SEARCHING FOR SHARED VALUES

The context into which I was appointed is a large, urban university where the faculty of education was undergoing major change. The students selected for the Intermediate/Senior program in which I taught were chosen on the basis of academic qualifications and experience in teaching the chosen age group. All students were required to have a minimum four-year degree, and the average age of students was thirty-two. Most students had had another career (banking, social work, law, engineering, public relations, etc.) before coming into teaching. When I began my work as a teacher educator/researcher in this context, I had worked with experienced teachers for a number of years as a curriculum and staff development consultant. I expected prospective teachers to value reflection, and be committed to developing the habits of mind, the practices, and the capacities for a career of reflective practice. Implicit in this view, and explicit in my teaching, was the expectation that learners recognize the interrelatedness of all aspects of the person, (the social, moral, affective, cognitive, aesthetic, and physical) in the learning and teaching processes, and that they learn to work collaboratively with others in order to focus on the development of their own understandings, those of others, and on the creation of good learning situations and settings for students in schools. This was the view of teaching I had enacted in my work with experienced teachers, and I viewed my role as one who stimulates, supports, and facilitates individuals' inquiries. As a consultant, I was accustomed to being able to refer to and to draw on the wealth of practical knowledge experienced teachers bring to inservice education. As a beginning teacher educator, I experienced major surprise at the extent to which I had to adapt all I knew about teaching, in order to be successful in this environment. I kept a record of my thinking in a professional journal, describing the changes I made in my practice, the ways in which I adapted to a different clientele, and the successes and failures of these ventures. I wrote about individual students who made significant changes to their understandings of themselves as teachers, who had come to the teacher education setting with expectations that they would teach as they were taught, and came to understand their roles in new and more complete ways. I wrote about how much I learned from reading these students' accounts of the "unlearning" and new learning they did, the ways in which they examined the structures of their experiences, and came to understand how they were shaped by the societal, gendered, political, and philosophical settings in which they lived. My professional understandings were enriched by reading students' accounts of professional learning and changed practices, and the ways in which they made distinctions between becoming a teacher and learning how to teach. Their writing showed me how they responded to my teaching, and they taught me how to teach them to create communities of inquiry for their own students. As I was an assistant professor without tenure, the professional journal enabled me to find ways to deal with the ongoing tensions and dilemmas inherent in my situation, and with the difficulties that grow out of a long-standing dissatisfaction with teaching situations that provide neither the spaces nor the time "for the development of sustaining relationships, for the nurturing of ideas, or for the fostering of creativity" in either the students' or teachers' lives (Beattie 1995, 19). It gave me a framework for dealing with the paradox that as part of our efforts to reform teacher education these settings call for prospective teachers to be creative, reflective inquirers, but do not always provide the conditions and time frames to do this for either the prospective teachers or for the teacher educators who instruct them. I learned to live with this paradox and with what I have understood as major obstacles to the creation of a setting for inquiry in my own teaching life. I noticed that when prospective teachers reject opportunities to inquire, take control of their own learning, and be creative, I experience this as the suppression of my efforts to be creative and innovative and as having negative effects on my own learning. In such an environment, I feel frustration, discomfort, and dissatisfaction, but can use the reflective writing for each new attempt to reconcile the dilemmas and confer order on chaos, "to put things in balance, to create harmony" (Eisner 1985, 28).

During these years as a teacher educator I lived in a constant state of overload. I taught four or five groups of thirty-five students each year, and found that being in a meaningful relationship with approximately 150 adults was challenging, exhausting, and overwhelming. I was also aware that my teaching was only one part of my life as a teacher educator, and that my research and writing supported and enriched my teaching. My teaching life left little time for research and writing but I made spaces for these, and lived with the unhappiness I felt at my inability to do the kind of extended work in these areas that was satisfying to me, or that I felt would satisfy the expectations of any committee set up to review my scholarship. I was anxiously dealing with too many agendas at the same time, playing too many roles—teacher educator, researcher and writer, responsible faculty member—and felt that I was living in the eye of a storm.

During this time, I was constantly reminded that I was experiencing what Schön (1987) so aptly described as the paradox of learning new competencies and the discomfort associated with this. Schön points out that the learner "cannot at first understand what he needs to learn, can learn it only by educating himself, and can educate himself only by beginning to do what he does not yet understand" (93). I had to learn everything in a hurry, without time for experimentation, playing with the process, or enjoying the new learning. In retrospect (and with the benefit of the documentation), I can now see that it was through the establishment of relationships that I tried to work through this paradox and deal with it in the only way that made sense to me. The relationships that sustained and helped me were with students I taught, from whom I got feedback and responses, and colleagues with whom I collaborated on research, writing, and community service projects. These became frameworks for collaborative work that enabled me to gradually gain control over my life and my environment, to bring about some changes and to do so creatively and constructively.

One of these collegial relationships was with Liz, a colleague with whom I corresponded for two years. I suggested to Liz (also a beginning professor in another institution) that we could support each other if we began a correspondence where we wrote on a regular basis, and responded to each other's concerns, dilemmas, and difficulties. I draw from this correspondence here, and present a letter written in February 1992, when I was in my third year as an assistant professor, to provide insights into the issues I was dealing with then. I present it here because it provides a window into the feelings, thoughts, and inward realities I was experiencing at the time, and the ways in which I decided to deal with them. The letter shows the level of "disharmony" I was experiencing, and the pressures being felt between my internal values and my perceptions of the external expectations and realities of others.

Dear Liz:

I have just finished reading and responding to nearly 100 student writing assignments and it has taken me an untold number of hours to do it the way I want to. Many of the students submit all their writings (journal entries, stories, images, metaphors, critical incidents, details of practice teaching, etc.), and some submit selected pieces for my response. I respond to what they have written by giving them feedback on the patterns I see in the writing, asking questions, and providing new ideas, suggestions and resources. This takes an untold number of hours but I think it helps them as many of them are very grateful and they express this openly. My problem is that I don't know how not to give too much in the teaching part of my life, so that there is something left for the other parts! I teach four classes of approximately 35 students this year (5 next year) and I find that the preparation, the responding to individuals, the marking and the administration of all this takes so much of my time during the teaching session. The sheer number of personal contacts (4/5 classes of 35 students) reminds me of high school, it is emotionally draining, and it leaves little time for research and writing other than at weekends and in the summer.

What I am trying to do with these students requires that I know them as persons—not as one in a hundred and fifty people with whom I occasionally make eye contact! I feel the constant pressure associated with the reward system of the academy which requires me to be doing a lot more writing. The issue here is the tension between our internal stories of who we are, and the external stories of who others think we should be—which way do we go? Which pressure do we respond to? I think the answer makes all the difference to who we are becoming.

To what extent are we changed in unacceptable ways when we allow the external scripts to unbalance the creation of the internal one, especially if it is important to us to remain authentic? It is only when we have strong, well-developed inner voices that we can redress the balance. How we deal with these pressures is *critical* for our professional development at every phase (preservice, induction, in-service, leadership development, graduate studies) of our careers. I need to hear how others have dealt with these issues and to learn how to deal with them successfully in my own life.

The way each of us deals with this issue, defines who we become and it structures our future selves. I worry about becoming someone that I don't want to be. That would not be a success story—to be successful in other peoples' eyes and a failure in my own! I know the kind of teacher/researcher/faculty member I want to be, but whether I can get tenure as this kind of person is another matter. I live with this ambiguity, imperfection and anxiety . . . but being true to myself counts for something at the end of the day. To be continued at another time. Now—to respond to your last letter to me . . . (Professional Journal, February 1992)

Looking back now, I see how the process of writing to a colleague helped me to articulate the dilemma I was experiencing and to work out how I would deal with it. The writing provided a venue for expressing the tensions between my internal value system and my perceptions of external expectations. The act of writing about them forced me to acknowledge the extent to which teaching, and being successful as a teacher, is fundamental to my professional identity. The writing helped me to begin to reconcile the difficulty of being a responsive, caring teacher educator who treats students as individuals, and of addressing external expectations by writing about and researching my own practice. It enabled me to make connections between the creative dimension of the writing process and my image of teaching as a creative act, and to see how a reflective journal could help me confer order on my professional life. I had described my image of teaching as creative and artistic in an earlier journal entry in response to an assignment I had set for my students. There, I had written about the way I know my teaching when I feel successful.

I see my role as the creator of settings where my students will question, inquire, explore their assumptions, beliefs, values and their origins, as I explore mine. . . . and to create these settings for their own students. . . . I wonder about the relationship between Teaching and Art, and about the times when I have felt that there is art in my teaching. Artists show us things from new perspectives, they shake up our preconceived understandings, and we can never see things in quite the same way again. Good teachers do this too. Like artists, they make settings and spaces where others enter and make something of their own. When learners are helped to make new meanings, to see new patterns and to come to new understandings, they can be transformed by the process. This kind of teaching is an Art. (Professional Journal, September 1992)

The process of putting the various pieces of writing together and allowing them to resonate with each other, and of searching for patterns and ways to make meaning, provides new strategies for re-forming and transforming what is known, and for conferring order on the world. As Eisner (1985) says:

> The aesthetic is not only motivated by our need for stimulation; it is also motivated by our own need to give order to our world. To form is to confer order. To confer aesthetic order upon our world is to make that world hang together, to fit, to feel right, to put things in balance, to create harmony. Such harmonies are sought in all aspects of life. . . . [The creation of which] is a very high aesthetic achievement. (29–30)

By examining the writing over time I began to see that I interpreted success and failure in teaching according to my ability to work with groups of individuals in a way that acknowledged and respected how they wanted to learn, while at the same time remaining true to myself and to my own values and beliefs about teaching and learning. The patterns in the writing show that it is through relationship with colleagues and students, and the creation and recreation of communities of inquiry with each new group of students, that I have achieved success and new levels of harmony and balance. It shows my growing awareness of the connections between the reform of the self, the reform of teacher education, and the reform of the university and school settings that provide the context of our work. This theme has shaped my actions as I have worked to create a new order in my classroom teaching, to make changes to the context and the culture in which I work, and to extend my work and ideas into the wider community.

LEARNING FROM STUDENTS: RECIPROCAL RELATIONSHIPS

> Where languages and naming are power,
> silence is oppression, is violence.
>
> —Adrienne Rich

> Educators can help [those they teach] to develop authentic voices if they emphasize connection over separation, understanding and acceptance over assessment, and collaboration over debate; if they accord respect to and allow time for the knowledge that emerges from first hand experience, if instead of imposing their own expectations and arbitrary requirements, they encourage students to

evolve their own patterns of work based on the problems they are pursuing. (Belenky et al. 1986, 221)

The creation of communities of inquiry in settings for teacher education requires the establishment of trusting relationships and an environment for honest and authentic inquiry. This requires that traditional power structures, conceptions of knowledge, and attitudes toward the learning process change; that collaboration replace competition; and that empathy and understanding replace judgment. Those who will teach in the schools of tomorrow need to unlearn many of the lessons of received knowing and of individual learning. They need to acquire sophisticated listening and hearing skills, to develop the abilities to understand and value others' ways of knowing, and the capacities to work collaboratively with colleagues to bring about change. If classrooms are to be comfortable learning environments for all learners, prospective teachers need to be able to create settings where individual students feel that what they know is valued, and that they have a contribution to make to the learning community. A respect for multiple kinds of intelligence (Gardner 1983), the values and beliefs of other cultures, and the many ways in which the world can be known and respected, will have to be learned. Many lessons will have to be "unlearned," and as Ursula Le Guin (1989) says: "I am trying to unlearn these lessons, along with the other lessons I was taught by my society, particularly lessons concerning the minds, work, works and being of women. I am a slow unlearner" (151). Prospective teachers need to be good learners, adaptable and flexible, and capable of learning what they need to know. For them and the students they teach, the lessons of yesterday are not always appropriate in a rapidly changing world, where "the central survival skill is surely the capacity to pay attention and respond to changing circumstances, to learn and adapt, to fit into new environments beyond the safety of the temple precincts" (Bateson 1989, 231).

   In authentic communities of inquiry, teacher educators and their students learn with and from each other. Prospective teachers learn to see how real teaching involves tensions and contradictions and how these realities are dealt with in a reflective practitioner's life. They learn that good teaching cannot be prescribed; that it takes place within relationships and that it requires the adaptive responding to constantly changing phenomena; that it is attuned to people, to the concrete and to the particular, and that it is focused on student learning. The art of teaching is filled with deliberating, discussing, and making choices; teacher development takes place when individuals share the complexi-

ties of what they are trying to do and collaborate with each other to resolve difficulties and manage dilemmas. This kind of setting enables
professionals to make music together, to improvise on shared themes,
and create something that no one individual could create alone. It is a
setting where the risks of exposure are high, and where trust, honesty,
empathy, and genuine commitment to one's own inquiry and to those
of others, is an absolute necessity.

Belenky and her colleagues (1986) point out that it was only
through finding their authentic voices, and developing the courage to
use them that the women they studied moved from positions where
they lived according to received knowing, into a place where they constructed their own meanings and took control over their lives. In professional education, prospective teachers need supportive relationships
and a safe place to identify their authentic voices and receive helpful
feedback, advice, and support for the construction of their professional
knowledge. They need opportunities for individual and collective reflection on the details of everyday practice, opportunities to examine
and assess them, and plan future action. Through reflective writing the
process of reflection can be documented, and the writer has the opportunity to reflect again on that which was first reflected upon, and to
track reflections over time. Thoughtful responses and constructive feedback from a teacher educator can enhance the student's learning and be
a source of learning for the teacher educator also. The development of
voice can be supported, as can the capacity to hear other voices, and
that within. Such reciprocal relationships with the students enable
teacher educators to create conditions in which they themselves develop the capacity to hear others' voices, and increase their capacities to
be more responsive and develop their professional knowledge and
practices.

A conceptualization of professional education and development
as the re-forming and transformation of the whole person who is becoming a professional, requires that individuals continually make and
remake the understandings necessary for movement from the limitations of the actual, toward the realization of the possible. This conceptualization necessitates continuous involvement in the process of creation
which itself energizes and creates the desire for continued involvement,
and continued personal and professional growth. In the absence of a
balance between the exploration of internal and external theories, the
strong, powerful voices of external others—theorists, experienced practitioners, and educational reformers—have the potential to drown the
less confident and less developed voices of teacher candidates. Sometimes, the voices of these external others are so loud, so strong, and so

certain that they overwhelm and silence the altogether personal voices of teacher candidates. The resultant condition is one of voicelessness, powerlessness, and lack of confidence in one's ability to teach or bring about change in one's own life or in the lives of others. The sheer complexity, difficulty, and multifaceted process of becoming a teacher makes teacher candidates especially vulnerable to this condition, open to doubting their own knowing and easily overpowered by the knowledge and expertise of others. I am concerned about teacher education programs where this language is used but where the personal, internal voices of teachers are not recognized and the focus is on exposing student teachers to the voices of others with their theories, philosophies, and instructional strategies for teaching embedded in them.

Many of these issues were raised for me in the context of reading and responding to students' writing. One student in particular caused me to reflect on the extent to which I was helping students develop their authentic voices and construct a professional knowledge that was uniquely theirs. When Mary came to the teacher education program we met as teacher and student for the second time, for I had taught Mary twelve years previously when she was a student in one of my grade nine English classes. She wrote extensively about her struggle to become the kind of teacher she wanted to be, and her writing enabled me to support and assist her in her meaning making and to provide private and detailed feedback to her on her questions, dilemmas, and difficulties. The process of doing so caused me to reflect on my professional practice over time, and wonder about my ability to create settings where my strong teacher voice did not overwhelm students' voices. Mary wrote about the difficulty of finding her "teacher-self" in the current situation, and of her past educational experiences in schools and universities, where "it is so hard to hear your own voice when it is being swamped by the loud voices of others." By the end of the teacher education year, Mary was describing her success at linking the person and the musician she had always been, to the teacher she was becoming. Using a musical metaphor, she explained how for the first time she had maintained her authenticity and personal power within a relational and educative setting. Her words are excerpted here with her permission.

> Pachabel's canon in D is one work that will always haunt me and is a framework for my narrative of becoming a teacher. . . . The canon starts with a single lone voice which throughout the composition gets joined and influenced by an increasing number of voices, each with a specific function in propelling the work forward. Although the main voice does change, it is never lost as it re-

mains recognizable as such, the main voice. In the end this main voice stands, stronger than ever. My voice is like this, changed because of what has taken place and those I have been influenced by, but it is my voice and it is now stronger than it was before. (Mary Wells, Unpublished Professional Journal, 1991/1992)

Mary's writing helped me to think about the role of the teacher's voice as one that influences but does not overwhelm, that empowers but does not overpower, and that encourages prospective teachers to author the script for their own lives, future classrooms, and school communities. Her writing reminded me of the importance of nurturing the uniqueness of each prospective teacher's voice, and reinforced my belief in the importance of reflection in preservice teacher education, and of the importance of a trusting learning community to support genuine inquiry.

In the context of my inquiry into my practices as a teacher educator, Mary's words held a special significance for me, creating a powerful bridge between my past and present teaching situations. Her writing raised questions I could examine in the context of two different periods of my teaching life—comparing, contrasting, and juxtaposing one with the other. I remembered Mary as a quiet student who did not say much in my grade nine English class. I had a vivid memory of her as an accomplished flute player in the junior high school band. Mary had seemed much more alive as a member of the school band than as a member of my English class. I had not made this observation at the time, but now with the benefit of hindsight, I thought about how I might have done things differently in that setting. As a prospective teacher, Mary explained that as a junior high school student, she had been a shy, nonvocal member of her classes. For her, music was a form of expression that sustained and satisfied her; the music class was the only place where she felt that she gave voice to her own meanings. For Mary, music was the language through which she had made sense of her world and created meanings, and as her former English teacher, I did not feel content that language and literature had not given her the same frameworks.

She wrote about it this way:

Music has been an integral part of my life for as long as I can remember, a means to express the joys and sorrows I could never find with the use of words. In the land of music, I could create what I felt was right . . . when I was making music I was in control. (Mary Wells, Unpublished Professional Journal, 1991/1992)

Mary's writing raised issues for me about ownership, control, and power within the teaching-learning relationship, and about the powerlessness of those who are not encouraged or allowed to develop and use their voices. Relating these issues to my role as a teacher educator, I wondered to what extent I was currently enabling students to be actively engaged in their own inquiries, to develop confidence in their own knowledge making, and be inspired but not overwhelmed by my teacher's voice. I wondered to what extent I was still controlling students' learning, taking away from them the opportunity to make their own music and be responsible for and in control of their own learning. When Mary wrote, "In the land of music, I could create what I felt was right . . . when I was making music, I was in control," her words were a source of inspiration and encouragement to me to teach others to bring order and harmony to their lives, and teach their students to do likewise. They reminded me that the art of teaching teachers is intimately connected to enabling them to create knowledge and relationships, and classroom settings where students can be in control of their learning, and imagine, create, and express their own meanings.

Mary's voice had a significant influence on my teaching; so too did the voices of other students who expressed negative things about my teaching, and rejected a reflective, inquiry approach to teacher education. Some of these prospective teachers had well-developed belief systems grounded in their experiences, and in an understanding of teaching as the delivery of knowledge from the teacher to the learner. They rejected a classroom setting where it was expected that they should work interdependently with colleagues, engage in collaborative projects, and question their beliefs and understandings. For some students, the reconstructed power relationships between the student and the teacher in a collaborative classroom was not what they expected. For some, professional knowledge was something they expected to have passed on to them, and they expected generic strategies, systems, and formulas that would guarantee success in all classrooms, and with all students. When invited to give feedback on my teaching in year-end assessments, these voices spoke of "reflection and inquiry as irrelevant to becoming a teacher," of expecting to be "given the strategies to become a good teacher," wondering why initial teacher education courses did not involve more of "the recipes for success." One voice in particular stood out, as it appeared (unsigned) on one of these end-of-year assessments of my teaching:

> You could be such a good teacher. You have so much experience and knowledge that you could pass on to us, but you refuse to

give us the strategies to be successful, and to tell us how to teach, even though you know how to do it . . . (Anonymous Student)

The comment struck me forcibly, as does any negative comment, but it so clearly articulated a philosophy of teaching that was in opposition to what I was trying to do—continually modeling and discussing teaching strategies, the appropriateness of a particular strategy for a given situation, and continually drawing students' attention to the analysis of teaching—my own and that of others—that it gave me much food for thought. Universally, teachers speak of the tendency to hear only the negative comments about their teaching and to discount the positive ones when they receive student feedback. In my own experience, I know this to be the case and I am aware of the way in which negative feedback from students brings self-doubt and shakes self-confidence. I am also aware of the necessity to look at negative comments as material for reflection, and to place both positive and negative comments into the larger context of my goals as a teacher educator. As an assistant professor without tenure, I was also aware of the risks involved and well aware of ways to avoid any negative comments on my teaching. Ironically, I knew that the adjustment of my teaching goals and methods to achieve high ratings on the student assessment forms would simultaneously have lessened my workload and anxieties, but it would also have lessened my sense of authenticity and honesty, and sense of self. To opt for higher ratings rather than professional authenticity and integrity, I would have had to opt for certainty, predictability, and the polished presentation of ideas worked out in private, rather than the public exploration and sharing of ideas, of the questioning, risk-taking, tentativeness, and unpredictability of authentic teaching.

Teacher educators need to keep their voices strong and well developed in order to participate fully in their professional lives, as well as modeling this for those they teach. Without strong empowered voices, we cannot engage actively and authentically in conversations with students and others, and in the conscious and critical meta-level thinking that allows us to continually reflect on our understandings, and balance them with those of others in the service of our own professional development. Our professional voices are as unique as our fingerprints; they need to be nurtured, respected, and developed so they can be used in directing our professional growth with creativity and integrity. Using my teaching journal to do this, I continued to express the ways in which I experienced the dilemmas of my practice, and drew from past experience and research, and continuous feedback from students, the strategies and understandings I needed for ongoing situations.

I draw from my teaching journal now an excerpt written in March 1994, that includes an excerpt from a letter I received from a student in February 1994 in response to a request for feedback on my teaching. I had stapled the student letter inside my professional journal as I did many other kinds of feedback. My own journal writing and the feedback from Carol is presented here to show how writing and feedback enabled me to balance the negative and the positive and move forward in a way that was authentic to myself and my values. The first part of the excerpt here comes from my own professional journal (March 1994); the second is from Carol's journal (February 1994).

> I know from past research about the powerlessness, anxiety and dispiritedness experienced by a mature, experienced teacher when the only voices she could hear were those of others; her own voice having been overwhelmed and silenced. I have described this internal condition as a "cacophonous soundscape" and recall how it had the effect of draining the energy, the sense of potential and the capacity to act, in the life of the individual. Now, I am experiencing this same phenomenon, feeling a sense of alienation and a distance from the source of my own knowing, and the attendant feelings of powerlessness, of passivity and of sadness. The inner landscape is bleak and there's no prose, no poetry and no music. The feeling is one of being "unfocussed," "out of sync," "fragmented" and "unfulfilled." I hear blurred arrangements of sounds but there is no distinct pattern emerging. I feel a pressure to find a pattern and a structure that makes sense to me. I'm between two islands and I need to build a bridge between them to stand on. . . .
> . . . . The bridge will be my place, as I will hear the sounds from both sides as I stand there. I need to re-read Carol's letter and to return to it occasionally. I need to remind myself to maintain a balanced perspective, to place both positive and negative feedback into the larger context of my principles and goals. (Professional Journal, March 1994)

> Dear Mary:
> Your little tick marks throughout my writing show that you have taken the time to read the mountains that I have sometimes painstakingly written. I say this because no other professor here or during my undergraduate years ever took the time to get to know my personal self and to help me to understand it as a tool in my learning. Your references and suggestions for further reading

help me to answer many of the questions I sometimes don't get around to asking, or that I am afraid to explore. Your encouragement doesn't go unnoticed and is probably the reason that this writing has never been a chore for me. You're never judgmental and have demonstrated a sincere and genuine interest in my development as an educator. Sometimes I get the feeling that you cry and laugh along with me in my experience of teaching and learning and words cannot express how much this means to me. My philosophy is generally about connections, bonds and relationships between students and teacher. You have definitely set the stage for what I aspire to be in my own teaching. You have treated me as a colleague throughout and for that alone, I'm eternally grateful. (Carol's Professional Journal, February, 1994)

These excerpts show how reciprocal relationships with students, in which honest feedback, both positive and negative, is freely given, can be a source of professional learning and growth. The self-doubt, anxiety, and loss of self-confidence teachers experience in response to negative feedback can be placed in perspective and balanced when it is viewed within the totality of the inquiry. Through the analysis of the writing in the professional journal, I have come to understand that writing and feedback from trusted others can support professional learning and the struggle to make sense of life's experiences, to choose among the possibilities available and construct a future from among them. I have come to understand these reciprocal relationships as frameworks in which teachers and students together enable each other to gain control over their lives.

Within reciprocal relationships and communities of inquiry that are nonhierarchical and collaborative, teacher educators and their students can construct and reconstruct the stories of their lives, hear the voices of their inner consciousness, and balance those voices with those of external others. Here, prospective teachers learn to question, explore, and develop the confidence and competence to transform themselves and the systems to which they belong. When they share the process of doing so with their teacher educators, they allow us to participate in their learning, to learn from and with them, and to engage in the creation of shared values, shared meanings, and shared stories. The value of shared stories, of voice and of relationships, is not underestimated in some cultures. Laurens van der Post (1962), for instance, explains the importance of these for the Kalahari Bushmen he studied:

The story was his most sacred possession. These people knew what we do not: that without a story you have not got a nation, or a culture, or a civilization. Without a story of your own to live you haven't got a life of your own. (9)

CREATING COMMUNITY: LEARNING FROM AND WITH COLLEAGUES

The music of a people, or even a cohesive group, is peculiarly its own. It is a particular musical style that permits a group's life style, its incipient musicality, to express itself in full dance and song. The connection is of course reciprocal: the musical style in turn molds the life style. But it cannot be an altogether alien mold. There is a beautiful paradox in the peculiar intensity with which a person responds to music which is his own. Even if he has not heard it before, it is familiar, as though something is sounding in it that he has always felt in his bones; and yet it is something new. It is his own style revealed to him at an otherwise unimaginable level of clarity.

—S. Crites

For teacher educators to create learning communities in their classrooms and to model collaboration and collegiality in their professional lives, they need to work in communities where these conditions exist for them also, and where the culture and the context enable them to work collaboratively and creatively with their colleagues. Documenting the need to belong to a community that allows me to hear and develop my own voice, to hear voices that influence and inspire me, and that influence and shape the community itself, I wrote about membership in such a community as giving and receiving, as hearing and being heard, and as making music together. Reflectively, the collegial project I initiated, can be described as a community-building project, but when it began, I understood it as a way of "giving back" to the community of which I was a part and of collaborating with a group of trusted colleagues to work for the development of teaching in the university. We called our group "The Faculty Development Group," and we organized a program of seminars and events focused on the development of teaching in higher education, and on providing support for colleagues who wished to develop their teaching and make connections between teaching and research. Our purpose also was to work toward raising the profile and status of teaching in the wider academic community, and create a venue where colleagues could share pedagogical practices, and talk about difficulties and dilemmas in a supportive and collegial environment.

I have documented the work of this group and have written about it elsewhere (Beattie 1996). I excerpt here from this writing to show how the work of the Faculty Development Group enabled me to extend my interests, in teaching, in relational learning, and in the creation of community, into the wider community. I excerpt here from the document I wrote at the outset of the project to explain the purpose of the initiative and to set guidelines for the work and direction of the group. I follow this with a retrospective piece written two years later, when the work of the group could be seen from a new perspective.

The initiative began in 1994, and on behalf of the other group members, I wrote the following to explain our purpose and direction:

> The purpose of our collaborative work will be:
> - To provide institutional support for the new and experienced faculty who wish to develop their teaching;
> - To provide a forum and support system for faculty who are interested in the study of teaching as an academic pursuit in itself (rather than as an activity which is separate from our research);
> - To provide interested faculty with a community of colleagues who are involved in studying their own practice—teacher educators studying their own teaching—and who would be willing to collaborate in joint research projects;
> - To provide faculty with information on events, conferences, publications, etc., which have the improvement of teaching in higher education and research into teaching as their foci.

In 1996, drawing from the documentation of the project kept throughout in a professional journal, the larger dimensions of the initiative and the benefits of collaborative, collegial interactions could be seen. Through the analysis of the documentation, I began to see the familiar patterns and themes that had informed and guided my past experiences—the reciprocal relationships, the search for community, the desire to learn from and with others—as patterns that were also guiding this initiative. The collegial relationships of the Faculty Development Group were providing a framework for individual and shared learning as we worked together toward common interests. Our meetings became occasions for deliberation, discussion, argument, and improvisation, for sharing perspectives and adjusting and adapting our own interests and understandings within the context of the work of the group as a whole. Reflections on the initiative showed me how individuals can learn from and with each other in professional situations, by creating a cohesive group who are responsive to each other, and whose shared music changes the landscape to which they all belong.

> Planning seminars together and discussing the ways in which we could best support our colleagues as they developed their teaching, were occasions for reflection and analysis of how we were doing this in our own lives. Our planning sessions provided new information, new ideas and occasions to interact and to learn from colleagues. Although frustrating and difficult to deal with, the restrictions we experienced with regard to lack of budget, time and resources, also provided us with a framework within which to examine our core values and beliefs and to focus on what was important for us to do, in spite of all obstacles. The situation forced us to be creative with all available resources, to consider the strengths and areas of expertise which we ourselves and our colleagues already possessed, and to be improvisational, adaptive and alert to new possibilities throughout. To do this with a group of trusted, respected colleagues was itself a learning event and a source of ongoing professional development. (Beattie 1996, 176)

EPILOGUE

I began by looking at the ways in which the process of coming to know the self as teacher or as teacher educator is intimately and profoundly connected to developing and using one's own voice, acknowledging and responding to the voices of others and integrating them in the creation of reciprocal relationships, shared values, and community. I have suggested that teacher development and faculty development take place within responsive, reciprocal relationships where individuals learn from and with each other, and that the development of professional knowledge is enhanced when individuals collaborate to extend the sphere in which their voices are heard, and create communities where there is commitment to the transformation of both the self and the community.

Fullan (1993) says, "Personal change is the most powerful route to system change" (140). Currently, the debates surrounding educational reform, the reform of teacher education, and professional reform rarely make links between these fields, and treat them as if they were separate entities. The debates rarely focus on the human dilemmas and realities of professional learning, or on teaching as an art that is centrally concerned with interpersonal matters involving beliefs, values, and matters of the spirit. Rarely are professional learners thought of, in Heaney's (1995) words, as "hunters and gatherers of values" (29). Rarely is educational reform conceptualized as a process where individuals re-form and transform their own understandings, and collaborate with others in ways that are transformative for all those involved, and which result in positive changes to the communities and societies to which they belong. The kind of reform I have outlined here begins with individuals and with one's own practice. It calls for continual adaptation, flexibility, and improvisation in circumstances and situations that are continually changing. I hope this self-study will resonate in the lives of other professionals, that it will enable them to gain insights into their own professional lives, to collaborate with students, colleagues and others to achieve a shared vision and find new words for old songs.

3 *Enhancing First-Time Teaching at the Postsecondary Level*

A Story of Collaborative Mentorship

Katie Flockhart and Vera E. Woloshyn

The concept of mentoring is an ancient one dating back to early Greek civilization. In Homer's *Odyssey*, Odysseus appointed Mentor to guide, protect, and educate his son during his absence. Although there is no single definition of a mentor, it is generally agreed that mentors are persons with relevant experience who are willing to share their knowledge and model their skills. Furthermore, effective mentors provide their protégés with emotional and moral encouragement (Gaffney 1995; Luna and Cullen 1995).

The ultimate goal of mentorships is to empower and develop protégés so that they become self-reliant and accountable in defined environments (Luna and Cullen 1995). Ideally, the process of mentoring provides opportunities for protégés to gain understandings of organizational structure, practices, attitudes, and values, as well as access to formal and informal networks of communication (Luna and Cullen 1995; Valadez and Duran 1991). Mentors, in turn, typically benefit from the intellectual stimulation and sense of personal satisfaction associated with assisting protégés (Luna and Cullen 1995).

According to Kram (1985), mentoring is structured around career and psychological functions. Career functions occur when mentors sponsor, coach, protect, and challenge protégés so that they acquire knowledge and gain status within the organization. Mentorships based on career functions are businesslike and serve to facilitate both mentors' and protégés' career goals. Psychological functions occur when the mentors model, counsel, affirm, accept, and interact with protégés—functions that in turn facilitate trust and rapport. Mentors who provide both career and psychological functions are perceived to be caring, unselfish, and altruistic.

Today, mentoring programs are used extensively in business and industry to help attract, retain, and promote junior employees (Luna and Cullen 1995). Wilbur (1987) found mentoring to be a significant predictor of career success. Individuals who have been mentored usually earn more money, are better educated, are more likely to follow career plans, and experience greater work satisfaction than their unmentored peers (Roche 1979; Short and Seeger 1981).

Mentoring programs have also been used extensively in primary and secondary school education. For instance, teacher candidates are required to complete practica under the supervision of experienced teachers in most preservice programs (Cole and Watson 1991). There is also a growing trend for experienced teachers to mentor beginning ones (Cole and Watson 1991; Strobe and Cooper 1988), with both reporting increased reflection on their teaching styles and refinement of their teaching strategies as a function of this mentorship (Krupp 1987; Warring 1991).

Mentoring programs at the postsecondary level tend to be more elusive; they can either be formal or informal, long-term or short-term, planned or spontaneous (Luna and Cullen 1995). Long and McGinnis (1985) concluded that graduate students who formed positive relationships with their mentors tended to secure academic positions. Queralt (1982) concluded that faculty who had mentors while in graduate school were more likely to publish, receive competitive grants, accept leadership roles in professional organizations, and experience greater career satisfaction than faculty without mentors. Having a mentor may be especially beneficial for female faculty. Research indicates that women with one or more mentors report greater job success and satisfaction than those without mentors (Dreher and Ash 1990; Riley and Wrench 1985).

Unfortunately, many females are unconcerned about finding a mentor, believing that hard work, perseverance, and skill alone determine career success (Hollingsworth 1992; Ragins 1989). Such beliefs may be especially limiting in academe where new professors are required to balance teaching, publishing, and committee responsibilities. New faculty often report feeling overwhelmed, inadequate, isolated, and unsupported (Boice 1991). Most relevant to this study, new faculty have limited access to role models when teaching and tend to rely upon student memories of effective instructors.

Female faculty tend to experience greater social and intellectual isolation (Clark and Corcoran 1986) than their male counterparts and are more likely to leave before applying for tenure (Rausch, Ortiz, Douthitt, and Reed 1989). Thus, having a mentor who can help overcome these barriers may be especially important for women who select academic careers (Adams 1993; Maack and Passet 1994). Similarly, it may be particularly important that females are mentored by other women who share similar professional and family experiences (Luna and Cullen 1995).

We are two women educators. Katie is an experienced former junior-intermediate teacher, who is in the advanced stage of completing a doctoral program. Katie intends to pursue an academic career in education. Vera is an associate professor in a faculty of education. In this chapter, we describe our experiences as postsecondary instructors in the context of what we have come to call a "collaborative mentorship." We identify the benefits associated with this mentorship and provide insights about the factors that were critical for its success.

OUR RESEARCH

We first met when Katie enrolled in a research course taught by Vera. The course was a requirement in the masters program in which Katie was enrolled. We subsequently discovered we shared many academic interests and personal experiences. For instance, we were both interested in teaching adult learners and in developing teaching methodologies that would enhance the learning process. We also discovered that we lived in the same community and had children of similar ages.

After graduating, Katie enrolled in a doctoral program at another institution. Throughout the course of her studies, we maintained contact socially. Vera enjoyed hearing about Katie's graduate experiences, and Katie was interested in Vera's life as an academic. A few years later, a sudden increase in student enrollment required that Vera's research course be divided into two sections. She recommended that Katie be invited to teach the additional one, because she was aware of Katie's academic aspirations and believed she would be a competent instructor. Katie agreed to accept this challenge with the provision that Vera be available as a resource person.

Throughout the duration of the course, we carried out several in-depth phenomenological interviews (Hollingsworth 1992; Merriam 1988; Seidman 1991; van Manen 1991). Specifically, we explored each other's teaching practices, beliefs about effective instruction, and experiences within the mentorship. We agreed with Seidman (1991) that the interviewing process should begin by establishing the context of each participant's experiences, progress by clarifying details, and close by reflecting on their meaning. Each interview lasted approximately one hour, and was audiotaped and transcribed for subsequent analysis.

Analysis consisted of coding and categorizing data as described by Bogdan and Biklen (1992), Strauss and Corbin (1990), and Kirby and McKenna (1989). We independently reviewed the transcripts for themes, and then met to present our interpretations and arrive at a shared understanding. Through this latter process, we attempted to ensure negotiation and reciprocity with respect to data analysis (Cole and Knowles 1993; Hunt 1992). From this final analysis, several themes emerged including: (1) teaching as a rewarding and reaffirming practice, (2) shaping personal pedagogical beliefs based on prior academic experiences, and (3) developing a mentorship founded on the principles of collaboration. We address the first two themes from the perspective of each participant, and the third from a combined one.

TEACHING AS A REWARDING AND REAFFIRMING PRACTICE: KATIE

For Katie, teaching the research course under the guidance of a mentor provided an opportunity to enhance her knowledge of research methods as well as her curriculum vitae. She was especially excited about teaching in the department from which she graduated and where she hoped to return as a professor.

> I treasured my years as a graduate student in this department. While the courses and research were challenging, they were also fun. Now I have the chance to teach here and I am very excited. I

have worked towards this for a long time and I hope that teaching this course will lead to other teaching opportunities.

Refreshingly, Katie's experiences were not typical of those of many new instructors. Specifically, Katie found the teaching experience to be positive and exciting. "I love teaching this course! It's motivating, challenging, and highly rewarding." She expressed confidence in her ability to teach course content, communicate effectively, and be available for students.

> I believe that I am a good teacher. The responses that I have received from the graduate students in this course have been positive. I remember introducing myself on the first night. I told them that I was completing a doctoral degree. I told them about my research interests, my family and what I hoped we might accomplish during our time together. I also told them that they could contact me either before or after class. I even gave them my home telephone number.

Katie believed that she had sufficient time both to prepare for her course and to meet her family obligations. She also acknowledged that she received recognition from her students as an instructor.

> I think that respect comes from the rapport that instructors establish with their students, the interest they take in them as individuals, their availability, as well as the effective preparation of lessons and the provision of prompt and constructive feedback. I really believe that my students respected me as their instructor.

Unlike many women in academia, Katie did not experience the "imposter syndrome" (Brookfield 1992). That is, she was not plagued with feelings of doubt or uncertainty about her position at the university. Rather, being mentored while instructing the course reaffirmed her passion for teaching, her caring for students, and her regard for herself as an effective educator. Like many females (Hollingsworth 1992; Ragins 1989), Katie attributed her positive experience as a new instructor to "hard work." She spent many hours preparing and rehearsing for class and willingly accepted her dual positions as "instructor" and "learner."

> I spent three days a week preparing for each class . . . reading and rereading my notes, practicing them and phoning you for answers

to my questions. As an instructor, I needed to be ten steps ahead of my students. But first, I needed to be a learner. I needed to see and experience what you had done so many times. Next time, I will be more independent.

According to Murray (1991), the ideal protégé is one who is willing to assume responsibility for his or her own growth and who is receptive to constructive feedback and coaching. Consistent with these behaviors, Katie sought greater challenges and responsibilities throughout the course.

Katie also attributed her positive teaching experiences to the rapport she established with her students. Katie believed she could readily relate to their academic concerns and struggles as she too was completing a graduate program. "They sensed that I was not removed from graduate research and that it was still close to me." Her dual roles of learner and instructor may have rendered her as especially "approachable"—a perception that Katie wanted to reinforce. She adamantly believed that "an effective teacher is an available one who cares deeply for his or her students. It's all about being committed and having a real passion for what you're doing."

Finally, Katie attributed her positive teaching experience to Vera's availability and "experienced knowledge" (Hunt 1992). Katie's confidence was enhanced knowing that Vera had used the course materials before and that she was readily available for assistance. Vera provided Katie with ongoing encouragement, empathy, and support. In such a caring and supportive mentoring environment, Katie was "empowered" and flourished as an instructor (Luna and Cullen 1995).

> I could call you any time to ask you questions when I was uncertain about the course. Going through everything with you before a class was a great asset. It was important to talk about what we were going to teach and how we were going to teach it. These discussions made me aware of potential pitfalls and helped me overcome any hesitations or obstacles. Debriefing after the class was also great as it encouraged reflection and allowed us to plan for the next one.

> I remember the first night of the course. As I stood up to begin the lesson, you told me to "break a leg." Those few words gave me a real jumpstart. The butterflies in my stomach were quickly replaced by overwhelming self-confidence, enthusiasm and a strong desire to succeed.

TEACHING AS A REWARDING AND REAFFIRMING PRACTICE: VERA

Like Katie, Vera also perceived this mentoring experience as an enjoyable and rewarding one. In some ways, mentoring Katie was a natural extension of teaching the course. Working with Katie provided a unique opportunity for Vera to review course materials. Specifically, Katie's questions and concerns required Vera to conceptualize and discuss course content at a higher level than she was accustomed to with her students. These discussions often challenged and deepened her understanding of the curriculum, while alerting her to potential areas of difficulty for students. Vera was very much reminded of the cliché, "The best way to learn something is to teach it."

Working with Katie also provided Vera with an opportunity to share her pedagogical knowledge of adult education. Although Katie was an experienced elementary school teacher, she had not instructed adult learners. Effective teaching methodologies for mature learners often differ from those used with children, or even undergraduate students (Cranton 1989). Thus, Vera spent considerable time sharing teaching methods she believed were effective for facilitating adults' learning.

Consistent with the reported experiences of primary and secondary school teachers (Warring 1991), mentoring required Vera to be reflective of her own instructional practices. An unexpected and pleasant outcome of this reflection was the development of new teaching approaches.

> Each time you asked a question about either the content of the course or my teaching approach, it made me stop and think about the ultimate purpose of the activity and whether there was a better way to achieve it. It was great to hear your ideas and develop new materials based on both our perspectives.

Vera also found Katie's excitement and enthusiasm for teaching "contagious." Because she worked so closely with Katie in the planning of the course lessons, Katie's positive teaching experiences became an extension of her own.

> I have always enjoyed teaching this course. I feel very strongly about the importance of research and it's great to get students started on the research process, especially when so many of them believe that they "cannot do" research. However, working with you was exceptionally rewarding! Every time you believed that

you had completed a lesson successfully, it was like I had taught the class. I was being reinforced twice: once from my students and another time from you.

Hence, the mentoring experience reaffirmed Vera's commitments to her own students and to the provision of high-quality instruction. The process of mentoring "exhilarated" Vera and provided her with a greater awareness of both her profession and her role within it (Luna and Cullen 1995).

SHAPING PEDAGOGICAL BELIEFS BASED ON PRIOR ACADEMIC EXPERIENCES: KATIE

Fundamental to Katie's beliefs about effective teaching were the concepts of availability and caring. Specifically, Katie believed that a critical component of exemplary teaching was committing time apart from class to meet with students and listen to their questions and concerns. "Building positive relationships with those whom I teach is a primary goal; relevant and meaningful content comes next." More importantly, Katie believed that successful instructors present themselves as open-minded, nonjudgmental, and genuinely concerned about their students' well-being. In other words, these instructors practice the art of "invitational education" (Novak 1992).

Regretfully, Katie recalled having undergraduate instructors that seemed anything but "inviting." These instructors appeared to have little time to meet with students, and one, in particular, did not support her decision to seek a career in education. "I didn't feel a lot of warmth. I wasn't comfortable there and I wasn't motivated. . . ."

More positively, Katie recalled her graduate years as ones in which she was able to develop positive relationships with some of her instructors. Katie perceived these instructors to be genuinely interested in her as a person and as a scholar. Not only did these relationships reinforce Katie's basic beliefs about the qualities of effective educators, they also encouraged and sustained her confidence to continue graduate studies and seek an academic career.

I've had all the comfort and all the support that I could ask for with every graduate instructor. My thesis advisor encouraged me to start the doctoral program. Shortly after, I was invited back to the university as a guest speaker. It was then that I decided to pursue a career as an academic.

The positive qualities Katie attributed to her graduate instructors are consistent with those of effective mentors (Warring 1991; Welch 1996). It is likely that Katie benefited from the guidance and support of more than one mentor—a factor that has been positively associated with achieving career aspirations (Rozenholtz 1989b).

Katie reflected that both her positive and negative experiences were instrumental in her decisions about how to interact with students. Indeed, Katie expressed a desire to become a mentor to other students. Such aspirations underscore the power and the cyclical nature of mentoring (Luna and Cullen 1995). In this manner, mentoring programs may promote "cycles of goodness" within academia (Swartz 1996).

> I think you need to learn from the negative experiences too. . . . I'm trying to keep all my experiences in mind when I am teaching now. . . . I had a good teaching environment in graduate school and I want to extend that or provide the same to my own students.

SHAPING PEDAGOGICAL BELIEFS BASED ON PRIOR ACADEMIC EXPERIENCES: VERA

Vera also developed positive relationships with many of her instructors while in graduate school and acknowledged that they were instrumental in her decision to become a professor. When Vera accepted an academic position, she was committed to providing her students with a positive learning experience. "I loved my years in graduate school. . . . My instructors, especially my thesis advisor, ensured that I was well prepared for a research-oriented career in academe. I will always remember—how important my advisor's support was in graduate school. It was this support that made me later want to provide the same quality of support to my own students."

Vera's graduate training was in a discipline and department that, in many ways, differed from the one in which she accepted a position. Most relevant to this study, Vera had no experience teaching adult learners. This led to unexpected teaching difficulties.

> The transition from graduate student to faculty was not an easy one. I was unaware of the needs of many adult learners and tended to use a traditional, teacher-directed method of instruction. I failed to take their prior experiences into consideration and I was genuinely surprised and devastated when they expressed concerns about my course. I questioned my abilities as an instructor.

Fortunately, Vera was able to resolve these issues by experimenting with different teaching methodologies, consulting with her students, and confiding in trusted colleagues. Seeking advice and support from colleagues can be described as an informal format of peer mentorship. Harnish and Wilds (1993) concluded that peer mentors can improve teaching for inexperienced faculty and abate feelings of isolation and incompetence. Vera perceived her subsequent teaching experiences more positively.

> In retrospect, first-time teaching was an incredible learning experience. It forced me to get to know my students, respect their needs and familiarize myself with their learning styles. More importantly, I discovered that I had a tremendous respect for these individuals, that I admired their decisions to continue in their professional development and that I had a lot to learn from them.

Collectively, these experiences contributed to Vera's desire to facilitate others' first-time teaching experiences at the postsecondary level. Human developmental theorists such as Erikson (1963) and Levinson (1977) contend that mentoring can be a critical component of a healthy life cycle. By being mentored, and in turn mentoring, individuals can fully develop and value the concept of "care" (Luna and Cullen 1995).

> Working with you provided me with an opportunity to give back. It was important for me to guide another person's initial teaching experiences at the postsecondary level and to share with him or her all that I had come to learn about teaching. In many ways, I am just giving back to a system that gave to me.

DEVELOPING A MENTORSHIP FOUNDED UPON THE PRINCIPLES OF COLLABORATION: KATIE AND VERA

According to Elliott and Woloshyn (1997), collaborative projects require rapport and respect among partners, compatible goals, negotiation of tasks, and a commitment to both the project and the partners. Similarly, effective mentorships require mentors and protégés to be willing, open-minded, encouraging, respectful, and committed to each other (Bower 1991; Nagel, Driscoll, and Grimala 1991). Thus, we came to regard our experience as a "collaborative mentorship."

Because we knew each other through previous experiences at the university and within the community, we had some familiarity and trust for one another before entering this teaching mentorship. Through the process of teaching the course, however, we were pleasantly surprised at the extent to which this rapport was further developed and strengthened. Establishing rapport may be especially important for women who are often socialized toward developing caring perspectives in their relationships (Gilligan 1982; Gilligan, Ward, and Taylor 1988). As we came to know one another better, we were able to trust each other completely with our personal and professional thoughts and struggles. The connection between us became truly powerful.

From our previous discussions, we knew we shared professional interests (facilitating student learning) and career aspirations (being productive faculty members at a postsecondary institute). Furthermore, we realized that our participation in this mentorship would facilitate the probability of attaining these outcomes. Elliott and Woloshyn (1997) concluded that in effective collaborative ventures partners usually hold either identical or mutually compatible goals. Explicitly developing and stating mutual aims and objectives is also associated with effective mentoring (Luna and Cullen 1995).

Throughout this mentoring process, we also benefited from each other's unique areas of expertise, and negotiated tasks based on them. For example, Katie relied on Vera's working knowledge of course materials, and trusted her insights about how best to present this information to adult learners. "It was nice to know that her materials were organized and helpful to the students. I knew this because of the positive response the students continually gave her." Vera, in turn, benefited from Katie's application of alternative teaching methodologies, approaches to establishing and building rapport with students, and her overall enthusiasm for teaching.

> I was extremely interested in your reactions to the course and to the lesson formats that I had used in the past. I was also very interested in your relationship with students—how you interacted with them, how you responded to their questions and concerns, and how you combined your teaching responsibilities with your family life.

Katie used the term *balanced* when reflecting upon the teaching mentorship. Balance, or what otherwise can be referred to as reciprocity, is a critical element for effective mentoring and the empowerment of protégés (Luna and Cullen 1995). According to Gray (1989), protégés usually rely on their mentors for advice and solutions when confronted with challenges during the initial stages of a mentorship. As protégés become more skilled and experienced, effective mentors adopt a "back seat" approach and restrict their input. This process requires that mentors respect and trust their protégés' abilities and decisions.

Finally, we remained dedicated to our students and to the mentoring relationship throughout the course. Each person's commitment to teaching was a source of inspiration to the other. "It was wonderful watching each other. It provided us with the opportunity to integrate some of the other person's teaching techniques into our own practices." In addition, each person willingly contributed to the planning of the course, as well as to the other's success in teaching it. "We did everything in consultation, from creating the course outline to assigning final grades. We made it a priority to fulfill our individual responsibilities as they affected both of us." Consistent with the findings of Elliott and Woloshyn (1997), respect and caring for each other appeared to motivate us to fulfill our commitments to the course, the mentorship, and each other.

> It is like exercising with a partner. There are days you just don't want to do it. . . . But if someone is counting on you, you go. . . . Best of all, you have a wonderful time and are thankful that you went.

FINAL REFLECTIONS

Katie's positive teaching experience represents a sharp contrast to those of most new professors (Boice 1991) and can be attributed partially to her participation in this collaborative mentorship. We have come to realize that the timing of the mentorship with respect to our careers may have been especially critical to its success. Specifically, Katie's flexibility as an "all-but-dissertation" doctoral student, and Vera's security as a tenured professor allowed us to focus considerable time on this endeavor.

While analyzing the transcripts that described our teaching experiences, we realized that we were reliving the mentoring process during the writing of this chapter. Vera modeled the writing process, which facilitated Katie's role as an author. Collectively, these teaching and writing experiences have inspired us to continue in our collaborative relationship and seek out new ones.

Furthermore, we, like others (Luna and Cullen 1995), acknowledge that our rapport and commitment to each other made the collaborative nature of this mentorship possible. However, we realize that these relational qualities cannot be mandated or delegated. Rather, both prospective mentors and protégés must assume active roles in seeking mentoring relationships that will satisfy, sustain, and fulfill them. In order to facilitate mentoring programs, faculty may need to adopt more open and collegial approaches with respect to both their teaching and research practices. This does not imply, however, that institutions do not have a role in the delivery of mentoring programs. Rather, academic administrators need to recognize and support (physically, monetarily, and emotionally) mentoring as a valid occupational function.

Many people believe that the cliché "sink or swim" accurately describes most graduate programs. We contend that collaborative mentorships between graduate students and faculty can positively change this perception. Indeed, such mentorships may be instrumental in facilitating a sense of community within postsecondary institutions. Community building may be especially beneficial within faculties of education where the majority of graduates either seek or return to practice "in the field." We contend that graduates who participate in collaborative mentorships will be more likely to sustain positive relationships with faculty and encourage their colleagues to pursue advanced studies than graduates who participate in more traditional learning formats. Finally, although we acknowledge that collaborative mentorships are not a panacea, we believe they can serve as an effective vehicle for professional development—a concept that is consistent with the educational objective of life-long learning.

Note

This research was supported by a grant to the second author from the Social Sciences and Research Council of Canada. The authors are indebted to all those, especially their students, who made this research possible. The authors would like to thank Ann Hollingshead for her technical assistance.

Part II

FOCUS ON PARADIGMS

In Part Two our exploration of individuals building community continues as contributors use different paradigmatic lenses in order to describe the process, tell their stories, and step back from them to reflect.
Chapter 4 presents a dynamic view of the concept of community in the
posttraditional era, as Lorraine Ling and her colleagues suggest that in
the future each of us will belong to multiple communities that are
unique in their diversity. Teacher educators, therefore, will need to find
new metaphors in order to describe the practices of community in education.

   At their institution, Hans Smits and David Friesen became members of a community of practice when they taught two sections of a preservice course in teacher education. Using a hermeneutic lens, they
reflect upon their collaboration, and explore the question of teacher educator identity (chapter 5).

   The Centre for Teacher Development at the Ontario Institute for
Studies in Education, University of Toronto, has been a gathering place
for narrativists working with Michael Connelly for over a decade.
Chapter 6 describes the lived experience of five students at various
stages in their doctoral work. Here Florence Samson and her colleagues

explore the reciprocal relationship between narrative inquiry and community.

Part Two closes with a postmodern interpretation of community
building in teacher education through arts-based inquiry. The authors
of chapter 7, Carol Mullen and Patrick Diamond, encourage readers to
become "educational artists" as they ponder some of the ideas therein.

4 *The Posttraditional Community*

A New Concept for a New Era

Lorraine M. Ling, Eva Burman, and Maxine Cooper

We human beings have a great need for one another. However, at the end of the 20th century this instinct to be together is materialising as a growing fragmentation and separation. . . . We are using the instinct of community to separate and protect us from one another, rather than creating a global culture of diverse, yet interwoven communities.
—Wheatley and Kellner-Rogers

Our opening citation captures some of the sense of fragmentation, discontinuity, and disempowerment that is facing groups and individuals as we enter a new globalized millennium. We perceive a rise of new social movements and social discourses, and a decentering of the human subject, linked with a stretching of time and space. In the posttraditional era some sense of community is perhaps more necessary than in previous eras but it will not be a sense of belonging to a community, so much as a sense of belonging to multiple communities.

A posttraditional community is marked by contradictions and disjunctions and by constant and dynamic change and renewal. Members are required to live at one and the same time as members of a local and global community; there is a fragmentation at the same time there is globalization; there are multiple discourses and meanings abounding in the posttraditional community; there is a need for a sense of enclosure at the same time as there is a drive to open out to the wider social world. The posttraditional community is about dealing with uncertainties and unremitting change that is constantly causing traditional boundaries between people and places to be blurred and broken.

In posttraditional society, citizens are required to be at one and the same time part of a local and global community, and it is demanded of them that they function effectively in both simultaneously. To be able to do so demands a range of skills, knowledge, values, and attitudes that need to be taught, practiced, reflected upon, and internalized. In this chapter, the new sense of community demanded in the current era and into the new millennium is explored through two case studies. Posttraditional and critical perspectives are employed as a means to interpret the current era and the concept of community inherent in it.

There are many nuances attached to the concept of community. In most commonly used definitions of community there is a sense of coherence, a sense of group, and a concept of belonging through a commonality of interest and identity. In a posttraditional community, both groups within it and the community as a whole will be volatile. In a posttraditional era, communities can be seen as existing within multiple domains—global, macro, meso, and micro. Individuals can be simultaneously members of multiple communities in and across multiple domains.

In a posttraditional society there are multiple identities, multiple social, political, and economic groups, multiple interests, and a diversity of definitions as to what it means to belong. In such a context, a sense of enclosure is lost and human beings, grieving for the enclosure that gives them identity and security, search for new enclosures and groups to join. In Australia, for instance, exclusive social and political movements have developed during the past two years, capturing the imagination and loyalty of many. Pauline Hanson's One Nation Party, which based its philosophy on narrow, racist perspectives of culture, provides one example of such a movement.

Within the Australian educational context as we begin the new millennium, explicit efforts are being made to recreate a sense of community, citizenship, and civic pride. In 1994, an Australian report entitled *Whereas the People: Civics and Citizenship Education,* was produced by the Civics Expert Group, and was commissioned by the Commonwealth Government.

This report highlighted the need for Australians to gain a better understanding of government, constitutional citizenship, and civic matters. The report emphasized the need for education to play a major part in educating and informing the Australian public so that they may also better understand their rights and responsibilities as citizens.

> There are many reasons for the decline of civics as a component of teacher education. We believe that universities should review their pre-service teacher education program in the light of our report. If civics education expands in the schools, as it surely must, then employing authorities are likely to recruit teachers whose courses have included substantial components in civics and citizenship education. (76)

Many of the professional development or inservice programs currently being designed for teachers and principals within the school system, have as their main focus civics and citizenship education. This drive to privilege civics and citizenship education may be seen in the current context as an attempt to reestablish a strong sense of community and thus to strengthen the Australian national identity.

It is difficult within the context of economic rationalism not to perceive this new drive toward community in a somewhat cynical light. It is assumed that the stronger the national identity, the stronger the loyalty of citizens toward the nation and, therefore, the stronger the drive to work and produce more with less. In an era where market forces dominate world trade as well as local trade, it is essential to gain a market edge, be competitive, and produce a multiskilled, highly competent work force. With these demands at the forefront of the movement toward the new millennium, a sense of community and belonging becomes an important platform in the political, economic, and social policy agenda.

The concept of community does not necessarily give rise to attitudes of togetherness and negotiation. On the contrary, it can provide an arena for the playing out of struggles and tensions and for the micropolitical activities of society and organizations to be carried on. Thus, a community can also be seen as a container for micropolitical activity. In communities, as in all social organizations, there is likely to be an ongoing tension between individual goals and motivations, and group goals and motivations. In organizational theory, it is traditionally held that the greater the fit between individual and group goals the more successful the organization will be in achieving the results it seeks. Within any organization, as within any community, there are multiple meanings that are brought to bear on any given situation, and it has been traditionally perceived that it is not until a negotiation

process occurs as a means to establish common meanings within a
group, that a group can function as such. This negotiation process concerns elements such as values, norms, attitudes, myths, legends, metaphors, rituals, artifacts, and all of those other threads that weave
together to form a culture. Within a community, however, there will be
a plethora of multiple, contesting, and competing agendas, and it could
be held that this diversity is essential to adaptation in a dynamic environment.

In order to explore the concept of a posttraditional community in
terms of the consequences it has for education in particular, we will
apply some of the ideas so far raised to the context of classrooms and
teacher education through two case studies. In seeking to prepare learners to be simultaneously citizens of a global and a local community, educators are faced with a dilemma. This dilemma centers around the fact
that the means to create a sense of community at a local or micro level
focuses upon exclusivity of purpose, enclosure, and exclusion, and thus
is opposite to the means by which a sense of global community will be
fostered. A sense of global community relies upon inclusiveness, per-
meable boundaries, movable enclosures, and a broad definition of belonging. It is necessary for educators to consider how to address the
notion of multiple community participation and to acknowledge and
confront the tensions this concept embodies. The following section of
this chapter recasts traditional educational concepts and practices in
posttraditional forms while being constantly aware of the tensions of
living and functioning in multiple community domains. A case study of
a multicultural classroom follows here as a means to gain some insights
into a posttraditional classroom community.

CELEBRATING DIVERSITY—A CASE STUDY

The following discussion is informed by data from an ethnographic
study carried out in one primary school classroom in Melbourne,
Australia. An exploration is made here based on the question, "In what
ways can a classroom in the present era prepare students and teacher
education students for living and learning in a posttraditional society?"
Students, teacher education students, and teachers have multiple interests, contesting and competing agendas, and a diversity of definitions
of what it means to belong to the classroom community. By looking at
some elements of one classroom in a school attempting community
building in a situation of diversity, we may gain a sense of the way these
students, teachers, and a teacher education student are moving toward

some of the possibilities and exploring some of the contradictions of a posttraditional educational community. Furman (1998) attempts to unravel the paradox of postmodernism and community in schools, suggesting that, "in particular, research is needed in specific settings in which community building is being attempted in the midst of diversity" (323).

The data drawn on for this discussion were part of an ethnographic study that focused on one classroom over a school year. The data were collected by weekly classroom observations by the researcher, informal discussions with two classroom teachers, a specialist, a substitute, and a student teacher, and were supplemented by interviews with the classroom teachers, journal extracts, and written comments from the student teacher.

The classroom chosen as the site of this study was a composite Grade 3/4 in a primary school located in a densely populated and culturally diverse inner city area of Melbourne, Australia. The children in this class were between eight and ten years of age and were representative of eight different ethnic backgrounds—Anglo-Australian, Hmong, Turkish, Macedonian, Chinese, Japanese, Vietnamese, and Somalian. The two cooperating classroom teachers were Mike, from an Anglo-Australian background, and Athena, a teacher with an Australian Greek background. Kyoko, a student teacher with a Japanese cultural background, was attempting to develop a sense of common understanding with the diverse backgrounds of the students in the classroom setting. She was also aware of some of the alienating aspects of being "other." Kyoko was trying to facilitate communication, a sense of trust and caring for others, and enhancing personal and agreed meaning as part of her rapport building and teaching role in the classroom. Aspects of both local and global community building were part of this ongoing dynamic.

One of the paradoxes of community, it appears, is the "need to recognize difference and otherness while finding a purpose or meaning for bringing people together" (Shields and Seltzer 1997, 429). In addressing this need, Shields and Seltzer call for "a notion of unity within, and not from, diversity" (435).

In the analysis of fieldnotes collected during the research study, student responses to the question, "What can we do to make our classroom a happy place?," commented on aspects such as "listen to others," "respect other people and their work," "consider other peoples' feelings," and "help others."

The teacher was engaging in dialogue with the class about "appropriate" ways of behaving in the classroom and building on previous discussion with the students about ways of having a "happy" class-room. The word *others* was used frequently by the students. Many children contributed to the discussion and none of them disputed the contributions made by one another although the teacher used his position to rework some of the ideas and to request students to try and phrase them in positive, rather than negative ways. Nevertheless, the students' knowledge, values, and attitudes were taken into account in the phrases the teacher wrote on the board.

In terms of feelings of belonging, trust, and safety, the classroom teachers attempted to take reasonable account of these elements throughout the year. Furman (1998) argues cautiously, but optimistically, that a concept of community that would fit the current era, would mean that

> a different type of belonging, trust and safety needs to be developed—belonging based on a sense of guaranteed inclusion in spite of difference, trust in the consistent adherence to the ethic of acceptance of otherness and in the consistent application of processes that promote inclusion, all of which create a safe environment. (313)

Mike, as well as Athena and Kyoko, is continually working on the acceptance of otherness and reflecting constantly on his teaching approaches and the classroom processes of inclusion. Mike focuses on involvement in the decision-making process regarding the rules of acceptable behavior in the classroom. The students indicate an understanding that they share agreed-upon ideas about common practices, and indicate that they trust that the classroom teachers and the other students will abide by these. The students have acknowledged their collective relationship and their responsibilities to one another. There is a sense they are to be valued for being themselves and that they have a "longing to belong" (Noddings 1996, 248), to share in something larger than their own small friendship affiliations, and to contribute to the community within the classroom. There are hints though of "the dark side of community" (Noddings 1996, 258), in the exclusion of a few girls by some boys, based on particular constructions of femininity. Exclusion of one boy with a learning disability and another with poor social relationship skills was also observed. These concerns, though, were being worked through by the classroom teachers. The sense of shared agency, of support for the vulnerable, of caring for others and a willingness to respond supportively to others' legitimate needs is the most obvious emphasis in this classroom throughout the year.

As well as the processes that teachers use to establish agreed-upon understandings of acceptable behaviors, there are also the structures and processes of establishing and maintaining working/learning groups and interpersonal relationships within the classroom. It is important also to consider these in the light of the idea of posttraditional community. Furman (1998) suggests that one particular challenge for schools in the current era is to ensure that school and classroom structures and processes promote a sense of community:

> The experience of these feelings is clearly related to the ethics for postmodern community—acceptance of otherness and cooperation within difference. Belonging and safety are promoted through inclusion in the deliberative discourses of the community and through the guarantee of acceptance despite differences. Trust develops from the consistent adherence to these ethics and deliberative process. (321)

Mike appeared to use various ways to build a community in the classroom, through utilizing both structured and random social groups and encouraging a variety of social relations, small group building, cooperative group work, actual lessons in cooperation, sometimes forming pairs of similar ability, at other times forming pairs of complementary ability, and at other times forming pairs of contrasting abilities.

In his interview Mike used the metaphor of "shuffling" the class to form "random" working groups. Mike purposely "shuffled" the students to make sure classroom working groups crossed friendship groups, gender, ethnicity, class, ability and disability, religion, ways of learning, ways of being, and any other possible divisions or boundaries that he discerned in the class.

Mike explained his approach to diversity by using the metaphor, "a full class shuffle."

> What you try to do is you try not to let them become little social and cultural groups in the classroom which will happen if you let it happen. . . . All the children who have come from a background where education has been really valued and they've had a lot of grounding . . . before they come to school. . . . They will all come together. I think you have to make sure that you break down those barriers a little bit and that you treat everyone as an equal. . . . So I think you have to intervene there and that's why you have a seating arrangement that is flexible and changes often, that encour-

ages children to work with different children and to talk to different children at their tables. (Mike, Interview 3/7/98)

The main working groups in the classroom were reorganized every six weeks or so and this came to be expected by the children and was deemed a normal part of the classroom processes. Each child drew a number from a box and was then assigned to a seat at a table on the basis of the number drawn.

Mike's emphasis on inclusion of all "without fear of derision" is important as it shows how the teacher encourages students to try out new ways, to question old procedures, to take a chance, to take a risk without feeling concerned about being derided or made fun of. It is important to consider the issue of risk and trust together. Hargreaves (1994) states, "Risk is something to be embraced not avoided. Risk taking fosters learning, adaptability and improvement" (254). Along with this is the "challenge of building confidence and connectedness" (254) among students and teachers. The particular construction of the culture of the classroom studied appears to be designed to strengthen these elements. Mike, Athena, and Kyoko all take risks while at the same time encouraging the students to do likewise.

Shields and Seltzer (1997), in arguing for a more adequate concept of community for the current era, suggest the need for a "more complex, dynamic, public [concept]—grounded in notions of dialogue and processual strivings" (435–436), but they point out that much dissonance and conflict may ensue. They continue:

> The community that emerges will . . . be a unique combination of the values, beliefs, personalities and situations of its members. Through the synergy that emerges from this combination, it is hoped that all participants will be able to develop a deeper sense of self and of each other, a sense of community within which students may learn to overcome the gulf between the past and the future. . . . (436)

On the basis of these data collected from the classroom in the case study, there was, overall, a sense of energy in belonging to a learning community that was made up of diverse elements. It was a sense of concern for self and for others, for tolerance of difference and concern for everyone's physical well-being that the children and teachers showed to each other in the classroom. Diversity was valued, with mutual respect and regard evident among children, teachers, and parents.

The participants in this classroom work together, and take risks in an attempt, like the schools discussed by Apple and Beane (1999), to connect the school curriculum to the intricacies and multiplicities of ethnicity, gender, and class diversity of the students and their communities. Furman (1998) calls for an education and school-wide culture

> that recognizes and promotes acceptance of differences, proactively teaches staff and students to cooperate within difference, incorporates the metaphor of global community, and attends to members' feelings of belonging, trust and safety. (318)

In highlighting the concept of diversity and "otherness," the case study brings out the distinction between a traditional community and a posttraditional community. We are all inevitably "others" in a myriad of contexts. By establishing a community we inevitably create "others" and outsiders and exclude those who do not "fit" the narrowly defined norms of a group. We see in the case study a microcosm of society where there is diversity and where, in an effort to bring about a "stable" state, the teacher "shuffles the deck" of student groups.

STRIVING FOR COMMONALITY—DISCIPLINE POLICIES

In contrast to the celebration of diversity apparent in the case study above, the authors' experience of working with schools on discipline policy has indicated a quest to find some common values that will include as many as possible in a community of learners in a classroom, but that necessarily exclude others. Strike (1999) claims:

> No community can be united by shared values and be infinitely inclusive. The very act of erecting some set of values as those that are to be shared by community members will create a membership in which those who share the community's values are preferred to those who do not. Either non-sharers will be excluded from membership altogether or they will in some way be second class members. (54)

In attempting to define the relationship between individualism and collectivism, Charney (1994) states:

> In today's world, it is particularly urgent that we extend beyond the domain of self and the lessons of self control. We need to find

connections to others, and to feel ourselves members of many groups—intimate groups, community groups and a world group. (14)

The links between the role of the individual within an educational community in a posttraditional era and issues relating to individual and group power may be exemplified by a brief analysis of the role school discipline plays within global and local communities. Discipline and management issues in schools inevitably reflect the concepts of community held by those who hold power within the school. Currently in schools, the notion of community is integrally linked with the rhetoric of citizenship and social responsibility.

The word *discipline* is derived from the Latin *disciplina*, which means learning, and it is what students learn from the disciplinary processes within schools that helps determine how they view themselves both as individuals and as members of a group. Discipline may be viewed by educators and community members as having both a managerial and educational function in a school community. The managerial function relates to the development of order in a school so that teaching and learning can occur. This function focuses on individuals developing the ability to make rational choices about their needs and the needs of others, and the understanding that by making sound choices, effective learning can take place.

The educational function of discipline relates to inculcating in students a sense of responsibility while preparing them for active participation in both a school setting and the wider community. The educational function of discipline, therefore, characterizes school discipline as a learning experience by which students learn about the rights and responsibilities of individuals, particularly individuals who are in conflict with others. Linked to the notion of rights and people in conflict are issues relating to power, control, authority, and decision making. Discipline, therefore, is a curriculum issue; if schools focus on the need to foster particular knowledge, skills, values, and attitudes to their students then the "disciplinary curriculum" needs to be addressed as carefully as does the academic curriculum. Ingersoll (1996) argues that of all the experiences students have at school, disciplinary interactions are the most potent. Through disciplinary interactions, students learn about the distribution and potency of power relationships, obedience, control, solidarity, and conformity.

The three major disciplinary approaches commonly employed in schools are: the interventionist approach, which fosters compliance and conformity; the interactionist approach, which fosters a sense of group cohesion; and the noninterventionist approach, which fosters a sense of individual responsibility. These approaches to discipline are in turn categorized by Lewis (1997) as models of control, management, and influence. The approach considered most appropriate for a particular educational setting depends on how the school community views such issues as the role of the individual in relation to change, the role of the individual in a local and global context, how the notion of community is interpreted in a particular setting, how power is to be distributed within groups, and how active citizenship is seen to be best developed.

In some educational contexts for example, the term *active citizenship* may be interpreted as the development of citizens who learn to obey authority and engage in decision-making processes led by a legitimate leader. If citizenship is seen in this light, then an interventionist, teacher-oriented approach is the most appropriate disciplinary process to adopt. Within this approach, the adult in authority has the power to make decisions for the whole group, as he or she is considered to have the knowledge, skills, and ability to make the most appropriate decisions.

If, however, active citizenship in a community involves individuals who are decision makers, risk takers, and who have the ability to seize opportunities within a communal or group structure, then an interactionist, or group approach, to discipline is the most appropriate model to implement. Within this approach, power for decision making rests with the group, and individuals within the group learn about the rights and responsibilities of group membership. In a school setting, involvement in an interactionist disciplinary approach develops in students a sense of empowerment as the students are the decision makers with more power to bring about and control change.

Belonging and a sense of community are perceived differently within the noninterventionist approach where power rests with the individual, and it is the individual who is the decision maker. The aim of this approach is to develop self-disciplined, independent individuals who know what is right for them and are able to make rational decisions about their own welfare and future. The teacher's role within this approach is that of motivator and facilitator, and the teacher is there to influence rather than control or manage students' decisions. The approach supports the implementation of respectful conflict management processes within schools and stresses the importance of student / teacher negotiation. A number of these features of the disciplinary approach may be seen by school communities as essential elements to incorporate in their disciplinary approaches if they are seen to be contributing to the development of critical, active citizens of the future. Within the noninterventionist approach, the power for decision making rests with student, as it is the students who are to make decisions about their futures.

Belonging to a group or community may be based on compliance or genuine involvement. Community based on shared purpose rather than shared, common behavior, according to Wheatley and Kellner-Rogers (1998),

> changes the entire nature of the relationships within that community. . . . Belonging together is defined by a shared sense of purpose, not by shared beliefs about specific behaviours. The call of that purpose attracts individuals but does not require them to shed their uniqueness. (15)

This concept changes the traditional understanding about the place and purpose of discipline in school communities, in that it overcomes the traditional emphasis on conformity and compliance, and stresses the values of uniqueness and individuality when based upon a concept of community through shared purpose. This accommodates a more posttraditional view of the role of discipline in school communities, and allows for the concept of "otherness" to be incorporated.

It is important in the context of the posttraditional community, that the disciplinary processes that aim at developing in students a sense of belonging and a sense of community are implemented in a positive manner so that the students can develop the ability to simultaneously exist in a number of communities at both local and global levels with a well-developed sense of belonging. If new learning communities both at a local and global level are to develop, then relationships need to be changed, so that risk taking is supported, community input is valued, and new alliances are created.

Preparation for life in multiple and dynamic communities might be sought through the application of the concept of democracy to discipline policy. Pearl and Knight (1998) argue that students also need to have an understanding of general democratic theory and related skills and knowledge if they are to tackle contemporary issues and develop an understanding of universal rights and their associated responsibilities. This knowledge would allow for cultural support for decisions made and would help ensure that those decisions were democratically responsible. Whether teachers provide a comprehensive preparation for communal participation, or provide students with limited access to decision-making processes, school discipline may be seen as playing a part in the development of future citizens and community members.

In terms of education and teacher education there is a need for more vibrant and vigorous approaches to exploring the multiple possibilities of teaching and learning, more risk taking at local and global levels, more networking and professional dialogues at the multiple levels in which we learn and work. Fullan (1999) reminds educators that there is a need to work collaboratively both "inside-out" and "outside-in" in terms of the school in relation to its local community and the global community (45).

THE NEED FOR NEW METAPHORS

A posttraditional dilemma occurs here in that when we attempt to define a set of values to constitute the basis of a group, we are, by the very act of defining those values, being exclusionist, elitist, and judgmental. We, on the one hand, speak of tolerance for difference and diversity, but then attempt to manipulate values to form some kind of consensus to which those who wish to "belong" must subscribe.

Communities in a posttraditional era will be infinitely variable, infinitely inclusive and exclusive, and endlessly dynamic. Communities will be so not because of their recognition of sameness, but because of their acceptance of difference without insisting on "others" becoming mainstream. Shields (1999) claims:

> Communities of otherness or difference, then, would not be based on tradition or unchallenged assumptions about their members; rather they would emerge through careful listening to the cacophony of voices of those who together, make up the school community. (106)

A posttraditional society is a community of others in which we are at one and the same time included and excluded, accepted and rejected, controlled and controlling, empowered and disempowered. Rather than feeling abnormal, antisocial, or deviant, we need to acknowledge our right to be different, and thus to belong not to a community of sameness, but to a community of difference.

There is a multitude of metaphors associated with the concept of communities, which include families, rustic settings such as villages, musical metaphors such as a jazz group or an orchestra, a living organism, a shopping mall, a garden, a bank, a sports team, and a democratic community. Kirkpatrick (1986) claims that because of the enormous flexibility in the word community, we often [are] either confused by its use or, more likely, so inured to hearing it used in a multitude of ways that it eventually collapses into a meaningless term evoked more for rhetorical or emotional reasons than for illumination or explanation. (2)

As educators then, we are confronted with the need to formulate new metaphors to attach to the term *community*. The new metaphors will need to accommodate such elements as continuous change and restructuring, manufactured uncertainty, diversity and fragmentation, local and global relationships, inevitable conflict and struggle for power and supremacy, and competition and entrepreneurialism. Thus, warm, fuzzy, touchy, feely concepts of community belong to a past era. As educators, we must ensure that we do not also belong to that past era.

COMMUNITY AS A COMPUTER GAME

In a posttraditional era where simulation, simulacra, and imagery are dominant elements in the social context, it is common to find that it is almost impossible to detect where imagery starts and whatever passes for reality stops. So blurred is the line between imagery and reality that these states constantly make and remake each other. Computer games that rely on simulation and imagery have perfected, in sophisticated ways, a means to act and "live" in a world of imagery and imagination. It is the metaphor of such computer games that is used here to describe the community of the posttraditional era.

Computer games rely on the user having skill in manipulation of the controls to make the images move in the desired manner; they demand high levels of concentration, patience, and time; they are often based upon a playing out of the risks and fears of real life in an imaginary setting, thus involve frequent violence and fighting; they are competitive whether the player is playing against the computer or another player; they involve ongoing learning and skill development especially where skills used in one game are transferred to another, thus giving the player an advantage; the programming for computer games is extremely complex; they are protected from being copied unless by experts who do this illegally; they are dynamic, fast moving, continuously changing, and graded in difficulty; they can encourage compulsiveness and addiction. Computer games are the product of a consumer age where people continuously upgrade, renew, and redevelop products to seduce consumers.

To apply this metaphor to posttraditional communities, then, provides us with a new way to analyze an old concept. Communities are controlled by those who have the skill and expertise to manipulate them and shape them in ways that allow for benefit to privileged individuals and groups. With the age of expert and abstract systems, knowledge and skill bring power and control to those who possess them. To be a member of a community demands patience, time, and tolerance and thus one has to be prepared to work at being accepted and being seen to belong.

A sense of community and belonging is necessary for most human beings, and thus it is inevitable that a concept of community will continue to exist, but the new community cannot bring back an old era with modernist assumptions. The posttraditional community, like the computer game, is unpredictable, dynamic, sometimes violent and risky, and exhilarating when we learn to play the game and to be at one and the same time both a winner and a loser.

COMMUNITY CHANGE

Throughout this chapter, change has been implicit in that the very concept of posttraditionalism incorporates a notion of change and renewal. One cannot posit a concept of being "post" anything without implying that change is inevitable. As teachers and teacher educators, the changing, uncertain, and fragmented nature of community impacts upon us insofar as we see that the only constant is change and the only certainty is uncertainty. In such a context, we see change not as an exceptional event, but as the norm. Such is the world of teachers and teacher educators in the posttraditional era. Scott (1999), in addressing the change process in education as we move into the new century, comments:

> Understanding and achieving successful change in education and training does matter. It matters because relentless change in every sector of education is inevitable; it matters because the pressures for continuous change are increasing, not decreasing; it matters because failed change brings with it not just economic but significant psychological and social costs; and it matters because how well we manage educational change right now will, in large part, determine the directions which broader societal changes take in the twenty-first century. (199)

This chapter has addressed the way in which a critical view of community and diversity demands a change in perspective from a traditional to a posttraditional one for teachers and teacher educators. Hargreaves (1994) claims:

> Teachers know their work is changing, along with the world in which they perform it. As long as existing structures and cultures of teaching are left intact, responding to these complex and accelerating changes in isolation will only create more overload, intensification, guilt, uncertainty, cynicism and burnout. . . . The rules of the world are changing. It is time for the rules of teaching and teachers' work to change with them. (261–262)

We need to change not only our ways of perceiving community and what the posttraditional community means for teachers and teacher educators, but also change our perceptions of what constitutes knowledge, and change the metaphors through which we describe and illustrate community in relation to education. This chapter has focused upon dynamic and constant change and thus it is in keeping that the new metaphor proposed here as a means to picture the posttraditional community is centered upon dramatic and at times violent movement, risk taking, imagery, and pseudorealism.

Collaboration among educators at all levels, across sectors, across institutions, and across borders of time, place, and space are obviously called for in a posttraditional world. The writers of this chapter have been collaborating with each other and with other educators as a matter of course, and as such are constantly in a dialectical relationship with one another such that each one is changed by, at the same time as she changes the others. It is not possible to be part of any system and not make a difference, thus when we actively and formally enter into collaborative ventures, we do so with a view to maximizing the skills and attributes each of the members brings to the task. We inevitably change interaction, and thus, as community is a dynamic and in a constant state of becoming, so are we as educators. When we are able to say we have completed the cycle of becoming, we will cease to be humans, let alone educators.

Note

We would like to thank all the teachers and students involved in this study and to acknowledge the work of Andrea Allard and Kyoko Omachi for their invaluable assistance and support.

5 From "Common Grounds" to the "Rough Ground" of Teacher Education

Experiencing Teacher Education as a Collaborative Practice

Hans Smits and David Friesen

ARRIVING AT A QUESTION OF TEACHER EDUCATOR PRACTIVE

Teacher education has been dominated in the past by a technical rational orientation that presumes that effective teaching involves the application of technique to the problems of practice. With the more recent move to reconceptualizing teaching and teacher education within a reflective practice orientation, teacher educator practice needs to be questioned and critically examined. What is the place of teacher educators in the development of reflective teachers? Much has been written about teacher education programs that have been created to develop reflective teachers. Little has been written about teacher educator practice in a time of shifting approaches to teacher education.

This chapter reexamines teacher educator practice by reflecting on an action research project in which the authors were involved. The project focused on changing a third-year course in order for it to become more meaningful for our students in terms of their encounters in schools. We realized from the outset that our own practice as teacher educators involved much more than applying our authority and expertise to our students through course outlines, activities, and teaching. In a sense, our "authority" as teachers ourselves was not in question, although from past experiences we did understand that there was considerable dissatisfaction with the program in general, and our course in particular. Certainly this illustrates the ambiguous spaces we inhabit as teacher educators, and admittedly, it is difficult to capture the ineffable quality of teaching that we do with our students. In this chapter we use hermeneutics as a philosophical lens to view our experiences of attempting to make sense of our practice as teacher educators, and the collaborative work that occasioned such philosophical reflection on the meaning of being a teacher educator.

It is generally accepted knowledge in teacher education that students find their field experiences most meaningful while they "put up with" the on-campus courses. They often see coursework taught by professors who are not "real" teachers as disconnected from the realities of teaching. Teacher educators constantly face this dismissive attitude of students toward their work. The all-too-often response by the teacher educator in an effort to appease students is to try harder: revise the course, teach better, try to become more "practical." We know from long experience and research that teacher educators especially are caught in the ambiguous space of trying to live the discourse of the university—doing research, building theory, developing expertise—and the life of schools and teachers, to which we owe the responsibility for renewing the profession. If we accept and live this either/or space, however, what may be perpetuated is a technical-rational approach to teacher educator practice—a practice that also tends to be lived individually, or as emanating only from individually construed knowledge and expertise.

We too faced the problem of teaching a course that was thought by the students to be much less important than the field experience. For a number of reasons, however, we found ourselves—partly by inclination, and partly by necessity—working closely together to attempt to understand teacher educator practice as more than applying expert and technical-rational knowledge to problems. The hermeneutic philosopher Hans-Georg Gadamer has argued that this approach is really a diminishment of practice (Gadamer 1981,1996).

Given our situation, there was, firstly, a pragmatic need to provide continuity across three sections of the course by orienting two new instructors. Secondly, partly as a consequence of a generational change in the make-up of the faculty, there was more questioning and debate about the strong technical orientation of the course and program as a whole. Thirdly, there was a common desire to address student concerns about this course and its link to the field experience.

Given the reasons that led to collaboration in the planning and teaching of this course, however, a deeper question needs to be addressed. What really compelled the instructors to work together? Past practice legitimized the construction of the course outline for all three sections by the senior instructor. That course outline containing the required content based on the effective teaching literature was given to instructors for the various sections of the course. In a sense, it did not matter who taught the course as long as they followed the outline. This practice was based on the premise that there should be a high degree of uniformity across the sections to provide a common experience for all students before entering internship. Teacher educator practice was characterized by delivering the planned curriculum with roots at least two decades old. Although the course involved a high degree of student participation and activity, the curriculum was assumed as being the foundation—and legitimation of teacher education practice.

Our decision to enter into a collaborative action research project was thus driven, partly by desire and partly by necessity, to build a different understanding of teacher educator practice. We were interested in searching for a deeper understanding of the impulse toward collaboration that could allow us to live a teacher educator practice that could resist more technically rational and individualistic practices.

THE CONTEXT FOR THE PROCESS OF COLLABORATIVE ACTION RESEARCH

Educational Professional Studies (hereafter noted as EPS) 350 is a course taken by students in the third year of the undergraduate secondary program (first year for after degree students). The purpose of this class is to prepare students for the sixteen-week school internship that occurs in their last year of the program. To facilitate interdisciplinary understanding, each section of the course is organized into several "staff" groups, each consisting of the various subject area majors. EPS 350 is taken alongside Educational Psychology and two curriculum and instruction courses in the student's subject major. A unique aspect of this semester is a two and a half day Off Campus Residential Experience (OCRE) during which the three sections engage in a variety of activities to explore teaching and learning "beyond the classroom walls." A one week block and a two week block of high school field experience punctuate the semester.

Two EPS courses precede EPS 350 in the program. EPS 100, taken in the first year of the program, is a general introduction to education, whereas EPS 200, taken in the second year, is devoted entirely to the refinement of generic teaching skills. After degree students take 100 and 200 concurrently.

In the Winter 1998 semester, the three instructors[1] of EPS 350 decided to take a collaborative approach to teaching this course. In the past, the focus was on providing the students with specific instructional strategies such as cooperative learning, teaching for thinking, experiential learning, and so on. Over the past several years, however, the various subject areas have taken a greater responsibility for teaching instructional strategies that relate specifically to their subject area. EPS 350 often covered similar ground in a "one size fits all" generic approach. We wanted to shift the focus of the course from providing students with more technical proficiency to exploring their high school teacher identities formed in the context of their subject area specialities. Based on our growing understandings of an inquiry model and constructivist notions of learning to teach (Britzman 1991), we wanted to shift the focus of student learning from an "authoritative" discourse of prescriptive skills and strategies, to an "internal" discourse of what it means to become a teacher. Our work in action research led us to believe students could become more reflective about their practice by learning to inquire into their teaching.

Our weekly instructor meetings involving collaborative planning, delivery, and reflection on this course evolved into action research on issues of teacher and teacher educator identity and practice. Not so much a method as an orientation, action research provided a way of thinking about and engaging in our practices as teacher educators. It is a continuation of career-long inquiry into teacher education (Friesen 1994, 1995, 1996; Smits 1997b). As a "living practice" (Carson and Sumara 1997), educational action research concerns itself with research in education that "self-consciously attempt(s) to alter perception and action" (xxi) and in this sense is transformational research. Over the semester, each of us kept a chronology of our reflections on the project, which stimulated our weekly dialogue. Although students were aware of our deliberations they did not actively participate in them, but were surveyed at the end of the course to provide us with their perspectives.

During this action research, the content of the course became a series of activities intended to have students think about their experience as high school teachers and share that thinking with students from other subject areas in their staff groups. To this end, the course primarily focused on having students: generate questions related to the commonplaces of teaching (students, teachers, curriculum, context); explore some of these questions as individuals and staff groups; write and share narratives of their action research projects related to the questions they decided to pursue. Some of their research sites included: teenagers in the community; subject area groups; OCRE; schools and classrooms; community agencies.

The students kept track of their research in a "commonplace book." Rather than using the term *journal* we wanted to encourage writing that was more focused on the experiences of learning to teach. The term *commonplace* has a long history in literature, and refers to notations or observations a reader makes regarding a text. Thus, in keeping with an interpretative approach to reflection we were attempting to foster, we likened the experience of learning to teach as a "text" to be interpreted. The hermeneutic philosopher, Paul Ricoeur, for example, has written about the possibilities of understanding human action—in our case, the meaning of becoming a teacher—as a possible text for interpretation (Ricoeur 1992). It is possible to understand human action as a text, because like an actual text, human action is related in language, and the expression of its understanding lies in language. Thus, teaching is not just observed, but is an expression of a discourse, something that is lived in and through language.[2]

To further give meaning to the nature of the reflective writing we were attempting to encourage, we used the meanings of commonplaces suggested by Joseph Schwab (1983), namely, the elements that constitute an educational experience and situation—students, teacher, subject matter, and milieu or context. We will briefly refer to these commonplaces farther on in terms of their meaning for students.

THE LIMITS OF EXPERTISE AND CREATING AN OPENING FOR PRACTICE

In attempting to re-think, and revise, teacher education practice in terms of the experiences of our students, perhaps the major effect of the action research in which we were engaged was to realize the limits of our assumed expertise. We began to question the extent to which we could be certain about the efficacy of our existing practices: firstly, that we could convey understanding of teaching in all its complexities, and indeed reduce those complexities to more effective prescriptions for our students; and secondly, that we could sufficiently practice teacher education only in individualistic ways. Thus, in the collaborative action research process we began to live out, we also had to confront how the discourse of teacher education shapes our identities as teacher educators, and the difficulties of constructing alternative identities that challenged the conventional practices of teacher education.

As teacher educators in a professional studies program, we came to collaborate in our response to the anxieties about the limits of our understanding, and the desire at the same time to understand differently. Recognizing the voiced needs of our students to have a more practical orientation—particularly to satisfy their cravings for practical knowledge and assuage their anxieties about becoming teachers, we nonetheless saw the limitations of a highly rationalized and methods-based approach in the absence of providing a basis for questioning the grounds for becoming a teacher. One of the important consequences of the collaborative meetings we held to plan and discuss the course, is that we also created a space to give voice to the ambiguous role of being a teacher educator, caught as it were, between the "expert," detached, objective, discourse of the university, and the demands for grounded understandings of teaching required by our students.

Such questioning led to a concern about what constitutes the grounds that give life and meaning to teaching, not just for our students but also in our own work at the university. Yet we were still caught in what has been identified as a "modernist" framework for practice: that our understanding of practice grew out of what Toulmin (1990) terms the "three pillars" of Modernity: "certainty, systematicity, and the clean slate" (179). Taking up the question of practice as he does, Donald Schön's question captured our concern: "How comes it that in the second half of the twentieth century we find ourselves in universities . . . a dominant view of professional knowledge as the application of scientific theory and technique to the problems of practice?" (cited in Dunne 1997, xv).

Although the experience of collaboration provided the space to explore that question, collaboration was not in itself the goal of our work. Rather, and as our ongoing writing and dialogue showed, we stepped on the difficult, but "rough ground" of practice (Dunne 1997), questioning in the process the assumptions about expertise our places in the university accrue to us. Certainly we not only questioned the authority of the kind of knowledge evoked by the phrase commonly heard in university lectures, "the research says," or more timidly, "suggests," but how that knowledge should relate to our own practices—and that of our students. Perhaps rather than assuming our control over and exercise of teacher education practice, we were beginning to flirt with the kinds of questions the philosopher Hans-Georg Gadamer asks, "Is the application of science as such practice? Is all practice the application of science?" (1996, 3).

The evocation of Gadamer's name is not accidental or simply happenstance. Philosophically, we required something to help guide our thinking about and through practice—to inquire into the "meaning" of practice (Dunne 1997). In terms of conceptualizing "practice," we started from the critique of modernist practice that philosophical hermeneutics has undertaken, and that has found its most cogent expression in the work of Gadamer. In a more recent reflection on his life's work, Gadamer asserts that what is central to that work is the notion of practice and practical knowledge. As Gadamer notes about the centrality of practical knowledge and wisdom, "It is this practical knowledge which, in reality, assigns and opens the space for each scientifically grounded capacity to do things" (1997, 56–57). And, distinguishing practical philosophy from scientific rationality, Gadamer argues:

> Now certainly practical philosophy is not in itself such a rationality. It is philosophy; which means it is a kind of reflection, or to be more precise, it is a reflection on what a human organization and shape of life is or can be. In the same sense, a philosophical hermeneutics is not itself the art of understanding but only the philosophy of understanding. But both practical wisdom and philosophical hermeneutics arise out of praxis and are a waste of time without it. (57)

Our action research project started with a sense about the need to approach an understanding of teaching practice as something that incorporates and integrates discrete forms of professional knowledge, rather than viewing practice as being cumulatively defined by such knowledge. Although educational research has perhaps given a strong sense of what constitutes elements of effective teaching, it has not or perhaps cannot offer an understanding of practice as "vocation" (Huebner 1987) or in more lived and embodied ways (van Manen 1991; Varela, Thompson, and Rosch 1993). What is often missing for our students—and many expressed this in their feedback to us—is a sense of what holds things together in learning to become a teacher—in other words, what allows meaning and understanding to emerge in a more connected and grounded way. We knew from the existing teacher education research literature as well as our own experiences that for many student teachers it is "real experience" in schools that counts most in terms of meaning. Rather than denigrating or ignoring that belief, we attempted to take seriously the way our students valorized their field experiences over their university ones, and how that challenged our practices as teacher educators. At the same time, we wanted to resist the temptation to fall into a "practice makes practice" approach (Britzman 1991).

We were challenged to understand differently our practices as teacher educators, starting from the premise that the program we offer, and the fragmented approaches to learning to teach through discrete courses—curriculum, foundations, psychology, pedagogical methods, and even more discrete skills and strategies—although all necessary in some sense, do not necessarily lead to a stronger understanding of what it means to become a teacher. Indeed, it can be argued as some writers have (Briton 1995; Carson 1997; Felman 1987), that the assumed authoritative discourse of the university, in which knowledge is framed in theory, or in narrowly scientific-rational terms, may actually forestall the recognition of what one actually needs to learn to become a teacher, as much as "practice makes practice" (Britzman 1991) is a limitation. Although certainly not working from an impending sense of crisis, we felt the frustration of the limitations and difficulties that seem to be common to teacher education programs.[3]

The philosophical work that guided our reflections was based particularly on parallel reading we carried out in hermeneutics. Although hermeneutics does not offer an immediately practical orientation, it can help us think about practice in alternative ways (Smits 1997a). From a hermeneutic perspective, as Paul Ricoeur (1992) has written, practice can be characterized more globally as "a particular relation of meaning" rather than simply as the sum total of discrete tasks. Ricoeur provides some examples, which we think have some analogies to teaching:

> Just as farming (but not plowing—and starting up the tractor even less so) is a practice, in the sense of a profession, in the same way, household management—in the Greek sense of *oikos*, to which we owe the word "economy"—or holding public office in the government. . . . denotes as many practices, whereas the subordinate behaviors, such as putting together a menu or giving a speech at a public gathering, do not merit this title. Likewise painting is a practice, both a profession and an art, but not applying a spot of color to a canvas. One final example will put us on the path of a helpful transition: a shifting of a pawn on the chessboard is in itself simply a gesture, but taken in the context of the practice of a game of chess, this gesture has the meaning of a move in a chess game. (1992, 154).

Extending Ricoeur's analogies, we see that lesson planning, exercising classroom management, or developing effective means of assessment—all skills important for teaching—do not either individually or cumulatively constitute teaching as practice. Or, to use Ricoeur's analogy of a chess game, we can imagine someone making choices based on a rudimentary knowledge of the rules of movement of chess, but not understand in a larger sense either the meaning or purpose of such moves.

What is further developed in Ricoeur's work is that practice, and how one learns practice, also cannot be separated from the development of self and identity. As he notes, the question of what constitutes a "capable person," as for example a person who can act ethically (or play chess competently, or teach competently), involves "successively, the question of determining *who* can speak, *who* can act, *who* can recount, *who* can impute actions to himself or herself (1998, 89; italics in original). Ricoeur (1992, 1998) refers instead to "narrative identity" as something that emerges as possibility in a reflectively interpretive engagement with experiences, whereby one attempts to understand better—and act with more wisdom—in solving a problem or facing a challenge. Such a perspective is also integral in Hannah Arendt's work, *The Human Condition,* where she develops the distinction between *work, labor,* and *action,* arguing that human action—which includes what Ricoeur would call practice—cannot be described in discretely instrumental terms, but instead must be conveyed narratively. Such a narrative understanding of the relationship between self and practice again speaks much more deeply and holistically than a language that reduces practice to technique or the application of theory.

Charles Taylor, a philosopher who has also taken up the question of understanding self and human action, writes that "our agency is essentially embodied and . . . this lived body is the locus of directions of action and desire that we never fully grasp or control by personal decision." In discussing the central reality of language as a basis for human understanding, he points out the importance of recognizing "the capacity to speak [is] not simply in the individual but primarily in the speech community" (1995, 13). Hermeneutics is thus important to remind us that the very possibilities for understanding—and hence practice—lie in language, and that language is social and woven through human relations, thereby offering possibilities for understanding embodied as individual identities. When we speak of practice with these ideas in mind, we also begin to open up a sense of the purposes and possibilities inherent in collaborative encounters.

RESPONDING TO OUR STUDENTS' EXPERIENCES
AS REFLECTION ON OUR OWN IDENTITIES AND
PRACTICES AS TEACHER EDUCATORS

Through the process of action research, we have come to a recognition
that practice in teacher education—what we expect our students to
learn and understand, and what we ourselves understand as the practice of representing and teaching about teaching—that the work of
teacher education—is in many ways a set of ambiguities, perhaps even
"aporias" in the philosophical sense. Perhaps teaching others to teach is
even an impossibility, as Shoshana Felman (1987) has suggested about
teaching in general, since it is the desire of the other to accept learning
that is the critical quality required for learning.

   One ambiguity emerges when we attempt to articulate what it is
that we do, and the absence that opens up when we actively attempt to
deconstruct the position of the teacher educator; we come up against
certain limits of language and institutional boundaries. In part, those
limits are defined by the ways in which teacher education has been
framed in a modernist language of scientific practice, and within the
context of the university. The teaching about and learning of teaching
has been conceived and practiced as the correct application of univer-
salized and abstracted norms and rules.

   Enframing in the university and the language of scientific rationality has spawned, then, the notion of expertise we presumably represent and embody as teacher educators. But when we attempt to shed
this model of teacher education and what it implies for our teaching
work, we are somewhat at a loss to define clearly—either in theoretical
or practical terms—what it is we both represent and profess. This has
implications for how our students perceive and receive our work in the
university classroom, and how and what we represent as legitimate
teacher education knowledge.

   The second ambiguity has been discussed very well by other
teacher educators. We refer here to the problematic issues of how it is
that students learn to become teachers (Briton 1995; Britzman 1991;
Carson 1997; Carson and Briton 1997; Felman 1987). One of the questions the project opened up for us is, how do we begin to open up a
narrative space—in the ways that Ricoeur, Arendt, and Taylor have developed this idea—for the development of identity? And further, how
may a notion of identity be nurtured that is related to an understanding
of practice in a fuller and more connected sense, and at the same time,
one that may open up to what is not known, and not something already

readily available in terms of past experiences? Again such questions posed a challenge to our work and expertise as teacher educators. The attempt to have our students engage in a narrative fashion with their own biographies and relationships with others and situations, called on different ways of being teacher educators, at the same time showing the limits of our individual work and expertise.

THE ONGOING SEARCH FOR A "FOCAL REALITY" IN TEACHER EDUCATION

In his *Crossing the Postmodern Divide,* Albert Borgmann describes one of the qualities of late modernism as "hyperactivity." The more we attempt to capture the world and tame it to our perceived or constructed goals, the more hyperactive we become. It is not being busy that's the problem, but rather, the question of what is forgotten in the busyness. We become frantic in our efforts to construct a "reality" without having a sense or connection to what it is that ought to focus our attention, and focus our practices. Borgmann defines such "focal reality" as "a place-holder for the encounters each of us has with things that of themselves have engaged mind and body and centered our lives" (1992, 119). Of course, as Borgmann points out, the postmodern critique has sought to undermine, perhaps literally, the notion of "reality." For example, we may think of schools as being more real than university classes in terms of learning to become teachers; yet schools and classrooms in themselves are historical and cultural creations—their "reality" is as much a consequence and playing out of a kind of discourse, as is the teacher education class with its theories of teaching, and our roles in them as teacher educators. Thus, from a postmodern perspective we are enjoined not only to question the stableness and taken-for-grantedness of what we experience as real, but also to ask what stories and understandings are ignored, not told, or could be alternatively related.

The issue of what may constitute focal reality points to one of the major themes that have come out of our discussions. Borgmann notes that "people engaged in focal practices gratefully acknowledge the immediate and centering power of the focal thing they are devoted to" (122). In a way, that has been the nature of our struggle, but our writings and discussions reflect the anxiety and uncertainty about what constitutes focal reality for both our students and ourselves.

On a positive note, this may be indicative of a hermeneutic engagement with our work, students, and the program, but as well, with understanding our own identities as teacher educators. Somewhat counter to Borgmann's hopeful examples, however, it is perhaps rather more difficult to name what is focally real; in part because the realities we encounter are split so many ways, and it is difficult to identify and build in teacher education, to use Borgmann's terms, "a common order centered on communal celebrations" (116). We would probably agree with Vattimo, who notes that "the myriad forms of reality makes it increasingly difficult to conceive of a single reality" (1992, 7). Certainly we became more aware that although teacher education might be quite modernist in intent and structure, its reality is multiple, making it difficult to focus reform or change on one particular element. Through our collaborative discussions, we realized that each of us, in our own experiences, thinking, writing, and identities, was in fact singular in our qualities and activities, but that singularity did not preclude either the desire or necessity to construct more common and shared understandings.

THE INSTABILITY OF FOCAL REALITY—ENGAGING IN ACTION RESEARCH IN TEACHER EDUCATION AS "REPETITION"

For us, one focal reality has been the experiences of our students. Through this one course, we provided opportunities for them to write about their experiences in encounters within the commonplaces of teaching, an attempt to get at what is other than what is already strongly part of their memories and conceptions. That is also a way we have begun to examine our own identities as teacher educators. Through the process of hermeneutic action research, we attempted to arrive at a better (or rather, different) understanding of what it is that influences our thinking and what we understand as the "practice" of teacher education.

A major aspect of the interpretive process has been a development of what hermeneutic philosophers such as Gadamer, and pragmatists such as John Dewey (1934, 1938), call "experience": that is, experience becomes experience when what we know encounters perplexity and happenstance events in the world and we engage those events through inquiry and dialogue. Furthermore, experience occurs when we begin to attend to something that is "other" than our own already fixed understanding of the way things are. Gadamer's explication of experience is helpful here:

> Always present when we experience something, when unfamiliarity is overcome, where enlightenment, insight, and appropria-

tion succeed, the hermeneutic process takes place in bringing something into words and into the common consciousness. (1997, 29)

Carson and Sumara (1997) have described action research as a "living practice." What we are describing here is our living practice of experiencing experience, to put it awkwardly. But rather than describing this in methodological ways, we are pointing to the collaborative qualities of our engagement as a living practice of action research.

That experience of engagement in action research has been quite unsettling, in that we experienced a disruption in our identities, as defined more traditionally in our program. Despite the lack of hard results, there nonetheless has been movement in our understanding and thinking. The nature of such hermeneutic experience may be referred to as "repetition." An odd word, it seems, as it suggests no movement at all. But the experience of understanding implies movement: "Hermeneutics is about the awakening of life toward itself. Repetition, quite simply, is the name for this movement of life" (Risser 1997, 34). As well, repetition is not a process of recollection—that is, simply finding an affirmation of what one already knows, believes and understands. Rather, repetition is understanding differently. What we "repeat" is what we have come to understand, but through the language of dialogue and conversation—within the collaborative space—have come to understand differently.

And so, despite the fragmentary and unsatisfactory qualities of our action research thus far, we have nevertheless moved in our understanding; it would be difficult in the application of that understanding to go back to who we were and what we did before. The movement of repetition that action research has occasioned, points to some important areas for further thought and action, briefly summarized below. The thematic discussion that follows suggests that understanding our practices will require an ongoing struggle to discover meaningful focal realities in teacher education, and particularly, demonstrates the need to think about the nature of teacher education practice in terms of collaboration.

WHAT HAVE WE LEARNED ABOUT TEACHER EDUCATION PRACTICE?

The kind of practice in which we engaged becomes clearer as we look back on our experiences over the semester. The identifiable elements included surfacing questions, inquiring, dialoguing, writing narratively, and interpreting our own and our students' experiences. These elements were woven together into a tapestry—certainly not a seamless one—offering some tantalizing glimpses of the possibility of community as a practice of teacher education.

Collaboration did not by and in itself create a better practice, but rather the elements of practice identified above created a space for collaboration among teacher educators that was enacted in the form of action research. Collaboration was given room to emerge as the community of practice exercised its responsibility to explore the obvious challenges facing it. In this sense, teacher educator practice that reveals itself as collaborative is normative. A normative practice accepts the inherent complexities and contradictions of teacher education without capitulating to the "lure of technique" (Dunne 1997), and attuning oneself to the difficulties and decisions that must be made in practice. The normative quality of practice also means becoming more attentive to our colleagues and students and the difficulties they must work through.

Our heightened awareness of and ability to respond to situations of complexity and ambiguity that confront us in our work has sharpened our practical judgment rather than making us more technically skillful. Practical judgement means that although we do not abandon the creation of theoretical knowledge, and do not deny the importance as well of craft or technical knowledge in teaching, having such knowledge does not release us from the responsibility of relating such abstracted, universal knowledge to particular situations, and to the particular needs of our students. As Dunne emphasizes about the qualities of practical judgment, then, in terms of our work in teacher education, that work can never be simply reduced to application or the clever wedding of means and ends. It must be accepted that knowledge and understanding is

> realized always in concrete applications and never resolves itself into formulated knowledge that can be possessed apart from those applications (in an application we are never simply subsuming a particular with which we are now confronted under a universal which we already possess; rather, the understanding we reach through it contains a unique determination of the universal and particular together). (127)

Although we think we can now produce a better course outline, and improve our teaching by means of more appropriate activities, it is the capability of attending to the other—in his/her specificity—that changed our understanding and commitment to practice. We do not pretend to offer a new set of guidelines for better teacher educator practice but simply point toward that which we already do when we recognize our limitations in puzzling situations and join with others to try to understand them. In the normative quality of practical judgment, there is also the recognition that practice requires social support. But, there is no collaborative program to lay out for others, only the taking up the responsibility to make sense and meaning of the common questions that face every teacher educator and that demand multiple interpretations to understand.

Our collaboration was thus a resistance to the egocentric focus we often bring to our teaching experiences. Working together on the course was marked by a tension between the technical impulse to implement the planned program versus the hermeneutic impulse to engage in a more critical dialogue about the meaning of what we were doing. And, in terms of practical judgment, it involved coming to the realization that a course could not be a simple, "expert" application of knowledge and prescriptions. On the one hand was a curriculum to be effected, and on the other our individual and idiosyncratic experiences with our students. Collaborating with one another allowed us to live in this tension without reverting solely to the technical through the sharing and interpretation of our experiences, or becoming overly theoretical because of the urgency of delivering the course.

For us collaboration has become an experience; it is not an abstract idea that can be theorized but a lived experience that is better narrated. As an experience it was an evolving, shifting, and indeterminate way of living together that grew into a commitment to each other. The questions for continuing action research are now: "How do teachers, students and the other instructors experience our practice? What does our practice have to do with them? How is such collaboration sustained within the demands of universities that tend to pull us back into individualistic pursuits? How can the community of practice be extended beyond teacher educators?"

SOME FURTHER REFLECTIONS ON THE COLLABORATIVE EXPERIENCE

Reading back through the experience—as chronicled in our journals and discussions we had with others, as well as presentations to faculty and conferences—reveals ongoing questions and concerns about our action research journey over the semester.

It is interesting, and as well something that serves as a caution, that with a change in content from prescriptive instructional strategies to a more inquiry-oriented approach came a sense of hyperactivity. That is, even with the best of intentions to overcome the limits of technical rationality, we still tended to fall into old habits and ways of doing things. We needed to replace the traditional content with something. The class activities were to be the basis for student narratives employed to make sense of their learning. Trying to provide experiences other than in school classrooms to deepen understanding of the commonplaces, however, led to a proliferation of class activities that seemed to pass by in a flurry. It was difficult to provide coherence to the course from day to day. Student feedback indicated many of them also experienced this discontinuity.

Borgmann (1992), writing about the difficulty of achieving the "focally real" in postmodern times, suggests that "patient vigor" is necessary to resist hyperreality or an alienation from that which is real. In our weekly planning, we searched for what is "focally real" for our students. Often the ideas we exposed students to, such as the commonplaces, were taken up in an abstract way by our students. We were not sure that their action research, as a process for their own work, would help focus them on making sense of their practice. Making up the course on the run was difficult because we soon realized that there were no sure-fire activities that could guarantee specific change in the students in their journey toward becoming a teacher.

We were reminded by this sometimes frantic process of course development that becoming a teacher is a messy if not unpredictable process, and that being a teacher educator, once released from the certainty of prescription, was also messy, and indeed often insecure. Detached from the familiar moorings of a skills and strategies curriculum, we began to realize that in the context of the whole teacher education program, the impact of our practice was somewhat limited.

Related to our struggle to re-think content was an emerging realization of the limitations of our expertise as teacher educators. Our weekly dialogues reveal ambiguity around our identities as teacher educators. If we could no longer be rooted in our knowledge of teaching to be transmitted to students, then what does this mean for teacher educator identity? Leaving the familiar curriculum behind stimulated us to seriously take up thinking about the kind of teachers we wanted to be and the impact this would have on our students. What was our responsibility to prepare the students for the internship in the context of the overall program? How could this be balanced with our responsibility to address the reality of our need and responsibility as teacher educators to get beneath the surface of preparing teachers by transmitting the knowledge base to our students?

Throughout the semester we struggled with the degree of control we could exert through this one course. Were we trying to do too much? Was it in contradiction to student experiences in other courses taken concurrently? This tension was particularly apparent when we discussed our desire and subsequent difficulty of building relationships with our students, their cooperating teachers, school principals, and the subject area instructors so the learning experience could be more coherent and cohesive.

Our relationship to students was at the forefront of our conversations. We began to ask questions about what is conveyed to them about student-teacher relationships by the way we treat them: spelling out expectations for assignments; assigning rooms to them at OCRE; arranging the mandatory computer skills lab. What kind of community is being created? Why were certain students engaged in the course and not others? How could we address the fears some students expressed about their impending first experience as student teachers in high schools? We recognized that we had a closer relationship with our students during the Off-Campus Residential Experience than in the on-campus classes. A tension we experienced was our place with students who were more strongly committed to their subject area majors than EPS. The OCRE experience, held early in the semester, helped relieve this tension somewhat.

Our relationship to teachers was also a topic of concern throughout the semester. We met the cooperating teachers at a dinner meeting that included teachers, student teachers, subject area, and EPS faculty, and principals. During the school experience we also continued to develop relationships with the teachers in our EPS role as university liaison to high schools. We sensed some degree of community with the teachers involved through the contacts with them. Many of the teachers had participated in previous semesters and generally supported the program.

In terms of our experience of working as an EPS team, there was a strong sense that the day-to-day challenges, tensions, and struggles that were a result of the nature of EPS 350, were shared; each of us lived a common experience. The weekly meetings were not onerous because each of us brought a different perspective to them. For example, in a presentation about our work, one of the instructors, after reading our weekly journals, suggested that one of us often focused on the critical aspects of practice, another on relationships, and the third on student teacher identity. The weekly dialogue to him was more of a reading of our experience from different perspectives than an assessment of how well we were delivering the course.

Yet, the admission of complexity and ambiguity itself says something about how we are thinking about practice, or more accurately, attempting to live practice. In questioning the modernist assumptions of teacher education—questioning the epistemological model of knowledge deeply embedded in Western thought (Taylor 1997)—we also came to question practice as the work of the solitary expert. Such a move also calls on us to question knowledge as abstracted theory, and the desire to impose uniformity and certainty. As Stephen Toulmin suggests, "The present state of the subject marks the return from a theory-centered conception, dominated by a concern for *stability* and *rigor*, to a renewed acceptance of practice, which requires us to *adapt* action to the special demands of particular occasions" (1990, 192; emphasis in the original). As we are discovering, such a form of practice, and the demands of the particular, also calls on us to think about living differently in our places of learning and teaching.

Notes

"Common Grounds" is the name of a coffee place at the University of Regina where the writers met once a week, the experience of which forms the basis for the discussion presented in this chapter.

"Rough ground" refers to the messiness and indeterminacy of lived experience, and suggests a different approach to practice than one based on certainty and the correct application of technique and theory. The term is from Joseph Dunne's book *Back to the Rough Ground: Practical Judgement and the Lure of Technique*.

1. Although three instructors were part of the collaborative action research discussion group, the present discussion reflects only the views of the two authors.

2. More particularly, we were concerned about the following issues: (1) the relationship between university program and field experiences, and the way that field experiences become privileged as being more authentic learning; (2) the relationships (or lack of relationships) among different courses, particularly subject-area curriculum and instruction courses, and more general "professional studies" courses, as well as educational psychology and foundations courses; (3) in terms of the secondary program, the tension between subject-area specialization, and understanding teaching and learning in more integrative senses; (4) how to help students become "reflective practitioners" and

encourage a capacity for inquiry; and (5) how we could develop a meaningful orientation to such issues in the schools as increasing cultural diversity.

3. Of course, this in itself is problematic; that is, one of the experiences we became more attuned to is that student teachers have very different ways and needs for expressing their understandings. Thus Schwab's commonplaces of student, teacher, subject, and milieu, given student teachers' relative lack of school experiences were taken to be too theoretical and abstract, suggesting the need for commonplaces that speak to the actual experiences of learning to teach.

6 Situating Ourselves within Narrative

Reeducating the Educator

Florence Samson, Bev Brewer, Angela Chan, Maureen Dunne, and Vicki Fenton

There is a responsive, reciprocal relationship between narrative inquiry and community building. Narrative inquiry engenders community; community nurtures narrative inquiry. This statement is rooted in our lived experiences as five graduate students in the Centre for Teacher Development at the Ontario Institute for Studies in Education, University of Toronto (OISE/UT). Here we were introduced to narrative as phenomenon and narrative as research methodology. We came to understand narrative research as a process through which we explore our teaching and learning—a "study of how humans make meaning of experience by endlessly telling and retelling stories about themselves that both refigure the past and create purpose in the future" (Connelly and Clandinin 1988, 24). In time, narrative led us to within ourselves, outward to our external conditions, backward to our histories, forward to our futures. All perspectives were examined within the context of community. During doctoral studies, each of us used narrative inquiry to come to understand the way we experience the world and to imagine new possibilities, new ways of living and teaching. The result was, and continues to be, an ongoing transformation—the reeducation of the educator.

The questions we invite you to ponder with us in this chapter are: What is the interrelationship of narrative and community? What is the meaning of community to our work in narrative? What is the role of the interrelationship of narrative and community in the reeducation of the educator? We approach these questions as puzzles within Dewey's dialectic of the personal and social dimensions of situation. We understand situation as the experience of the interaction between external conditions and the internal response to these conditions. In this chapter, the contextual situation is located in the interaction between the doctoral degree requirements and our personal responses to meeting these requirements. This is not a quest for certainty, but rather a conversation among five women exploring the tensions we experience as educators and researchers in the process of our reeducation within the research community at the Centre for Teacher Development (CTD), formerly the Joint Centre for Teacher Development (JCTD).

CONTEXT

The JCTD was created in 1990 to foster cooperative endeavors among faculty at Ontario Institute for Studies in Education (OISE), the Faculty of Education of the University of Toronto (FEUT), and the cognate departments of the University of Toronto. From the beginning, the students who came to study at the Centre worked diligently to build community. Formal and informal structures were established and sustained over the years: brown bag lunchtime seminars, the Among Teachers Journal, the Centre listserve, afternoon teas, thesis defense parties, works-in-progress seminars, and seasonal celebrations. These venues offered and continue to offer students the opportunity to gather to discuss their research interests, debate research issues, problem solve, and, sometimes, simply offer or receive personal support in the rigors of the research process.

The Centre students have been encouraged and supported in their endeavors by its director, F. Michael Connelly. His support has come in many ways: the provision of the actual physical space for our gatherings; his continual and enthusiastic attendance at these functions, and his funding for resources. Michael Connelly and D. Jean Clandinin, as co-researchers and narrative collaborators, within their own respective centers, promote and support the notion of community as an important external condition for the learning situation in which we find ourselves.

Research in education places narrative inquiry in the domain of teacher thinking (Connelly, Clandinin, and He 1997). As such, it explores the personal practical knowledge of teachers (Connelly and Clandinin 1988; Elbaz 1983)—the personal understandings we have of our practice, the way we learn, and what we learn. Narrative inquiry allows us to explore the relationship between the knower and the known (Fenstermacher 1994), what it is that we know and how it is that we know it. As "narrative inquirers [we] tend[ed] to begin our inquiry not in theory but with experience as lived and told in stories" (Clandinin and Connelly 1999, 128).

NARRATIVE AS BOTH A PHENOMENON AND A METHODOLOGY

Grounding our understanding in the work of Connelly and Clandinin (1990), we believe narrative is both a phenomenon and a method of inquiry. After grappling with this notion and its meaning for us and our work, we embrace narrative as stories of experience and the meaning making with which we reconstruct a new understanding by which to live. Connelly and Clandinin (1990) state that the distinction between phenomenon and method exist in story as phenomenon, and narrative as inquiry. People by nature lead storied lives and tell stories of those lives, whereas narrative researchers describe such lives, collect and tell stories of them, and write narratives of experience (Connelly and Clandinin 1988, 24).

Narrative inquiry is nested within Dewey's philosophy of education (1938). For Dewey, experience is both social and personal, and narrative as a method of inquiry studies experience in context. Education is life, life is education. Dewey's notions of experience and education form the backdrop for the recovery and reconstruction of meanings of our stories. Recovery of stories, in a narrative sense, explores the meaning of experience. Reconstruction gives new meaning to our stories of experience—our lives, our curriculum, our past, present, and future.

As beginning doctoral students involved in narrative research, it was important for us to acknowledge and embrace the notion of negotiation of narratives between ourselves as researchers and our participants. In the process, we moved from a traditional concept, of research as participant being acted upon, toward an understanding of participants as co-researchers. In narrative inquiry, researchers and participants work together to reconstruct and interpret their stories of experience.

NEGOTIATION OF ENTRY INTO THE COMMUNITY

Individually, we entered the field of teacher thinking through narrative research. Our collective relationships with narrative inquiry evolved through a nine-year history of the Centre for Teacher Development (CTD). Florence began her full-time doctoral studies at the inception of the JCTD in 1990, taking a leave of absence from her elementary school administrative position in Newfoundland. Maureen began part-time studies in 1991 and continued as a high school administrator in Newfoundland, taking occasional semesters to study. Bev and Vicki both came to the Centre in 1995. Bev came from the Ontario community college system and Vicki arrived at the Centre from an elementary mathematics position in Ontario. Angela was drawn to the Centre as a result of her involvement in a narrative inquiry. As members of this narrative community, we are each at different stages in our lives and thesis journeys. Consequently, our stories of the Centre and community span the life history (Clandinin and Clandinin 1995) of the Centre. That history, too, is also a work-in-progress. As we live as students in the Centre community we shape it and it shapes us.

In retrospect it seems fair to say that those of us who entered the Centre at the beginning were exposed to newness on several different levels. As we were learning to articulate our stories of experience, we were involved in another articulation—that of the process of narrative inquiry, for it, too, under the advocacy of Connelly and Clandinin, was in its initial stages. We were coming to know the relational issues that were part of narrative inquiry, and that underpin the entire process (Clandinin and Connelly 1999). Narrative inquiry as a method of research is evolving. Concepts are expanding and emerging that continue to shape the discourse in the Centre. The experience of those who entered the Centre in recent years is undoubtedly different from that of those who entered in the early 1990s.

Although different pathways brought us to study at the Centre, our common purpose was professional development. We soon discovered that professional development is not to be found in a course outline or a university calendar, but is a process lived in community with others through the negotiation of narratives. Community was vital to the process of developing a connected way of knowing, looking for commonalities within our diversity, establishing trusting relationships, and fostering openness and respect.

COMMUNITY: THE NEGOTIATION OF NARRATIVES

We believe that by embracing the notion of community as negotiation of narratives (Connelly and Clandinin 1994) our understanding of community is informed in an important way. The process of negotiation of narrative is essentially the shaping and being shaped by each other in a community. Dewey states that "we live in a community in virtue of the things which (we) have in common; and communication is the way that (we) come to possess things in common. What (we) must have in common in order to form a community, or society, are aims, beliefs, aspirations, knowledge—a common understanding—likemindedness" (1916, 47). We became members of the Centre for Teacher Development because we were educators in search of professional development, seeking to become more effective educators. We sought a place in our own journeys as learners that nurtured collegiality and conversation with like-minded persons, recognizing that we come from diverse backgrounds. We wanted to be with people who would question and delve into issues relevant to the dailiness of a life involved in teaching and learning. In that sense, we had an initial common understanding, a likemindedness (Dewey 1916).

Through our conversation related to this chapter on reeducating the educator, we came to realize that many of the activities within the Centre were and continue to be social experiences. Thus, learning is an act of communion, a spiritual, transformative, social process. The sharing of food, for example, created a special environment in which we connected. It afforded us time, place, and space to negotiate entry into one another's personal and professional lives, individual histories, and cultures. Activities within the Centre fostered and continue to promote our interpersonal communication and relationships. From these activities came our evolving narratives of the community within the Centre for Teacher Development. Thus, we entered into a process of negotiation of narratives (Connelly and Clandinin 1994) that is critical to the building of community. We were governed by an unspoken code of ethics; we had a "need to consult our consciences and our responsibilities as narrative inquirers in a participatory relationship" (Clandinin and Connelly 1999, 172). We were not to judge one another's stories, nor to repeat them outside of class. We were there to support one another on our journeys into our experience.

Both narrative and community are relational by nature. Narrative in the sharing of our stories explores the dialectic of the personal and the social. We become in-relation to others. We become a part of one another's stories through the negotiation of narratives. The interrelationship of community and narrative is in the place they have in shaping identities. This link is important to us and alters our thinking about the meaning of community.

Through our experiences with narrative inquiry we began to understand ourselves, our teaching and learning, our aims and beliefs, in different and more meaningful ways. Our new understandings were based in the resonances and dissonances of our stories of experience as we shared them with one another. Communication, in the form of shared stories and narratives, helped us build a community and hold a knowledge in common built on a respect for personal practical knowledge. The common themes and nuances of individual stories resonated through our shared stories and brought us together. This enabled the growth of trust, empathy, and validation. Equally important were the dissonances which heightened our awareness of how differences contribute to our personal and professional growth.

Dewey (1916) states that education is a process that shapes a person's thinking and actions, and that school is a form of community, where life, experience, and education are interrelated. As students in graduate school we certainly feel this is true. As we reflect on the kind of community we see as educational, Buber's (1957) community of otherness comes closest. For Connelly and Clandinin (1999), a learning community is, quite simply, a "community of otherness." It is the community that confirms otherness within climates of trust to the extent these are made possible by the educational structures and the persons working within these structures. "Real, uncurtailed, personal existence begins not when one says to the other, 'I am you,' but when one says, 'I accept you as you are,' in your otherness and uniqueness" (Friedman 1983, 153).

Our experience, the day-to-day tensions, struggles, and decisions with which we must contend, awakens us to the complexity of community. In our thinking about this chapter, we struggled with Buber's notions (1957) of communities of affinity and communities of difference. As members of the CTD we experienced tensions within this dialectic of having to define and sometimes even limit community. We found ourselves caught in the dilemma of wanting to provide a safe place for students to pursue the unfettered and enthusiastic and sometimes inherently risky development of narrative inquiry and, at the same time, needing to meet the challenges to narrative as a methodology within the academic community. In order for narrative inquirers to delve and push their boundaries farther in their work, there is predilection for a like-minded group. On the other hand, we know from Dewey that growth occurs when we attempt to resolve our dissonances and lived tensions. It is in the safety of community resonance that dissonances are resolved.

The resonances and dissonances in our shared personal and professional stories resulted in the reframing of our stories. As students of narrative inquiry we were on the leading edge; narrative was not accepted by all in the academy. Some questioned its value; even we ourselves questioned it. Then why did we continue? For all of us, narrative inquiry was so compelling we had to examine the reasons for its being. Story is such a powerful medium for understanding experience that we were irresistibly drawn to understanding the complexity of narrative inquiry. A desire to add to the unfolding knowledge about narrative methodology became an intrinsic part of our personal inquiries.

We struggled with the concept of narrative as a methodology. In a sharing of our struggles, we became closer. We needed to be affirmed in our beliefs; we needed to be supported by each other. We needed to be able to defend narrative to other researchers, to speak to its value and significance. Our struggles allowed us to discern the value of narrative and, at the same time, grow as a learning community.

As students in the Centre for Teacher Development, we respond to Clandinin and Connelly's discussion of community and their vision of what their Centres can be. Clandinin and Connelly write (1995) that communities of affinity are not what they hope their university centers will become, because communities such as these are marked by like-mindedness. Communities of affinity are built on a specific world view, and an intolerance for other views. We believe that community goes much deeper than likemindedness, to a bonding of the heart.

As we began to explore narrative as a method of inquiry we were introduced to Dewey's notions of experience and education. We told stories of our experience, for as narrativists we believe "that experience is the primary agency of education" (Eisner in Connelly and Clandinin 1988, ix). These formed the backdrop for the recovery and reconstruction of meaning from our stories. Recovery of meaning, in a narrative sense, is to ask ourselves about the meaning of this experience to our lives, our curriculum, our past, present, and future. Reconstruction of meaning occurs when we retell our stories with new understandings (Connelly and Clandinin 1988, 81). Community was vital to this process of reconstruction through developing a connected way of knowing (Belenky, Clinchy, Goldberger, and Turule 1986; Gilligan 1982; Hollingsworth 1994), looking for commonalities within our diversity, establishing trusting relationships, and fostering openness and respect.

As we attempt to define community based on our individual and collective experiences of narrative inquiry, resonances and dissonances are heard:

Angela: In recollecting my thoughts on the meaning of community and asking myself how I became part of the community at the Centre, Dr. Connelly's 1300 Foundations of Curriculum course sprang to mind. Many of my peers talked about the 1300 course as their "gateway to a community."

Florence: I think that has been the experience of many of us. It was as members of the 1300 course that many of us first experienced professional community to such an intense degree.

Vicki: The most important aspect I found in the community at the Centre for Teacher Development was the sense of connection and caring. In 1300, I felt that my text, my life, was read by an audience with what Noddings (1984), calls an ethic of care. When we read each other's texts or stories, we should read with an ethic of care.

Maureen: I think that what we found in the CTD was a place which connected both the "head" and the "heart," as Sergiovanni (1992) might describe them. It was a place where intellectual rigor was fostered but not without the affective support that is necessary for learners to take the risk of stretching the boundaries of their knowledge. For me, traveling more than two thousand miles to Toronto to study whenever I could get the opportunity, that sense of community and belonging was critical. I do not think I could have persevered without that personal support. After the first summer in which I completed the 1300 course, every time I walked through the doors of the Centre after a lengthy absence I felt like I was "home." The sense of belonging that the community afforded created a foundational continuity in the program.

Bev: For me 1300 was good while it lasted. After the course finished, everyone disappeared. I did not see anyone from my group again. Either they didn't continue or we followed entirely different paths. I found myself at OISE feeling quite isolated when I enrolled in 3303, the sequel of 1300. I was not with my original 1300 class. The students in my 3303 class, because they had just taken 1300 together, had already established groups. I experienced a sense of exclusion, a counter story to community.

What turned it around for me was that I got involved in works in progress, a seminar in which students share their progress in research and writing. There I felt heard (or listened to?) and the professor seemed to embrace my work.

I feel like I had to work hard at community—seek it out. Even as I participated in a number of small groups I continued to experience feelings of separateness. I was entering into friendship groups that seemed solid but I felt like a third wheel. It was the familiar story of "three." I had feelings of separateness. My story is the counter story of feminist pedagogy, and collaboration.

Florence: I can relate to what you are saying, Bev, but from the perspective of a member of a group who progressed from 1300 to 3303 only to find that in 3303 there were a number of new students who had not experienced 1300 with us. I was uncomfortable. The safe environment which I had come to know in 1300 seemed threatened by the entry of these new students. How could I share my stories with strangers? I felt no rapport with them. It had been such a difficult task in 1300 to learn to speak about my life. How could I once again find the courage to become vulnerable to become part of a new community, or to have new members become part of my old community? This is the dilemma of community.

Vicki: Community building is hard work. It takes time. Even in 1300 it took time to establish trusting relationships and become a caring community, a place where we supported each other.

Bev: I think many of us get pulled into a romantic notion of community. I did . . . and still do. Within my own romantic notion of community lies the assumption of the affinity between community and friendship. Do we mean community or friendship, or are we mixing the terms?

Angela: Isn't friendship embedded in community? When telling stories of our professional practice, we often found ourselves crossing that great divide which many of us had constructed between our personal and professional lives. In time, as we shared our professional and personal stories that rift was mended, and we realized that the personal and professional, like theory and practice, cannot be separated.

The Dialectics: A Conversation

Throughout our study of narrative we found that many of our previously held beliefs were challenged. We came face to face with concepts we had previously considered unrelated, even opposites. In time, we discovered that if we could view the relationship between these concepts as dialectical rather than appositional; we could actually explore the concepts in relationship and gain a more holistic understanding of them.

Before our introduction to narrative inquiry, many of us considered theory and practice to be unrelated. Theory belonged in the Faculty of Education, whereas practice belonged in the school. Theorists and practitioners were miles apart. Curriculum was therefore a course of study. However, our entry into narrative inquiry brought with it new understandings of curriculum. We began to realize that curriculum is not found between the covers of a book, but is the course of one's life. We teach who we are.

Maureen: When I arrived at OISE I came to study the experts. Instead I was asked to study my own experience and enlighten it with "expert" knowledge. Before this I had thought that there was "one true way." I had been raised in moral absolutism and had extended its perspective to all areas of my life. It took me some time to fully integrate the learning that I am my own best expert, that practice is "theory-in-action" and that good theory describes good practice.

Florence: I am from a similar background. In retrospect, I believe that background may have fostered the compartmentalization which I attempted to achieve between the personal and professional spheres of my life. Integration did not appear to be a possibility. However, when I came to narrative, inquiry, which, for me, also invited feminist studies, I was introduced to the work of the sociologist Dorothy Smith. With her theory of bifurcation of consciousness (1987), I began to understand why I felt I had to keep the personal and professional apart. It explained that on each landscape I was expected to operate in a different consciousness, one consciousness for home and family, the other for business, and my professional life where I was bound by society's institutions. When I came to narrative inquiry, I reflected on my life and saw the connections between the personal and professional. I moved them from a relationship of binary opposition to one of dialectic. I accepted that they, like theory and practice, are inseparable.

In addition to the dialectics of theory and practice—personal and professional—we addressed the dialectic of the private and public. The work of Crites (1971) introduced us to the concepts of secret, sacred, and cover stories and encouraged us to examine the stories we told. Were we, in our sharing, telling stories that made us look good in the eyes of others? Were the stories we told of our living and teaching the stories we knew others wanted to hear? Were they the accepted stories our society had taught us to tell, the ones that are never questioned, or were we sharing stories we had not told previously?

Our entry into narrative inquiry was an interesting adventure. At times we were frustrated, confused, afraid of change but we persevered, and became members of a community at the Centre for Teacher Development. It was that community that supported and sustained us as we studied and reconstructed our concepts of teaching and research. Transformation, as we lived it, altered the way we looked at our continuity of experience (Dewey 1938). It was the beginning of the reeducation of the educator.

How Do We Create and Sustain Community?

Narrative research situated us in a particular course and classroom. Part of the narrative process was to write and share a life narrative. First, we created time lines or chronologies of our personal and professional lives. Eventually, we shared our stories of life both in and out of the classroom. In doing so we entered into one another's lives. We came to appreciate that the intricate connections, like the theory and practice dialectic, the personal and professional in our lives, the private and public, are inseparable. We shared our experience of the human condition, the joy and the pain, and in doing so we bonded. We came to care for one another.

Florence: This goes beyond the 1300 to the practice of narrative inquiry within the academic/school milieu. For me, narrative invites a vulnerability which can only be protected through morally mandated care, and that care comes from community.

Maureen: The sharing of stories within community can create a depth of connection that we may call spiritual—a sense of union with another human being.

Florence: An example of that might be my experience, as a member of the narrative community, as we gathered at a classmate's house to celebrate the Christmas season. As Marilyn accompanied us on the piano we joined our voices in the singing of "Silent Night." Suddenly, in mid-verse, I became aware that the carol was being sung in at least four different languages. It was a powerful moment—one that transcended the everyday. This was a musical expression of what had happened to us in the living and sharing of our stories. We had transcended our cultures and were united in our humanness and our love of music.

Angela: I felt very vulnerable when I had to make my personal life public to strangers. I do not remember whether there were any ground rules mentioned by the professor, but somehow it felt like a safe place for me to share my life chronicle.

Vicki: I was very nervous. I felt very uncomfortable telling my stories because I had locked them away for a long time. My stories always made me feel different from other people. Their response was one of pity. I did not like feeling pity from other people.

Florence: I had always been a very private person. I was so scared that I chose the last possible class for my presentation. My hope was that we would run out of time and I would not have to present. Time did run out, but my professor promptly added another class.

Maureen: I was very nervous about presenting my personal chronicle in class. It wasn't just the telling of my story; I was anxious about how my classmates would respond to it. I gave my presentation in the second half of the class and finished the telling just as the class time ended. Dr. Connolly dismissed the class and said that there would be time to respond to my chronicle in the next class. I felt very vulnerable, as if I had laid my soul on the table and it had fallen into a void. I couldn't sleep that night and tossed and turned until morning. I discussed my response with Dr. Connelly the next day and he asked me to express my anxiety to the class. One of the learnings of that incident was that asking persons to reveal something of their personal lives brings with it the moral mandate to care for them while they do it.

Angela: I remember that on the morning of my presentation I was not concerned about being judged by the group. I was at a point in my life that I needed someone to listen to my story, to care about what had happened to me. I felt it as a space for my voice. It was a time when I felt very inadequate since the loss of my professional identity. My confidence as merely an individual, as a human being, seemed to have been buried together with my professional identity. I no longer knew who I was as a person, and there was no sense of purpose.

Florence: I remember there was music, singing, food, and celebration. Mary Beattie would play the violin, Marilyn would play the piano, and we sang. Dolores had the most beautiful voice.

Vicki: We did not have music but we had a great community of women who supported me and helped me grow. I remember the time we spent in the local restaurant celebrating one another's success stories. It felt like they were my older sisters always showing their concern, caring, and encouragement.

Angela: There were moments which I felt so alone but the caring experience felt as I was being asked about how things were. I did not feel connected with many, but with a small crowd.

LEAVING THE COMMUNITY: A CONVERSATION

It sometimes seems as if there is a reciprocal relationship between narrative methodology and community. In our experience the supportive community of the CTD was critical to the successful use of narrative as a methodology. We found that we could not have one without the other. This experiencing of community can cause problems for students, particularly when they have to leave the community.

Florence: Thoughts of leaving the community presented problems for some of us who had to leave Toronto to return to our teaching before completing the thesis. This was particularly true in cases where we lived outside of Ontario. Some months before leaving the Centre, I realized I needed to stay connected, and asked permission to have a student bulletin board and file folder system installed. Even if I was not physically at the Centre, information about my work and research interests would be there as a reminder for friends and students that although I was back home, I was continuing to work on my thesis. The bulletin board would keep me connected, for the plan was that students living away would receive the JCTD Newsletters and notes and thesis-related information from those students who were currently at the Centre. I sometimes referred to the bulletin board as an umbilical cord, my life-

line to the Centre. Back home in Newfoundland, I missed the friendship, the conversation, easy access, and the support of students and
professors. I was isolated. This was compounded by my choice of
methodology and the context of my teaching and administration. There
were few colleagues interested in my work. Narrative was so new—
leading edge—and the hours I spent at school left little time to visit family let alone the local university library, although I lived almost next
door. I really missed being at the Centre

Maureen: When I leave the Centre to return home to the workplace, work enfolds me and submerses me and cuts me off from academic pursuits. I also feel isolated and over a few weeks or months
become driven to connect with my OISE friends, usually in lengthy,
long distance telephone conversations. I feel compelled to travel to
Toronto as often as I can and a trip to the Centre is always on the
agenda. I need to connect with Dr. Connelly, with my friends, to walk
through the Centre just to reassure myself that it is still there and that I
still belong. The physicality of being there refreshes my soul and my in-
tellect. It's enough to keep me energized to the next visit. I haven't really
negotiated an exit because I still yearn to be involved in the intellectual
life of the place.

NEGOTIATION OF EXIT

We shape and are shaped by our community—by the process of negotiating our narratives within the context of the Centre for Teacher
Development. We bring our individual narratives into the community.
These, in turn, shape the community, and we understand that our own
narratives are also shaped by that community. The process is a reconstruction of identity. It is also a process of reeducation.

   Having lived through those tensions, we delved further into the
meaning of community in our lives. We recognized that we have had a
transformative experience; our identities are continually shifting through
our interactions within the community. We think to the future. We are
constantly aware of being ready to enter other communities, and for
some, the challenge lies in reentering our former communities, as new,
different persons.

   We see negotiation of exit as a process of leave taking that involves
tensions, uncertainties, and loss. The tensions and uncertainties arise in
thinking about returning to other communities or entering new communities. We recognize a shift in personal and professional identities.

As we have fashioned new identities within our community, upon exiting we lose part of the relationship that created that identity. There is safety here among the members at the different layers of our learning community. There is respect, trust, acceptance in our community of difference.

Recently we have been thinking about the process of negotiating exit within our research contexts. We think about it in terms of a multiple "I," that we are many people within the research relationship. This is particularly important in narrative inquiry. Exiting a narrative research relationship creates tensions and uncertainties. Those tensions exist within the blurred boundaries, the relationship we have within our research. Our identities shift as people within our community relate to us at multiple levels as we cross major thresholds, as in passing the comprehensive examinations, completing the thesis proposal, presenting at conferences, and defending our theses.

Another aspect of negotiation of exit is related to the concept of narrative space (Connelly and Clandinin 1998). We understand from this notion that narrative inquiry happens in three dimensions. The aspect we want to address is the temporality and rhythm of place. This is especially evident to us in this community when former members return. They enter a community that is evolving, living between old and new plots. Although the setting changes infrequently, there is movement in the characters and storylines. It is important to recognize that a place such as the Centre for Teacher Development has a narrative history. Its characters and their narratives enter a place as the history of the place continues to evolve. Hence, the need for ongoing negotiation within and among the different layers of our community arises.

The culture of the community shifts over time and with change in the larger institutional and social narratives. In our experience, the profile of students has changed as have tuition fees and university departments. There is a shift from full-time student to students who are part time. Course names change, even the name of the Centre has changed, secretaries come and go, students progress and move on.

REEDUCATING THE EDUCATOR: TRANSFORMATION IN OUR TEACHING

The Centre experience of journeying into narrative methodology and community building changes people. It re-educates. Not only have we been transformed but so has our teaching for we teach who we are. Although it is true that many of the ideals to which we aspired before the Centre experience remain part of who we are, we can now espouse them with a greater understanding of ourselves, our profession, and the context in which we live and teach. We are more aware of the relationship between the knower and the known and the value of living and learning within community. It is because of these new awarenesses that we can, after the Centre experience, return to our profession transformed and ready to make learning a transformative experience for our students and ourselves. Together, as students and teachers, we will engage in a process of continually learning and becoming.

7 *The Postmodern Challenge*

Using Arts-Based Inquiry to Build a Community of Teacher Collaborators and Selves

Carol A. Mullen and C. T. Patrick Diamond

In this chapter we, Carol and Pat, explore postmodern forms of inquiry and their role in teacher education and community development. We use images of change and combination to capture our sense of postmodernism and to describe how a new generation of researchers is experimenting together as teacher-artist collaborators. We offer arts-based inquiry as a postmodern way of developing innovative forms of research and community. Our readers are encouraged to see themselves as educational artists who can create their own arts-based research forms. They can promote their inquiries by collaborating with others and by building their own communities of teacher researcher selves.

BIRTHING A POSTMODERN CORPUS, BURYING A
MODERNIST CORPSE

To find our way out of the wasteland in which the glare of modernism
and one-eyed reason reduces rock, let alone the arts, to dust we invite
our readers to join us in William Blake's (1966) prayer:

> *May God us keep*
> *From single vision & Newton's sleep!*

Our senses had been dulled by the prevailing paradigm. Our social science training had put our imaginations to sleep. We struggled to
awaken, disheveled and led by dreams. These have suggested other
ways of seeing and engaging in inquiry and community that do not require surrender to rationalist models of knowledge. After first meeting
in 1990, we recognized that we were in similar states of flux and possibility. Through the process of gradually forming an arts-based community of two, we produced a dialogic journal. We wanted to get to know
each other as part of our study of inquiry and collaborative relationship
and felt encouraged to have our intimate approach published (Diamond and Mullen 1997). We shared an institutional self that had tired of
surveillance of personal creativity and that became enlivened through
the ritual of burying/interring the modernist corpse/corpus. We also
shared an emerging arts-based self that was ready for release through
experimental play with new and familiar research forms. We expanded
into a trio through using a metaphor of musical performance to describe
our improvising collaboration as teacher educator-artists (Diamond,
Mullen, and Beattie 1996).

Over time, we have strengthened our resolve both to explore art as
members of a postmodern community of inquiring educators *and* not to
defer to the modernist canon and its timekeepers, unless we chose to.
Modernists insist on a closed universe of neat correspondences and one
right answer in the face of otherwise chaotic/evolving/messy and
pieced-together experience. In contrast, we accept that there is no one,
whole story to be lived or told. There is no one viewpoint that is superior to all others, especially not about postmodernist, arts-based inquiry
and teacher development. The most we can do is to assemble pieces that
ironically serve to exemplify the motley fragmentation that we value as
postmodernists.

We dramatize pieced-together connectedness by using the Gothic
figures of the Frankenstein creature and Dr. Jekyll's double, Mr. Hyde.

We invite these figures to roam freely but clumsily throughout our inquiry landscape. They in turn allow us to explore the postmodernist self as non-unitary, multiple, and fractured even in the act of observing and representing itself, alone or with a collaborator. Like the Frankenstein monster, our community of arts-based researchers is a compilation of different parts of people stitched together into changing shapes. Our community is also constantly regenerating and deconstructing its multi-form body while seeking to develop a changing relationship with its creator(s) and its own self. We also use our patchwork coat of many colors as a metaphor for postmodernism and for the changing field of teacher education that is itself in mourning for its modernist guise.

For much of our careers the social science paradigm held hostage the artistic aspects of our teacher selves and those of our teacher collaborators. We sought relief and release. Sixteen collaborators helped us form a wider community by contributing to our patch-quilt studies, which have been published as our most recent book, *The Postmodern Educator* (Diamond and Mullen 1999). These developing educational artists consist of teacher educators, teacher researchers, students, and dissertation supervisors and candidates. This academic community spread across the borders of Canada and the United States and allowed us to join (and transform) our perspectives with those of others. We, Carol and Pat, both as a duo and as co-creators of a larger body of connected selves, were able to develop arts-based, textual strategies to represent and reflect on the experience. The use of evocative forms meant that others could share in, react to, and re-create their education and experience.

We continue to seek to understand and demonstrate how teacher-researcher inquiry and development can be rethought as transformation within people and places, including nontraditional sites such as the academy, schools, and prisons. Self- and other-study enable us to actively learn while functioning as parts of collaborating communities. In this chapter, we share provocative examples of arts-based inquiry and transformative processes (as well as the threat of decay). These examples are provided by ourselves and other developing artists who experimented with us in different postmodern settings. We use this chapter to re-stitch the complexities of arts-based practice and to freshly ponder the difficulties of its representation.

For us, Mary Shelley's (1818/1994) Gothic image of the Frankenstein creature conjures up postmodernism and its innovative combination of forms. This figure also represents the struggle of reflective pursuit and playful interrogation. We present our collaborative form of postmodern inquiry as a labyrinthine display of fragments of connections and discontinuities, of promising and misleading trails. We alert readers that the birth of a new pieced-together corpus, or at least of its "micro-becomings," have moved us toward "a less comfortable social science" (Lather 1997, 285). The difficulty is that postmodernism is not just a "new paradigm. [I]t is contradictory and works within the very systems it attempts to subvert" (Hutcheon in Readings and Schaber 1993). We explore postmodernism both for its ironic, irreverent, and contradictory treatment of the unified subject. We are drawn to its attempt to break away from yet continue to proclaim that history. For traditionalist critics, this kind of dialectic may represent a half-crazed Gothic or even a fiendish prospect!

We have shuffled off our modernist shroud, emerging from the laboratory of academe to take our first awkward steps. We two are the Frankenstein creation, that clumsy offspring of the postmodernist movement that is our art form. In our poem *Art Takes Its First Awkward Steps*, we cast art as a doubled character in the dual settings of a graveyard and an operating table. In this strangely coupled landscape, the emerging postmodernist "monster" first mourns the lost corpse but then lurches forth, displaying its ill-fitted, patch-quilt self:

Art Takes Its First Awkward Steps

Who's dead?
A new dug grave awaits
The in-ter(ra)nment of the pre-post body.
Its main part took a fatal blow.
Life ar-rested post-haste. Rigor mortis.
Stayed too long at its post. The last post.
"Pass the body bag, please."
Over the broken modernist body
the postmodernist "monster" now lurches.
Another stitched together Frankenstein,
the creation and not the Baron!

Postpartum, a body of opinion fears that,
even attaining fullness, the arts
cannot put/keep body and soul together.

The post-body etherized upon a slab of marble.
Time for its predelivery inspection,
the body cavity search, the logosectomy,
the dire-gnosis, and then out into the word-world.

> *Art takes its first awkward steps as inquiry,*
> *gasping, lurching forth, stretching newfound limbs,*
> *a patchquilt of ill-fitting parts.*
> *Head, heart, fingers, and tail*
> *all cast out from the dying zone.*

Like Shelley's inquirer, Baron Frankenstein, we deliberately produced a hybridized creation using grafted forms. The collaborative creation is cobbled together out of incongruous elements. It is the offspring of two different species—the modernist corpse and the postmodernist corpus. The grafting involves the artful sewing together of pieces of material that have been transplanted as dying and living tissue. Postmodernism provides not just a lapse of reason to be lamented but a means for scouting or at least lurching beyond the known.

We venture into the Gothic landscape/graveyard of arts-based inquiry and development where we are joined by other postmodern companions. One among them is Grace, the incarcerated "heroine" in Atwood's (1996) novel, *Alias Grace*. Grace, the part fictional, part biographical inmate, was granted a pardon after many years in a Canadian prison. As a reconciling memorial, this 19th century protagonist had sewed a quilt with a border of entwined snakes. Her central mandala, a Tree of Paradise, had leaves and apples assembled out of purple and red cloth triangles. But three of the quilt's key fragments were different: one was white from a petticoat belonging to a servant girl friend; another, faded yellow from the prison nightgown that Grace begged as keepsake, and the third, a floral cut from the dress of the murdered housekeeper. Grace "embroider[ed] around each of them with red feather-stitching, to blend them in as part of the pattern" (460). We understood this to be her artistic form for reconstructing events and for re-membering the women after she was set free.

As postmodernists, we also reach out to the forbidden and to the lonely, disillusioned, or reflective travelers who stumble along the slippery precipice without support. Such characters in our landscape resemble aspects of teacher self that have been unnurtured and forgotten, kept isolated and even remote. With our collaborators, we seek a home in our own fractures and discontinuities, pits and vaults, cracks and shadows, night terrors and growing things—all as parts of a new multiform creation. Now, if denied a research community that enacts and reflects on its own processes of creation, we would feel awkward and abandoned like the Frankenstein creature in the frozen waste.

Collaboration means that we still wander but differently and *with* a community of co-adventurers. Isolated self-consciousness can find relief in the experience of local and interconnected relationships. Joint expeditions help overcome the separations of different perspectives and selves while creating rituals of connection. Collaborative communities help us to live in and between the gaps—between what we want the social science paradigm to become and what we dread it will remain as, and between who we want to become as teacher researchers and who we fear to remain as. We are working in community to simultaneously lay to rest our earlier modernist selves and to enable their postmodernist re-imagining. This process involves renovation *without* ruination.

A LAST GASP OF MODERNISM:
UNLEASHING HYDE

> I compounded the elements, watched them boil and smoke together in the glass and when the ebullition had subsided, with a strong glow of courage, drank of the potion. —R. L. Stevenson.

Postmodernism has yet to impact the soul of teacher education. At its broadest, postmodernism represents an international movement in art, architecture, and literature that emerged in the West in the 1960s and became prominent in the late 1970s and 80s. It is a growing reaction against earlier modernist principles that either recycles classical elements of dead styles, or carries modernist practices to extremes. Postmodernism provides a moment of suspension at the edge of the new millennium, an acknowledgment that it precedes the future as a strange and hybrid interregnum that might be the last gasp of modernism. Postmodernism is marked by its refusal to privilege any one perspective, and recognizes only difference and fragmentation, disintegration and re-renderings.

As we found in our collaborative inquiries, implementing postmodernist approaches requires us to compound a strange brew of eclecticism and pastiche, a blend of art and fiction with philosophy, history, semiotics, and popular culture. These transformations or *"hydizations"* (Nabokov's introduction to Stevenson 1886/1987) are slowly beginning to be proclaimed in research and teacher education. The reception of such changes ranges from hostility through caution to enthusiasm. For some critics, postmodernism may resemble a schizophrenic Frankenstein monster whose appearance "besp[eaks] bitter anguish, combined with malignity, while its unearthly ugliness render[s] it almost too horrible for human eyes" (Shelley 1818/1994, 94). From this viewpoint, postmodernist discourse is feared as an unpredictable potion that may unleash another fiendish Hyde. Less extremely, postmodernism may seem to have "done little more than create a playground for frustrated poets who offer us their musings about the disintegration of knowledge" (Constas 1998, 27). Other educational researchers are watching developments without apprehension but still with reservation. For them, postmodernism is appealing in its elusiveness but disturbing as that which has not been named.

Together with the group of 16 arts-based researchers, we have viewed postmodernism more optimistically when it is combined with artistic inquiry and community development. We see such approaches as providing the spark for a new Romantic movement that champions the renewed value and use of ambiguity and incoherence. "Fumbling as it must over the creation of new forms, postmodernism now embraces all writers whose self-conscious structures can be defined as . . . narratives that are endlessly self-reflexive" (Dipple 1988, 47). As Barone (1995) writes, uncertainty or openness to possibility is enhanced rather than reduced by arts-based approaches to teacher inquiry and development.

A proliferation of postmodernist approaches continues to emphasize creative and eclectic forms of experimentation (e.g., Lather 1997; Richardson 1994; Slattery 1994), including approaches that are arts-based and affirmative (e.g., Barone 1995; Barone and Eisner 1997; Eisner 1997; Finley and Knowles 1995; Jipson and Paley 1997; Mullen 1999). Entire issues of several educational journals have been devoted to the relationships among art, teaching, and research (e.g., Barone 1995; Bresler 1995). Such postmodernist educators have been portrayed as importing "abstruse application[s] of the humanities to the field of education" (Constas 1998, 30). As postmodernists, we may be accused of wearing theory upon our sleeve, or, conversely, of indulging in antitheoretical lapses. We freely admit to personifying aspects of the unnamable in educational research by using "literary processes—metaphor, figuration, narrative—[which] affect the ways cultural phenomena are registered, from the first jotted 'observations,' to the completed [work], to the ways these configurations 'make sense' in the determined acts of reading" (Clifford 1984, 4). Postmodernist writers and readers occupy this paradoxical space that conjures up pictures of the elusive.

The Postmodern Genie

Although "the postmodern genie is out of the bottle" (Barone 1995, 171), the literary influence in educational research continues to encounter the modernist paradigm. In this traditionalist approach, meaning is construed as explanatory systems of human truth, phenomena, and experience that "should" not be pursued with feeling. Unequivocal recommendations to practitioners and policymakers are accepted as the "normal" outcomes of research that are produced by processes of reasoning. Even forms of narrative inquiry may have perpetuated this clear, plain form of explanatory text. Not surprisingly, the artistic aspects of narrative inquiry that portray radical ideas and irreverent feelings may have been underdeveloped (Barone and Eisner 1997).

As we show (Diamond and Mullen 1999; Diamond = Mullen 2000), postmodern educational inquiry and teacher development authorize experimentation with arts-based texts, such as stories, scripts, poems, and visuals. Depending on the particular form, there is a deliberate patterning and fragmentation of plot, character, tone, image, metaphor, meter, rhyme, color, distance, and association. These features are foregrounded to suggest a range of possible meanings, including ambiguity and messiness. Such purposeful (mis)shaping seeks to evoke not "truths" but emotions (Jones and Tydeman 1972). The role and effectiveness of postmodern arts-based activity may depend on the degree to which it channels awareness by recalling and arousing personally significant feelings and images that engage others. To respond, readers must draw on their own resources and reactions as educational artists and show what they have created.

As readers, our empathy is generally more engaged by arts-based forms than by the prose statements of dictionary entries or reasoned logic. Artistic images created by hybridized forms stir and inform us in ways that only they can. No matter how accurate a declarative explanation may be it can never evoke for us the qualities of the life experience that it summarizes. We encourage teacher-researchers and dissertation candidates to use arts-based inquiry as a form of research that values literary insight, reflective inquiry, and collaboration.

But how are arts-based inquiries and collaborative communities to be constructed? Some critics have accused current applications of narrative in educational research of informality, vagueness, lacking in discipline-based methods, and over-reliance on aestheticism (see, e.g., Constas 1998). Postmodern applications of narrative inquiry may draw even stronger criticism and arouse deeper suspicion. Although aesthetic value is not to be discounted, arts-based inquiry is not art for art's sake alone. *Arts-based inquiry is art pursued for the sake of an inquiry and the development, including communal, that it evokes.* Some provisional understanding or limited appreciation is reached. Like the doubting child heroine in O'Connell's (1998) New Gothic novel who asks, "What makes a really *good* horror movie" (276), we wonder what makes for a really *good* inquiry and community. For us, it is not the rules and categories but the experience and insight afforded by a particular inquiry and grouping that "dictate" value and meaning.

A student in an arts-based educational prison workshop (that Carol, the first author, coordinated with another teacher) developed a mask series that she performed with other inmates (Mullen 1999).

A Mask of Well-Cared for Plastic Flowers

My mask is beautiful and forever changing. It changes with the seasons. It can and does adapt to any changes that it is given. It is not watered. It will become dormant until life-giving rain falls. It becomes cold and goes into hibernation underneath a protective covering. When the warmth comes it is very fruitful and shows of its true beauty. When it is tended and picked it multiplies and grows strong.

My mask started growing when I realized that a lot of people don't slow down enough to take a look at what is really underneath. That's why I began to slowly grow my mask at an early age. When a flower is picked it exposes a little of itself. If I'm uncomfortable with that exposure, I can nurture that flower. My mask, when it is picked and pruned, does the same as Mother Nature does for her flowers when they grow back stronger and more prolific. Their stems and leaves are hardened and the flowers more difficult to pick. When a flower is picked it may grow back in its place. The more beautiful and radiant the flowers, the less likely anyone is to try and look past them. There are some areas of my mask where the flowers can no longer be picked. They have become resilient to any type of sickness and have almost become sterile because they've had to replace themselves so often.

When people see such a well cared-for mask, they often look but don't touch, which is why I first grew it. No one can see that there is anything wrong with my well tended mask. They don't care when a flower dies. They don't ask me questions because it looks like there isn't anything wrong. How can something be wrong when everything looks healthy? My flowers die more frequently now–their food is sometimes toxic.

I have learned to replace the dead flowers with plastic ones. I'm afraid that one day all my flowers will become plastic. When that happens I won't have to feel anymore because my mask will never need tending. No one wants to pick plastic flowers so they just look and keep walking. I used to have to work hard to hide my feelings behind my mask, now it comes naturally. There used to be feelings that tried to sprout and grow new flowers, now that barely happens anymore. I'm growing to like those plastic flowers because the only care they need is an occasional dusting.

How did this student know so unfailingly how to use literary devices to shape her account of the personal impact of social conditioning on women's identity? Her formal literacy level was not high and her exposure to arts-based learning and community development was new. She did not produce a work and then "give it a twist by inserting devices and techniques here and there like acupuncture needles. The work itself is the device" (Dillard 1982, 29). We invite readers either to find the arts-based form that will work for them or to learn to be more open so that it can find them.

ART IS FOR EVERYONE

We seek to avoid the charge of aestheticism by showing that art, like detection, is not limited to just a gifted few like Poe's Dupin, Doyle's Holmes, or Christie's Poirot. Arts-based inquiry and teacher development is not a hyperliterate game reserved for an elite. We view arts-based inquiry and collaboration as a fundamental drive both to expand present boundaries in research and education and to develop new understandings. Teacher-researchers are artistic storytellers and metaphor makers who can lift experience out of the ordinary through the use of arts-based forms. For example, *storia*, the Italian term for "history," is the same as that for "story." Both are considered to be "the gossip of diarists" (McCarthy 1959/1972), not in the sense of trivia but in the sense of writing about ordinary experience. The significance of personal knowing, as represented for example by "the teacher [or student] I now am," is not to be discounted.

Suggesting that collaborative narrative inquiry, teacher development, and students and teachers themselves are forms of "art," we return the term "art" to its older usage of "art as skillful fashioning of useful artifacts. The making of [texts] is artisanal, tied to the worldly work of writing" (Clifford 1984, 6). As arts-based teacher-researchers, we shape experience by using the artistic forms of elaboration, patterning, and disruption. Even if our artistic selves "went missing" during our childhood and formal education, their expression only awaits rediscovery.

TEACHER DEVELOPMENT:
ORDINARY OR GOTHIC?

Gothic describes an English genre of fiction popular in the last two centuries. An atmosphere of mystery and horror in a pseudo-medieval, desolate setting infused these works. Gothic classics include Ann Radcliffe's (1797/1968) *The Italian*; Mary Shelley's (1818/1994) *Frankenstein*; Edgar Allan Poe's (1841/1936) "The Murders in the Rue Morgue"; and Robert Louis Stevenson's (1886/1987) *Strange Case of Dr. Jekyll and Mr. Hyde*. In the original Gothic novels, a consistently supernatural atmosphere took precedence over all other features, speaking to "the mysterious fears of our nature and awakening thrilling horror" (Shelley 1818/1994, ix). The thrill of yet unrealized potential.

Like Shelley and Radcliffe, we seek to transcend the grisly paraphernalia of corpses to show our ambivalent admiration for many-sided, even threatening figures like postmodernism. For Shelley, this doubling of good and evil in human struggle was embodied in Baron Frankenstein's creature and for Radcliffe, in the monk Schedoni. Such a vision greatly influenced Stevenson's (1886/1987) Jekyll-Hyde image of "the duality of man" (104). In a melodramatic tale of hide-and-seek, Jekyll is presented as a composite of good and evil. But his fall is depicted as "wholly toward the worse" (109). The creator-genius-detective and his or her monster-nemesis are like oak roots and truffles that grow in symbiosis.

Our New Gothic story of arts-based teacher development unfolds as a community of (or contest among) different components of teacher self, constituting a meeting or clash of minds. For example, the differences between "the teacher I hope to become" and "the teacher I fear to remain" can be resolved into a provisional version of "the teacher I am." But this is only a temporary state of balance before another coalition of competing allegiances appears. In *The Postmodern Educator*, a new generation of teacher-researchers shared their stories of development and experimented with arts-based and rearranged forms from which some critics may recoil in horror. We engaged, illustrated, and explored various communities of teacher selves by using self-narrative, paradigm parable, photomontage, palimpsest and split text, pastiche, shape and space poetry, and Möbius strips.

As in this chapter, we stitched together our collaborative practices of art and education. What emerged is "an interrogative text that reflects back at its readers [and us as its authors] the problems of inquiry at the same time an inquiry is conducted" (Lather 1997, 286). Arts-based inquiry and development question and either reassemble or dissemble the taken for granted.

DEVELOPMENT AS MULTIPLICATION OF TEACHER SELVES

In *The Postmodern Educator*, we use the Frankenstein and the Hyde figures to dramatize the fragmentation of postmodernism and that of its most disputed progeny, the self. As something made and unmade, the postmodernist self is never in any final form. Creator and created, head and heart, consciousness and imagination, intention and intuition, self and community, all combine and recombine. While a postmodern self may seem a clumsy hodgepodge, it may also prove adaptive. There could be no form so powerful as that which overtakes and surpasses its creator in inventiveness (Vidal 1993).

As we operate within a postmodern context that is fractional and chaotic, our guiding but never totally coherent selves make the best of things so as to shape their inquiries and development in useful ways. How we feel and think is influenced both by those methods and choices we make as we represent experience and by the perspectives that we use to view our form and content. Development involves a shifting and transforming of self through arts-based, reflexive inquiry. In the act of discovering new forms, we can escape from our externally dictated and seemingly fixed teacher-researcher identities. A monolithic version of teacher self can be reconstrued as a multiple set of options or life forms.

Our story of teacher development involves the multiplication and collaboration of aspects of each teacher self. This process resembles the joining together of the different pieces of Baron Frankenstein's construction. In order to expand and deepen a self, teacher-researchers can look at more of its aspects, then at how they are viewing them, and finally at the effects of devising alternatives. When teachers use arts-based forms to represent their experience and to reflect on it, they are in effect assembling/dissembling and constructing/deconstructing their teacher selves. These efforts may further but do not guarantee development.

Like Pinar, Reynolds, Slattery, and Taubman (1995), we believe that "the self is an aesthetic creation, and the means by which the self is planned and 'built' are story-telling and myth-making" (494). When teacher-researchers work with refracted self-images and support from others, they can transcend static versions of inquiry and development to offer their own creations. Community allows teachers to experience and demonstrate the insights gained from such inquiries. But readers may still ask: "What is a teacher self? How does one begin experimenting with the different aspects of our teacher selves? How can different aspects of a teacher self be differentiated, represented, and multiplied? And, what difference can self-referential inquiry make to my own career and development?"

The Teacher I Fear to Remain

An uncomfortable prospect. Even as the murderous Hyde "trampled calmly over a child's body" (Stevenson 1886/1987, 40), O'Connell's (1998) kidnapper, when first seen waiting for his prey, shifted his weight from one foot to another, crushing under his shoe "the dry carcass of an eyeless sparrow" (1). After many hardening years of work in schools and universities, some teachers, supervisors, and researchers may seem not to have succumbed to evil but to have surrendered part of their humanity. As if under a spell, they seem to have lost joy and direction in their calling. Such a grim and unyielding version of teacher self is reflected in the "sinister block of building" where Hyde hides and in the gray stone of Gothic public buildings. Iron gratings on the windows seem to preclude any notion of development. Like Gwen and Sadie (O'Connell's 1998 child heroines) trapped in the villain's basement, teachers may sometimes feel cramped and held captive in the stony constraints of others.

Like O'Connell's (1998) bloodstained Santa, "monsters" who steal away children's dreams also steal hope from their colleagues—and themselves. But "the teacher I fear to remain" is not merely a heartless villain. In the context of an unruly classroom or a dysfunctional school, force and skill are needed to protect the teacher self and its different aspects against danger. When Agatha Christie began writing during the 1914 war, detective stories were no more than tales of the chase. Each "was very much a story with a moral; in fact it was the old Everyman Morality Tale, the hunting down of Evil and the triumph of Good. . . . The *enemy* was wicked, the *hero* was good; it was as crude and as simple as that" (Christie 1977/1996, 506). Our distrust of "the teacher I fear to remain" (or modernism) and loyalty to "the teacher I hope to become" (or postmodernism) should be similarly qualified.

The Teacher I Hope to Become

Self-directed development depends on teachers articulating and acting on a personal set of teaching ideals. But no one element in a community of teacher selves can provide more than a partial, and sometimes even deceptive, image of the whole. Compared to more traditional change management designs and approaches, arts-based inquiry and teacher transformation must seem like strangely unstructured strategies, half immersed in magic and wonder. As we, Carol and Pat, expanded our circle of understanding with the addition of other collaborators, we used arts-based approaches to escape conformity and even to transform our selves.

Our co-investigating teachers tapped into their own ideal aspect of self by reconnecting with memories of their sense of wonder experienced, perhaps, as children, dreamers, or even researchers confronting the unfamiliar. Such prompts helped them to re-enchant their teacher-researcher selves. Though they might have begun as apprentices in a world of wonder, they learned to weave spells. A renewed sense of magic provided not only an antidote to boredom and disappointment but also the synergy required for inspiring collaborative arts-based inquiries.

In contrast to the grim image of "the teacher I fear to remain" (the isolated modernist researcher), "the teacher I hope to become" may seem to resemble more the polychromatic fantasies of Gothic-Romanesque churches. Their green, white, and rose marbles merge in flamboyant, free-form designs. Arts-based practice similarly resists subjugation to any book of rules or "blueprints," let alone the "algorithmic writing produced in accordance with the style manual of the American Psychological Association" (Constas 1998, 30). In dismembering and layering space using split textual forms like palimpsest (for an example, see Diamond and Mullen 1999), arts-based inquiry escapes the boundaries of the traditional disciplines. But, as the fates of Frankenstein and Jekyll show, breaking away from traditional forms and reassembling new ones is not without risk. Developers of new arts-based communities may pay a price for improvising with the modernist canon and for lurching forward in their new shapes.

The Teacher I Now Am

The significance of personal knowledge as represented in the aspect of teacher self that we call "the teacher I now am" is not to be discounted nor taken for granted. In the community of teacher selves, it supplies the private (but never all-seeing) eye that sorts through competing claims and uses the first person to tell the stories of the conflict of wills (and canons). Like a fumbling postmodern detective, "the teacher I am" figures out things as s/he goes along. In the aftermath of the paradigm wars, we invoke the New Gothic thriller by considering "the teacher I now am" as forever on track but never finally nearer the truth. We each seek to catch up with and embody "the teacher I want to become" while keeping "the teacher I fear to remain" at bay.

In our book, the teacher-researcher contributors also question their earlier authoring experiences and versions of childhood, undergraduate, dissertation candidate, and personal-professorial selves. In one chapter of our 1999 book, Pat represents previously published and newer self-narratives together with a recovered poem as works in a retrospective "exhibition" of self. He re-views his exhibits, making connections to his developing selves and his writing over time. In these fragments, Pat challenges the words of the baronial fathers, and struggles to rescue his self-threads from the imposed fabric of who they want him to be. The monologic father, in this account, resembles the teacher whom Pat fears to resemble. In this story of breakout that Pat wrote as part of a larger composition with Carol, he shows how some in authority are threatened by the least show of resistance.

Shelley's (1881/1994) cautionary horror story was subtitled *The Modern Prometheus*. We rework this Gothic figure to dramatize the galvanizing impact of artistic approaches as they subvert the rule of modernism. We also warn readers against the dangers of any promise of instant transformation and limitless, painless release. Arts-based inquiry and development with their pastiche of forms represent neither monstrous arrogance nor universal panacea! When teacher self is valorized as privileged and surpassing all standards, this implies a relentlessly superior hero/ine. But in inquiry and development the outcome is never so easily settled. Each consists of a contested space that is often uncomfortable, argumentative, and ambiguous. The challenge of postmodernism is knowledge of the death of ultimate meaning, of any one objective reality, and of any one individual's fixed interpretation.

The False or Idealized Teacher Self

"The concept of a child's autonomy is always a difficult sell" (O'Connell 1998, 324)—as is that of a teacher or prisoner. After surviving captivity, the character Gwen had to defend her version of the events! As she explains, "[My parents] want me to change so I can see it their way. My way is better" (324). The purposes of teachers are similarly not to be glossed over by those of others. In our present account, "the false (or Judas) teacher self" can be portrayed as delivering the "teacher I want to become" into the hands of over zealous, reformist teacher educators and their latest innovations. "They" are not the perpetrators of crimes, as in a New Gothic novel, but rather "they" are the perpetuators of myths about automatic and predictable teacher growth.

Always seeking to galvanize teachers with another fad, some teacher educator-researchers may resemble Baron Frankenstein with his grandiose plans of bringing the corpse (or the exhausted) back to life. Alternatively, they can be compared to Victorian English expatriates like Elizabeth and Robert Browning. While the English poets imposed on their readers an overly genteel version of Tuscany in the form of Chiantishire, some teacher educator-researchers may foist onto teachers an idealized notion of teacher education as universal remedy. This false or dictated version of teacher self may prove "bookish, synthetic, gushing, insular, genteel, and, above all, proprietary, [implying] a tyrannous resistance to change" (McCarthy 1959/1972, 21). "Situating the researcher as the 'Great Emancipator,' saying what things mean" (Lather 1997, 298) leads to the imposition of rigid definitions of growth on teachers.

Ironically, even our community of teacher selves may prove to be no more than another false lead unless teachers are empowered to devise and follow their own forms. Teacher self is not just a convenient corpus to be doctored by teacher educator-researchers into acceptable "advances." The developmental version of teacher education emphasizes the centrality of teachers as makers of an epistemology of their own practice.

The Missing or Kidnapped Parts of Teacher Self

In our 1999 book, one of the Brazilian teacher-researchers recovered previously missing aspects of his teacher self, including his problem-solving, pathfinder, quizzical, and writing selves. In another chapter, Carol explored multiple teacher identity construction for and with her Euro(white)american preservice students, including the "colors" of their teacher selves. Some students felt guilty, but most ignored the whiteness that they carried around. Carol's goal was to discover what aspects of teacher self were missing from preservice teacher development by using arts-based representations of cultural identity. In order to develop, teachers best "pattern" their selves as when they pursue an expanding or even artistic notion of their own transformation.

Over-reliance on any one perspective, whether in research or development, is confining. By extending arts-based invitations, teacher educators can encourage readers to locate aspects of their teacher-researcher selves that may have gone missing, or even have been kidnapped. When teachers explore the contributions of their many selves, they can counter the charge that a self-conscious teacher-researcher is necessarily pursuing a modernist project of unswerving and coercive unification. Teachers can use arts-based inquiries to experiment with permutations of self in community that can lead them to better appreciate their own "colors" and those of others.

In the example used in an earlier section, Carol alluded to how she had taught in an arts prison workshop. Incarcerated women were exposed to their multiple colors/selves in the context of collaboration as a form of aesthetic practice (Mullen 1999). Within this mixed racial setting, "expressive circles were used as the basis of our pedagogy, classroom spatial arrangements, thematic sequences, and artworks. Our circle of women helped one another in their transformation" (152, 159). The spiraling artworks produced by the participants and teachers included creative text/journaling, movement/live performance, and visual art/drawing.

BEYOND COMFORT TEXTS

Arts-based inquiry provokes us all as it stretches and recombines traditional and aesthetic forms. Committed to arts-based narrative inquiry, we, Carol and Pat, sought to represent and reflect on our own research and teaching worlds. Such activity "create[s] not argument but worlds, and a world, by definition, is an attitude toward a complex of experience, not a single argument or theme, syllogistically proposed" (Vidal 1993, 38). In providing examples of arts-based inquiry and community, we do not offer a comfort text but rather a provocative assembling of "proliferations, crossings, and overlaps, multiple openings, networks, and complexities of problematics" (Lather 1997, 299). We offer a multiple text that hopefully engages but that probably also provokes and unsettles readers.

Just as artists require special vision and acts of willed understanding, so too do we as arts-based researchers who are pursuing a kind of Gothic wantonness. Relinquishing the certain for the ambiguous, and the isolated for the communal, we seek advances in understanding that only increase doubt. The story of our research and writing has unfolded here against the dual figures of Gothic creature and detective-nemesis. We re-membered our experience of co-creation, cobbling it together as *bricolage* with all its roughly-sewn constructedness showing. Our images are intended to entice ourselves and others into entertaining yet further innovative constructions. We experienced our work as a kind of makeshift quilt in which words and worlds, material and method, overlap and support one another in mutual tension. We played with the creation of characters as our postmodern method and the stitching together of parts as our metaphor of art and community. Our work proclaims itself an artifact in progress.

As New Gothic fiction suggests, arts-based inquiry and teacher development may be challenged not just by modernist and easily identifiable forces. Rather than being besieged from without, we may face an inner Hyde or an apparently harmless other self who may unwittingly betray us! Conversely, Dr. Jekyll with his icy reserve and "slyish cast" was not merely an innocent connoisseur. Each of us "is not truly one, but truly two. [Each] will be ultimately known for a mere polity of multifarious, incongruous and independent denizens" (Stevenson 1886/1987, 104). Depending on the plot and characters that we each evolve for our story of teacher-researcher selves, we may experience our inquiries and development as a mystery, an adventure, a Gothic horror, a romance, a tragedy, a comedy, or a blurring of elements.

In this chapter, we have turned our communities of teacher selves into characters. We release them to wander across our landscape as the fumbling detective, the newly born monster, the magical or kidnapped child, the incarcerated and the newly released creator, and the struggling writer-artist. We seek greater meaning by combining isolated fragments not into a harmonious whole but into a stitched together montage of shifting parts. This process has the power to surprise even the maker and to evoke transformation where it is least expected.

While no arts-based genre can provide the last word, some of the threads in an inquiry, developing self or community may still occasionally "answer one another like notes in music [and] come from time to time together to make a picture in the web" (Nabokov's introduction to Stevenson 1886/1987, 25). Our collaborative, arts-based inquiry allowed us to reinvent our worlds. We played with and heard differently the "dominant chord" in teacher education, which is "analogous to transformation of perspective" (Diamond, Mullen, and Beattie 1996, 176). We hope that our readers will also use the arts both to reclaim and stitch together what previously were only bits and pieces of research ideas. New communities can develop as we tease apart and reassemble what had seemed to be unalterably stern teacher researcher selves.

Part III

FOCUS ON PROGRAMS

Part Three focuses on community building through new programs. Chapter 8 is a description of ways in which communities of learners are created online within the context of a graduate course in leadership. Ann Nevin, Antonette Hood, and Mary McNeil, professors from three American universities, argue that the Internet is changing the way in which community members communicate with one another.

The authors of chapters 9 and 10 examine the reeducation of the educator as they describe different kinds of partnerships in teacher education in their institutions in Australia. In chapter 9, Robyn Ewing and David Smith tell the story of the new Master of Teaching program at the University of Sydney. In chapter 10, Brenda Cherednichenko and her colleagues at Victoria University of Technology describe partnerships that led to changes in teacher education practice at their institution.

In the last chapter in this section, chapter 11, Miriam Ben-Peretz and her colleague Moshe Silberstein describe a study of community development among teacher education trainees at the MOFET Institute in Israel. In their study, they used Sergiovanni's adaptation of earlier work by Tonnies as a conceptual framework for their exploration of two polar opposites linked to the concept of community, *Gemeinschaft* (community) and *Gessellschaft* (society).

8 *Creating Community in Online (Electronic) Environments*

Ann I. Nevin, Antonette W. Hood, and Mary E. McNeil

EDUCATIONAL TECHNOLOGY IN TEACHER EDUCATION

Teacher education has a history of being influenced by a variety of disciplines. Social and psychological theories of human development influence the pedagogical practices in both the university and the public school classroom. For example, Deutsche (1949), a social psychologist, first reported a theory of cooperation and competition based on Lenin's (1935) field theory, which suggests there are three basic interaction patterns associated with achievement of goals among people in a group (such as a classroom) and that these goal structures are associated with a sense of group cohesiveness (i.e., community). A competitive goal structure exists when there is a negative correlation or negative interdependence among group members' ability to attain an academic goal. An individualistic goal structure exists when there is no correlation or neutral interdependence among group members' goal attainments. A cooperative goal structure exists when there is a positive correlation or positive interdependence among class members' goal achievement. David and Roger Johnson (1994) have shown the influence of these goal structures and the pedagogical guidelines that teachers practice to increase the goal achievement and social/ psychological progress of class participants. As participants progress through the stages of group development, an increased sense of cohesiveness is experienced (i.e., a feeling of being a member of a community of learners).

Similarly, technological innovations have influenced both higher education and public education practices. For example, the appearance of the printing press made text available to people other than scribes and monks, leading to the expectation of literacy. Similarly, the advent of the World Wide Web may be leading to the expectation of electronic literacy for both professors in teacher education as well as pupils in public schools. This raises the question of whether or not a class delivered via an electronic medium would elicit cooperative communication patterns similar to those elicited during face-to-face classes (Nevin, Hood, and McNeil 1998; Simonsen 1999).

Recent research on the impact of the Internet on instructional delivery in higher education is helping to define the elements and benefits of online learning. Owston (1997) concluded an extensive review of that research by stating, "a promising case" (33) exists to support the claims that the Web increases access to education, promotes improved learning outcomes, and contains the costs of education.

The advent of the World Wide Web provides an important new arena for teacher education faculty to consider. Teacher education researchers address this issue in a variety of ways. Husu (1997) discussed the pedagogical context of the virtual classroom through presenting a theoretical framework that capitalizes on education as experience-based and interpretive. In his view, the virtual classroom created by telecommunication generates an interpretive experience within learners as they encounter virtual situations, events, objects, and lectures. Distance educators, in his view, naturally create a network of interactions that are both intentional (i.e., guided by the course developer) and unintentional (i.e., emerging out of the interpretations by learners).

What is the learning theory that undergirds technology-based instruction? One explanation is related to the Hawthorne effect—any new instructional tool will (perhaps temporarily) positively affect the learning outcomes of students. Another explanation is based in the learning styles literature, which posits that students have a preferred mode of receiving and processing information. Those with a visual learning style may respond positively to the pictorial and color dimensions involved in Internet course delivery. Similarly, those with a verbal-linguistic learning style may respond positively to the lecture, reading, and reflective response approaches that Internet classes can provide. However, as Chisholm (1997) notes, there are cultural preferences in how to approach and organize learning that must also be addressed when designing Internet instructional activities. People from many cultural groups may prefer opportunities for thoughtful responses as distinguished from spontaneous contributions during class discussion.

In spite of several associations for educational technology (e.g., Society for the Integration of Technology in Teacher Education), there are very few colleges of education where teacher educators are systematically infusing educational technology into their programs of study. Although there are many teacher educators who are teaching specific classes using the World Wide Web (see the World Wide Web Lecture Hall), few are constructing programs of study to be delivered over the World Wide Web. Two exceptions are the vocational education special education teacher certification program offered by the University of Central Florida (Sorg and Truman 1997), and the series of courses on rural inclusion of students with special education needs offered by the University of Kansas (Chafin 1999). In their study of exemplary teacher education programs that use technology, Wetzel and Strudler (1998) identified key characteristics such as a common vision of technology use, leadership in implementing the vision, a history of incremental steps in technology integration, a culture encouraging faculty to use technology, user support, private sector partners or grants, technology integration throughout the program, and technology rich student practicum environments.

In the following examples, the authors share their experiences in using electronic media (e-mail and the Internet) to create a community of learners. The first example shows how electronic media can enhance and extend the community of learners that begins as a cohort within a campus-based leadership training program. The second example shows how participants in an online course created new collaborative roles as they used electronic media to conduct their cooperative group assignments. The third example explains how the professor and participants in an online course used the assignments themselves to create a community of learners.

**Example 1: Enhancing Face-to-Face Classes through Electronic
Journaling and Portfolio Development**

The Graduate Leadership Preparation Program at Plymouth State
College of the University of New Hampshire system (McNeil 1997) is
designed for professionals in the field of education who are interested
in becoming part of a new, dynamic, advanced-level system of coursework. Accepted candidates become part of a cohort group exploring
contemporary issues in education for all students, including those with
special needs. The Certificate of Advanced Graduate Studies (CAGS)[1]
addresses the needs of practicing educators who have completed a master's degree and who are interested in pursuing advanced academic
work in educational change and leadership. The program is built on a
foundation of human development and systems theories, critical thinking and reflection, advanced practice models, and democratic leadership skills. Program participants develop portfolios that address three
key questions: 1) What changes provide the most promise for improving schools for the benefit of students? 2) What strategies work best to
increase growth in individuals and organizations? 3) How can I work
with others to bring about best the effective changes that are needed?

EXTENDING THE COMMUNITY OF LEARNERS
BEYOND CLASS SESSIONS THROUGH ONLINE
ACTIVITIES

Many of the CAGS participants travel long distances to attend the class
sessions held every other week. In order to maintain communications
with one another and the professor, an electronic listserve is established
that allows participants to e-mail one another with issues of concern,
such as clarifying the homework assignments for the next session. The
professor acts as a facilitator who essentially asks participants to maintain an electronic reflective journal that includes questions about material presented in the previous class, assignments, and how to implement
what they have learned in their back home environments.

  In addition, CAGS participants are expected to create and present
many documents intended to demonstrate their mastery and appropriate use of electronic media. For example, they must create, present, and
critique a presentation on a select professional topic using PowerPoint
or HyperStudio. After they complete a Portfolio Development class that

teaches them explicitly how to create web pages, they are expected to contribute to the CAGS Home Page.

The overall outcome of these online activities is an extended sense of belonging to the CAGS community. Many graduates return to campus to show their portfolios to the new candidates; others have offered to mentor via electronic media; and still others have enrolled in a distance doctoral program that includes an online component. The fact that the doctoral candidates have maintained their electronic connections can be considered as evidence that the culture of the community of learners they created during the CAGS program has lived on. The experiences of these professional educators may be comparable to the school psychologists studied by Kruger and Struzziero (1997). They found that a computer-mediated peer support group (essentially maintained via e-mail) was effective in creating a professional community of ongoing support.

Example 2: Evidence of a Community of Learners in an Online Class

Nevin, Hood, and Thousand (1998) compared the learning outcomes for participants in an Internet section to outcomes for participants in campus-based sections using chi square contingency coefficients to show that the pre- and post-test responses of participants were statistically independent of the section in which they were enrolled. Gender and ethnic characteristics were typical of those enrolled in other College of Education teacher education classes, and match the demographics of the university as a whole, which includes 25 percent people of color. Those who enrolled in this elective class were a heterogeneous mix of undergraduates, matriculated teacher education candidates, and teachers who must take this class to obtain a "clear credential" from the California Teacher Credential system.[2] For six of the fourteen contingency coefficients that were statistically significant (< .01 level of significance), other variables such as participants' prior teaching experiences and instructor focus could explain the differences. A comparison of grade distributions across sections and a thematic analysis of the comments of participants regarding how they had changed their minds also indicated comparable outcomes across all sections. That comparable results were demonstrated across all sections indicated the viability of the Internet as an instructional delivery model for teacher education courses, and matched the outcomes of other Internet courses (e.g., McCollum 1997; Nevin 1997; Shutte 1996).

DESIGNING THE INTERNET OPTION

The self-paced course allowed elementary, secondary, and special education teachers to explore major issues in the education of children with special needs who may encounter learning, social, emotional, or behavioral difficulties in the classroom. The course also provided information on the current legislation, policies, terminology, and trends in special education. Characteristics of exceptional individuals and the implications for their learning were addressed, and suggestions on effective teaching techniques and strategies for accommodating for student diversity were provided. This practitioner-oriented course required at least two hours of observing a child in a minimum of two different school settings. Key design elements were adapted from Sorg and Truman (1997), such as structuring explicit online support for the learners as well as using principles of educational psychology such as advance organizers and focus questions to stimulate thinking and activate prior knowledge. Assignments were structured to be analogous to real situations teachers must address so as to increase instructional effectiveness and participant satisfaction as well as preserve the integrity of the learning outcomes intended for the course.

CREATING A COMMUNITY OF LEARNERS THROUGH ELECTRONIC TEAM WORK

Participants completed two team projects—one as a member of a team to decide how to support a child suspected of a specified disability and the other as a member of a "family team" to raise and educate a child with gifts, talents, and a special need. The professors as well as participants raised several questions regarding the viability of such a requirement given their own unfamiliarity with Internet-based collaboration tools. Some of the initial questions focused on the unavailability of body language and tone of voice, which are available for team members who meet face-to-face. Another concern focused on the coaching and eavesdropping that campus-based instructors can provide when scheduling some team meetings during class time.

In an attempt to address these concerns, a bulletin board system was established that allowed discussion topics to be threaded for easy reference (i.e., responses to the original message are stored sequentially so that a virtual conversation can be traced). Members of the Internet class were assigned to teams in much the same manner that teams are formed for campus-based classes. Direct instruction was simulated via a lecture on the stages of group development and the associated effective communication skills for each stage. The collaborative team meeting agenda format used for campus-based classes was reformatted for the electronic medium, with roles adjusted for the Internet. For example, the role of recorder of the minutes and public recorder were combined into one role of electronic synthesizer (a person who took on the responsibility of summarizing the information posted in several previous messages). Each team was asked to complete three agendas and the minutes, and to rotate the roles so that every team member had a chance to practice the roles of facilitator/coordinator and synthesizer/recorder. Teams were given private discussion rooms with user names and passwords so as to simulate the private meetings campus-based counterparts had when they met outside of scheduled class time.

To analyze the results of the collaborative interaction processes, all of the messages posted on each of the eleven family discussion rooms were collated verbatim. It was noticed that messages could be categorized as follows: Coordination (e.g., agreeing to or asking another to agree to a task, setting up a procedure for tasks to be completed); Feedback (e.g., making a comment or correction on another's message); Cognitive Contribution (e.g., posting a synthesis of a research article, making comments regarding the report to be submitted, expressing a difference of opinion); Compliments (e.g., praising, expressing appreciation, complimenting the message writer for the contribution); Technical Problems (e.g., commenting on the challenges involved in the writer's use of home computer or accessing the bulletin board); and Personal (e.g., commenting about a personal challenge, emotional state, or illness).

Of these families, all but one arranged at least one face-to-face meeting. Family 10 was comprised of two people who lived at opposite coasts, the most distant of the participants. They used the family discussion room to post their work-in-progress and to communicate their decisions asynchronously due to the three-hour time difference. Family 6 valiantly attempted to create a live chat room experience on the discussion room bulletin board. All families were able to use the bulletin board, their personal e-mail, and telephone calls to round out their communications and to meet their personal communication styles and preferences.

It should be noted that all families were successful in fulfilling the criteria for the family centered written report. In reference to the concerns about communicating via the Internet, several participants wrote about similar concerns. For example, a Family 5 team member wrote, "We all fit together well . . . we like face-to-face meetings!" (3/2/98).

Some participants were willing to try the "virtual" meetings via the Internet and forego face-to-face meetings. For example, a Family 4 team member wrote, "I just thought we could print off what we had found so far and chat awhile [rather than have a face-to-face meeting]" (3/1/98). All participants used additional signals to express the internal state or emotional intent of a message via the use of "emoticons" such as the smiling face consisting of a colon followed by a dash followed by the open parens (:-). Other signals used frequently included multiple question marks (???) to express confusion and multiple exclamation marks to show enthusiasm or happiness (!!!).

An analysis of the frequency of contributions per team member by team revealed an interesting pattern. The person with the highest frequency of contributions typically had the highest frequency of messages that were categorized as "coordination" although all members of all teams demonstrated the coordination function. Compliments, cognitive contributions, and feedback were evenly distributed among team members. Furthermore, all teams included participants with limited experience using the Internet and electronic mail and the bulletin board/discussion rooms. Those who detected how to use these media were generous in their online tutorials (and, reading between the lines, telephone and additional e-mail interactions) to help problem solve.

MEETING THE CHALLENGES OF COOPERATIVE TEAMING ON AN INTERNET TEAM ASSIGNMENT

A hallmark of good cooperative learning groups is the potential to work through cognitive controversy. This was evidenced in all teams except Family 4, where most of their work was achieved off line and thus not accessible to this analysis. Cognitive controversy was most evident for Family 9, where one of the four team members conducted additional research and volunteered to write the first draft of a particular section in order to represent a particular point of view subsequently integrated into the final report (i.e., accepted by the other three). Another form of controversy was evidenced in individual interpretations of the scope and intent of the assignment itself. Resolutions were achieved by checking for understanding with teachers, referring to the models provided for the assignment, and verifying conclusions with the instructor via e-mail.[3] Other communication skills typical of cooperative learning groups that were demonstrated in all families included division of labor, reiteration of agreements, task specific feedback, piggybacking and building on each other's ideas, and expressing praise and appreciation.

An unexpected outcome was the introduction of personal disclosures—a byproduct of face-to-face cooperative learning groups. Several teams were able to express warmth and support, compassion and friendship for individual team members who were facing particularly difficult life challenges. Some of those challenges ranged from temporary illnesses such as the flu, the heart attack of a parent, and the death due to cancer of a sister. In one case, the family named their virtual child to honor their team member's loved one. In another case, a team member agreed to take on extra tasks.

EMERGING (NEW) ROLES AND RESPONSIBILITIES

"New" collaborative roles emerged in all teams as they made adjustments to communicate via the Internet bulletin board format. One role/skill could be described as "resourcefulness" as team members used multiple methods to communicate (e.g., the bulletin board, e-mail to individual team members, phone calls, and face-to-face meetings). As one participant noted when transmitting the minutes of one of her team's meetings to the instructor via e-mail:

> We've actually been posting, e-mailing, and calling each other with the goal of getting this assignment finished. We've tried e-mail round robin but the system broke down. Some of us were not as motivated as others to get things done, just like a real family. Communication also broke down because of lack of checking the bulletin board frequently enough. (R, 4/9/98, Family 6)

Another role/skill could be described as "technical problem solution generator" for those people who had trouble accessing the bulletin board, remembering their password, and/or experiencing computer crashes on their home computers or having technical problems related to their Internet service provider. Still another role/skill involved being conscious of the internal emotional state and being conscientious in revealing the state via use of emotional icons or words to signal emotional state (smiling faces, question marks).

Interaction patterns indicate that participants used multiple communication tools to accomplish the academic task. They used the bulletin board, sent e-mail, called each other on the telephone, and, for seven of the eight teams, arranged for at least one face-to-face meeting. Two of the teams did their best to conduct virtual meetings on the bulletin board. As is true for face-to-face groups who complete cooperative assignments, both task and relationship concerns emerged in the content analysis of the posted messages. For all seven teams who used the bulletin board consistently, all members posted messages that focused on coordination of activities and agreements, praise and appreciation, and contributing ideas related to the cognitive content of the task. Unique to Internet teams, all teams addressed technical concerns related to accessing and posting messages on the bulletin board, Internet service provider problems, and/or computer hardware problems.

An interesting pattern emerged in that for each team, one person emerged as the "coordinator" by virtue of posting the greatest number of messages categorized as coordination. The ratio of the most frequent contributor was about two to one; that is, the team member with the most posted messages contributed about two messages for every one contributed by teammates. This outcome can be compared to the results obtained by Crawford (1998) who studied the ratio of contributions of organizers for an online conference and found that "the conference host must stay six and a half times more active in the conference with a result of only a little more than two additional posts created by participants for every organizer post." Crawford further stated:

> Many argue that online conferences have a life of their own and that unstoppable forces will drive their progress and allow them to develop into virtual communities. From my personal observations in participating in online conferences and an attempt to organize an online conference of my own, I have come to believe that the actual time needed to produce a successful conference is overwhelming.

Some participants of the 501 Internet class expressed a perspective similar to Crawford (1998). For example, a member of Family 1 wrote, "If the two of you are becoming overwhelmed as I am . . ." (R, 2/17/98), and a member of Family 6 noted, "I agree this [use of the bulletin board on the Internet] is time consuming . . ." (J, 3/15/98). Many participants also became aware of the broad scope of the task itself. For example, "There is a great deal of writing involved. . . . I read through the entire assignment last night. Wow! It's in-depth . . ." (R, 2/28/98). Another participant wrote, "We need to have this big report done to be posted by April 12" (Re, 3/12/98).

Adjustments to the electronic media were noticed in roles and communication skills. Family 5 messages appeared to be the most positive and contained the most frequently posted praise and appreciation messages. Upon successful completion of the project, one hundred percent of the participants expressed at least one positive comment about the experience of taking the family perspective and using the Internet. Some distress was evidenced by two teams, however, where individuals had a sense of time constraints and pressure that seemed to create personal anxiety and worries about getting the project completed. One person in Family 9 wrote, "I basically feel disappointed . . . about one team member's follow through on agreements. . ." (4/28/98). And a member of Family 6 noted, "We've found that working in asynchronistic time is very difficult. One person's [definition of] 'soon' does not match another person's" (4/9/98).

The concerns about electronic communication raised early in the semester decreased as it became clear that the bulletin board discussion rooms and adjusting for the electronic medium could compensate for personal communication preferences. However, electronic media have been successfully used by researchers for at least three decades, according to Hafner and Lyon (1996) in their history of the origins of the Internet. These researchers identify the people, events, inventions, and connections that transformed the Advanced Research Projects Agency (ARPA) communication system known as the ARPANET. ARPANET linked computer science researchers into the Internet which linked researchers in all subjects and the public. As noted by one participant:

> I think scholastic collaboration is what got the Internet out of the military and into the university circuit but that was back in the seventies :) Yes, we're the first college generation collaborating on the World Wide Web, but that just means we don't have to know UNIX on top of our subject matter, like our colleagues did in the seventies. (C, 3/4/98)

It seems that the majority of participants in this class were successful in creating a meaningful cooperative collaboration in order to achieve a major assignment. A community of learners emerged, which allowed everyone to achieve the group project.

Example 3: Building a Community of Learners in an Online Class

Over the past four semesters of implementing an online course developed by Nevin, Hood, and Thousand (1998)[4] there has been an increasing awareness of the unique communication relationships between and among participants. Informal observations and comparisons of communication relationships with participants in campus-based (face-to-face or F2F) classes of the same course show that the ongoing communication seems to be richer, deeper, more open, and more frequent in the Internet option.

NOTICING PARTICIPANTS

Participants who communicate with their instructors through electronic means and F2F are noticed, yet the factors contributing to that noticing are somewhat different. By their physical presence in a typical F2F class, participants generally become known or recognizable to an instructor during a semester. They may be seen as fully engaged, attentive, eager to share their ideas, leaders in group activities, or as followers, inattentive, nonparticipatory, and so forth. Instructors recognize them by their voices, by their appearance, and sometimes even by where or with whom they consistently sit during the class. Although university and college class sizes vary greatly, participants who participate on a regular basis are generally noticed.

Participants in online classes are usually not personally known to the instructor in the same way. Although it is true that some of them may have been participants in other F2F classes taught by the same instructor, this is generally not the case. The participants' "voices" become familiar through written communication using the electronic tools of the online class. The frequency of the communication certainly contributes to this familiarity; some participants even use particular greetings, such as "Aloha!" (as one recent online participant always did) to help establish a reciprocal warm and familiar communication relationship. Of course, the advantage of a name reference on each cyberspace exchange facilitates identification immediately!

MAXIMIZING COMMUNICATION OPPORTUNITIES

Participants in online classes tend to "speak" more. Although a future research agenda might include data comparing the actual number of times communication occurs by individual students in F2F classes, participants are not as forthcoming with comments as their online counterparts. In the Spring 1999 section of the online class, there were more than three thousand communication exchanges in the combined Class Mail and Bulletin Board tools of the course. That number represented a course that had been underway for only eleven weeks—and there are permanent records to prove it!

During a F2F class, depending on the topic and activities planned for the day, participants typically interact only when the structure of the class, or the instructor herself, calls upon them to do so. For example, in a commonly used cooperative learning technique known as "Jigsaw," participants read a given selection, become personal experts on that selection, and then meet in two groups. In the first (homogeneous) group meeting, they discuss the selection with others who have read the same selection. In the second meeting, participants are heterogeneously grouped, and they present themselves as experts on the content of their own selection, sharing in turn what they have read with others who have read different selections. By the end of a semester, however, many participants in such classes still do not know the names of many of their classmates. Nor have they openly responded during class to the comments made by others, unless prompted to do so. There will always be a few participants who enjoy the debate, want to put in their "two cents worth," or like playing the Devil's Advocate. However, generally speaking, a student makes a comment, and the class (activity, lecture, presentation) moves on.

This is not the case for the online class. When participants post their comments to the main Bulletin Board (to which all participants have consistent access), several participants enter the "conversation." Participants know, because of the recorded sender name on each posting, the names of the participants to whom they are responding, and usually and spontaneously they use the sender's name when they address their comments back to the sender. Other participants who join in often piggyback on another participant's response, and so it goes. There is sometimes a sequence of three, ten, or fifteen responses regarding a single topic. How many professors can claim that the same thing happens on a regular basis in their class discussions? The record of the communication is permanent (for the lifetime of the semester, at least), and participants who choose to respond have the luxury of time in which they may ponder, reflect, or otherwise consider how they will respond. Because of the constantly available visual record of each comment, there is little chance of what communications researcher and professor Haney (1992) calls "bypassing," or miscommunication. In his response to a question about which communication method is best, Haney states (294):

The best method depends upon the circumstances, of course, but there is no perfect method—each method has its limitations. A face-to-face conversation, for example, has many advantages. If you and I are sitting opposite one another over a coffee table, we have a good deal going for us. Beyond the language of words, we are also communicating with facial expressions, postures, gestures, and vocal inflections, to say nothing of subliminal clues that we may be sending and receiving. In addition, we have the immediate opportunity to assess one another's reception of our respective messages. If I say something and see a furrowed brow or a whimsical smile, I can ask for further feedback: "How do you feel about that?"

Haney goes on to say:

None of these extras would we have if I were, say, sending you a memo, letter, or a report. On the other hand, what we *don't* have is a *record* of our communication. And it becomes evident a week later that, despite the advantage of our face-to-face chat, we bypassed, can you visualize the futile, irreconcilable debate that would be likely to follow: "Don't you remember? You said this!" "No, I didn't. I said that!"

OVERCOMING THE ANONYMITY FACTOR

In trying to qualify or characterize the differences, and subsequently the advantages, of communicating online, perhaps the most significant difference between the two modes of presentation of the course is the *anonymity factor.* There is, no doubt, a cultural effect that influences how talkative we are in the actual presence of our peers—especially in a class in which we are in the process of gaining new knowledge and insights. Most of us have experienced those reservations about whether or not to speak up, give our opinions or contradict others in a F2F forum. Perhaps we are concerned with losing face with erroneous responses, seeming too forward, or hurting others' feelings. Perhaps speaking aloud is not within our "comfort zone," and some early childhood experience has made it difficult for us as adults to voice our thoughts.

In the online class, these concerns appear to be abandoned. Participants can maintain an anonymity to whatever degree they choose. They can "hide behind" their monitors, where no one is privy to their lack of public-speaking confidence, their dysfluency of oral language, or the passion with which they want to express their opinions. Of course, this is still conjecture, and certainly worthy of further study. But for whatever reason, participants seem to be more willing to engage in discussions, offer their opinions, and even correct errors made by the other participants—and the instructor. (In a recent online exchange, several participants showed a contradiction in the assignment due date when the instructor posted a reminder on the Class Calendar with a different date!) The point is: participants "speak." They speak passionately, respectfully, and frequently. They converse online with one another through personal electronic mailings. They converse with one another in whole group bulletin board postings, and communicate with the instructor in these forums constantly. Although their faces are not known to the instructor or their classmates, their words, ideas, and feelings are. We become a community of learners with many common purposes. We are supportive, we are collaborative, and we come to know one another well.

To illustrate more concretely how a community of learners appears in this online environment, two specific assignments are described: The "Getting to Know You" assignment and "Applause."

The "Getting to Know You" Assignment. An important task in the online class is that participants must complete in a given format a brief biographical sketch called "Getting to Know You," and then post their written self-portrait onto the electronic class tool known as the Main Bulletin Board. These are done during the first week of the course, and they can be accessed as soon as they are posted by anyone who has a password for this course.

In a recent class of thirty-eight participants (which was a double class, with twenty designated as the maximum for each section in our College of Education), all of the participants had shared about their lives, their goals, interests, current scholastic undertakings, class activity preferences, preferred professor attributes, and so on. As participants began to read one another's postings, common interests and experiences were noticed, and many of the participants began to spontaneously connect with the others in the class. This was an unintended outcome of the assignment, one we thoroughly enjoyed watching unfold in front of all our eyes. Participants realized they lived in similar geographical locations, had attended the same schools, had siblings with the same disabilities, and had similar hopes and dreams. Because the postings were available for rereading for the remainder of the semester, some participants began online conversations later in the semester when something prompted them to do so. Sometimes that "something" was initiated because participants were doing assignments relevant to topics about which they knew other participants had some knowledge or expertise.

In the online course, the "Getting To Know You" assignment has become much more than its counterpart in the F2F class. There, it is a first hour of the first class exercise from which few real connections seem to evolve. For the online participants, it has become a resource for those who want to make connections. And it has, therefore, and without intention, strengthened the sense of class community.

Applause. Another rewarding aspect of teaching this course online is the privilege to witness participants' responses to each other's work. Granted, some of these comments were solicited. That is, the professor asked the participants to respond to some of the work of their class-mates on the Main Bulletin Board. Nonetheless, their remarks are gen-uine, constructive, and generally positive and supportive. As an example, one such required response relates to a collaborative assign-ment that small groups of participants post on the class bulletin board for all to see. After viewing the Group Presentations (called the Family Centered Perspective), the participants were required to choose one presentation and provide comments and reflections on the Main Bulletin Board to the group members who did that presentation. The comments shown in Table 1 were taken verbatim from the Main Bulletin Board of the Spring 1999 section of the online class. Three things are demonstrated:

1. Participants fulfilled a required communication online and often went beyond expectations in their comments.
2. Participants appreciated overtly the comments of other partic-ipants in this forum.
3. Participants even commented on the comments of others!

Table 1: Threaded Conversations Showing Evaluation and Appreciation*

Article No 989: posted by T K. on Fri., Apr. 9, 1999, 13:55. Subject: Presentations

Sorry this is so late. I am living in Germany and have had some difficulties with the Internet service here. Response to Group Presentations by T K.

Family #1: Understanding the upside-down Kids I think your group did an ex-cellent job of creating a scenario of a family who has a child with Dyslexia. I re-ally felt your group described Mary very well.

She seemed very real in the story and I could empathize with the parents and their concern for Mary's well being. I like the use of the "we" statements in your story when talking about the parent's concern. I thought the group did a good job of presenting the series of events, which take place when conducting assessment of a learning disability. I liked the contrast between the symptoms of dyslexia and the "gifts" that Mary might have. The group also did a good job of conducting the prescreening of Mary's learning disability. I liked that the group discussed what an effective IEP would be in Mary's case.

The group did a good job of presenting what kind of educational environment works best for Mary and how to modify lesson plans. I think the concept of a "study buddy" is a good idea, which the group presented. The social relationships are such an important part of any child's education and especially someone who has dyslexia. I think it is neat that the family is so supportive. Having a supportive family makes all the difference in the world.

Finally, I think the group did an excellent job of presenting all the facts about dyslexia. The more we know as future teachers the more we will be able to help those we teach. I really have learned a great deal from reading these presentations and being a member of one of the groups. I have gained considerable knowledge of learning disabilities and dyslexia from the group presentations. Thanks.

To which the original family replied:

P B. on Fri., Apr. 9, 1999, 14:55. Subject: re: Presentations In Article 989 on Fri., Apr. 9, 1999, 13:55, T K. writes:

«>Dear T:»

This is Family #1. We would like to thank you for your thoughtful response to our presentation. With all your comments it is apparent that you took time to think about many aspects of our project. We also feel that it is a great disservice to those children that are labeled "lazy" who do have some form of a learning disability, and you were right when you said that teachers need to care about their participants to truly find a way to reach them . . . Again thank you for your insightful words. Peace, P

To which another student in the course who was simply reading the reflection of T replied:

V V. on Mon., Apr. 12, 1999, 22:55 Subject: re: Presentations
T, I enjoyed reading your reflections on Family #1. Your response showed caring and understanding! VV

*Note: Participants anonymity is protected by using initials only.

The applause given by classmates in the online class was frequent, sincere, thoughtful, and loud. Participants often initiated conversations about topics of interest to them related to the course. Sometimes they had an "A-Ha! Moment" they wanted to share, and thus prompted others to join in the thread of the conversation. In fact, when a student recently wrote about such an experience, the professor asked if others had had similar experiences and soon a dozen more "A-Ha! Moments" were posted to the Bulletin Board!

EXPERIENCING COMMUNITY: PARTICIPANTS' PERSPECTIVES

On the last day of class, the professor asked participants of the Spring 1999 cyberspace class whether or not they felt like members of a learning community. Several took the time to respond and of the eight who did respond all of them agreed. Evidence of being a member of the learning community ranged from giving and receiving help to appreciation for being recognized for contributions in discussions. For example, MS wrote:

> As a whole, I feel that I was part of this class. Are [sic] class was wonderful about helping each other out. If myself [sic] or someone else has a question, we were able to post it on the board. There was always someone that was able to answer our question, usually another student, sometimes TH [the instructor].

AC explained:

> I felt like I was a part of this course through the discussions and information that classmates and the instructor shared on the bulletin board. Whenever anyone had a question or something to share they were eager to post it for all to see on the bulletin board. When I posted anything I was always sure to find at least two or three responses from peers or the instructor.

Other types of evidence had to do with the communication tools and assignments. For example, BOG wrote:

> Our group activity, also, made me feel like a team member, even outside of my group. Our class mail tool and our chat room were also instrumental in making me feel part of a group learning situation.

JG commented:

> I felt like part of the class when I communicated online with either my group or other people in the class. There we got to exchange ideas and feelings just as in a regular class and feel that we weren't alone. It also helped to know several of the participants outside the class.

Surprisingly, the experience and process of conflict resolution appeared as an example of community. For example, JG wrote:

> I think for our [family] group we did the best in attempting to share information, but that it was rather difficult. Because of the time conflict with our participant from Germany, I felt that some of my information wasn't being heard by him; as I am sure he felt left out. It took attempting to get to know him and his experiences there to get past some of these feelings.

CW explained:

> Conversation and input were more detailed online as opposed to face to face. Thoughts were more specific online than face to face. Through comments and information that was contributed by individuals. Personalities reflected from their writings.

Although the majority of comments were of this positive tone, some comments pointed to some challenges to community. MS wrote:

> I feel that some people had too much to say, while others left me wondering what or who they are. I also feel that we could be more open because you didn't know everyone in the class and have to worry about what they thought of you.

And CO elaborated:

> I would much rather be in a face-to-face class, as that's my preferred learning style. I had a difficult time interpreting assignments without the oral directions. That's not to say I don't see the merits of an online class, I understand now that major universities like Yale and Stanford offer Master's programs via online, and it certainly was interesting and challenging for me being part of this

unique community of learners. . . . However, I prefer the face-to-face interaction and more "hands on" learning style. I was fortunate to have had a wonderfully supportive instructor that made tons of concessions for her online learners!

The experiences of these participants with regard to the advantages of the Internet format and e-mail communication seem to correlate closely with those reported by M. and C. Grabe (1992) who wrote,

> There are advantages to messages communicated using technology. Messages are automatically stored, so information collected this way can be reviewed, integrated, and forwarded to other interested parties. . . . Many creative projects based on the simple process of exchanging messages have demonstrated the educational potential of correspondence with other teachers, students . . . and potentially anyone in the world with access to a computer and a telephone. (194)

EXPERIENCING COMMUNITY: THE ONLINE PROFESSOR'S PERSPECTIVE

When first teaching via this new instructional delivery model, the professor was skeptical about whether or not the same, or similar, effective communication could occur. She doubted that teacher-student or student-student relationships could develop into or even approximate the level she had come to enjoy in her face-to-face classes. She thought that sitting at her computer typing responses to participants, evaluating their online assignments and supporting their learning could never be as rewarding or interesting. Her conversion was delayed for a brief time by a necessary growth in her own technical skills (and many of her students' skills still far exceed her own!). But she has come to that place of firm belief. The communities of learners she has met in cyberspace are indeed able to communicate their feelings, needs, and passions through their writings. From somewhat anonymous positions, they express themselves eloquently and sincerely. They demonstrate social grace and justice in their frequent dialogues, and the quality of their work is of high caliber. When all is said and done, the participants and professor have formed a productive and collaborative community of learners where insights are openly shared, debate is democratically conducted, learning is taking place, and relationships—professional and personal—often begin.

REEDUCATING THE TEACHER EDUCATORS

> The medium or process of our time—electronic technology—is reshaping and restructuring patterns of social interdependence and every aspect of our personal life. It is forcing us to reconsider and reevaluate practically every thought, every action, and every institution formerly taken for granted. Everything is changing—you, your family, your neighborhood, your education, your job, your government, your relationship to "the others." And they are changing dramatically.
>
> —Marshall McLuhan

These words, written more than thirty years ago, tell us that the promise of a transformation of teacher education via electronic technological media is yet to be fulfilled. We agree with Barbara Erdman (1997), a professor of library media education, who notes,

> Much of the real technology—in the anthropological sense—of the educational experience is interpersonal interaction—between student and teacher and between student and student. Everything you need to know about almost anything—from basic math and reading, to the work of most careers including brain surgery and rocket science, is available within the books in the libraries in this country—in its public libraries, academic libraries, law libraries, and medical libraries. It's all there, organized by subject. Not even the much touted Internet provides this huge, elegantly organized document service on every topic of the human imagination. Libraries are the greatest single educational resource we have. Given that this is so, why don't we just drop all our country's 5 year olds off at these libraries every day and let them have at it? Because learning is not about information; it's about answers and it's about questions, it's a cyclical process—all those many questions that students ask in the process of learning, and all that guidance, direction, selection and nurturing that teachers provide. (Retrieved 4/25/99 from the World Wide Web)

We enthusiastically agree with the sentiments expressed here especially in the sense that the most powerful learning seems to be *mediated* by people. We think there are at least four activities that seemed to directly impact our own reeducation in adapting the Internet as an instructional delivery model for mediating the learning outcomes for our school professionals. First, we ourselves had direct and meaningful access to online resources including our libraries. Second, we experienced incentives such as internal grants and one-to-one tutorials with those who had the skills to use online resources. Third, we actively created new partnerships and affiliations with other departments in our respective universities (e.g., between the college of education and the instructional technology department). Fourth, we acquired new methods to deal with frustrations and overcome barriers to using a new medium. In particular, we have enjoyed the advantages of the mutual collaboration from coast to coast—from New England to California and southwestern Arizona. The original intent of our coursework was to make our cognitive content available to others at a distance. Participants have provided explicit feedback about their appreciation of how we modeled good instructional practices and how they developed friendships and personal relationships—in short, a community of learners—in what was initially perceived to be an impersonal medium.

Earlier in this chapter we stated that teacher education has a history of being influenced by a variety of disciplines, raising the question about the role of learning theories that might undergird technology-based instruction. We then shared our experiences in using electronic media (e-mail and the Internet) to create a community of learners. Many of the benefits that other researchers have suggested are possible outcomes of online learning were observed; to wit, online learning is effective, efficient, and successful in establishing a sense of community.

The technological influences that are contributing to the rapidly changing global scene of teacher education today can no longer be considered additive. Indeed, they are part of the formative process of teacher education, and as such, we, as teacher educators, must find ways to accommodate that new reality. Developing communities of learners in an online medium provides us with a powerful opportunity to complement the social psychological framework of education. Our experiences confirm this possibility. Including the Internet as an instructional delivery model in teacher education in full partnership with face-to-face teaching will, we believe, be a commonplace practice in the new millennium. In fact, we predict that it will be a "best practice."

We hope other teacher educators will be inspired by our experiences in exploring the Internet as an instructional delivery model and in creating online communities of learners. We hope all of us can become dedicated to a reeducation process that encourages wise use of the technological support available to establish a viable, meaningful, and continuing community of learners.

Notes

1. A Certificate of Advanced Graduate Studies or CAGS is an advanced graduate level program in education, typically 30–36 credits beyond a Masters Degree, and often the necessary credential for superintendent of schools.

2. The California Teacher Credential System requires that a teacher complete a course related to education of students with special needs within five years of receiving a provisional license. This is colloquially known as "earning a clear credential."

3. In keeping with a constructivist approach to knowledge development, the instructor consistently referred such questions to the team with the suggestion to rely on their professional judgment.

4. Available Online: http://ww2.csusm.edu/thousand/501cover.html in the College of Education at California State University in San Marcos, California.

9 *Building Communities in Teacher Education*

The M.Teach Experience

Robyn Ann Ewing and David Langley Smith

Currently, teaching as a profession has a problematic status in Australia. Many teachers have reported an ambivalence about their profession, and a number are, in fact, quite negative about their capacity to cope adequately with the increasing demands of the community (Kelly 1995). Some beginning teachers have even reported a high degree of cynicism from the teachers who supervise their work, which has intensified over the past decade. The demands made on teachers to cope with rapid changes, together with the "greying" of the profession over the last twenty years, have contributed to a projected increase in resignations and predicted shortages of teachers across Australia by about 2002.

In addition, teacher education continues to receive much critical attention with many teachers describing their preservice preparation as neutral at best and useless at worst (Department of Employment, Education, and Training 1991). Some Australian research has suggested that initial teacher education programs do little to enable the developing teacher to think critically about changing the nature of learning and school knowledge to meet the demands of the twenty-first century (e.g., Hatton and Grundy 1994), whereas others claim it can actually provide a "watershed" (Martinez 1992) to encourage the development of reflective practitioners, critical of their own, and others' practices (Smith 1997).

This chapter reports on an exciting new graduate model of teacher education at the University of Sydney, Australia, that attempts to address the recognized problems in teacher education (Faculty of Education, University of Sydney 1999). The program aims to orient student teachers to become change agents equipped to help young learners prepare for the demands of the twenty-first century. It focuses on facilitating student teachers' learning, and an understanding of learning as a basis for changing classroom practices within the whole education community. One of the key features of its planning, design, and delivery is the partnership being developed between educators in the postsecondary institution, the schools, and the employing bodies. A second feature is its case-based methodology.

CASE-BASED METHODOLOGY AND PROFESSIONAL EDUCATION

The use of a case- or problem-based approach to professional preparation has become widespread (e.g., Morine-Dershimer 1996) in a range of courses including medicine, social work, and engineering. The approach aims to ground the knowledge and practices of a profession in cases based on authentic workplace experiences. At the University of Sydney this radical change in pedagogy was happening at the same time within the faculties of Medicine, Social Work, and Education. Partnerships within the community of Sydney academics provided an important basis for arguing for a new way of structuring professional education.

In education, four principles have been suggested (Shulman 1986) as characteristic of all case- or problem-based approaches:

- Students are expected to be actively involved in their own learning and formulate relevant questions to explore;

- Students are encouraged to work collaboratively to support each other and challenge each other's ideas and knowledge;
- Students will be reflective about how and why they are learning using this approach; and
- Students will be nurtured within a community of learners in the field.

The M.Teach Degree at the University of Sydney has attempted to incorporate all four of these principles in its underlying philosophy, course structure, and teaching practices. First offered in 1996, the degree currently has seventy-five elementary and 165 secondary student teachers in Year 1 and more than two hundred in Year 2.

In the past, criticism of teacher education in Australia has centered on the claim that the theoretical study of the processes of teaching and learning at the university or postsecondary institution does not adequately prepare prospective teachers for the reality of classroom and school situations (e.g., National Board of Employment, Education, and Training 1995). This is often linked to the suggestion that preservice education has not confronted prospective teachers with their often unarticulated and unchallenged beliefs about teaching and learning based on their lived experiences in schools and other learning contexts (Morine-Dershimer 1996). In addition, a traditional largely competitive university structure, including assessment grades based on the normal curve, discouraged student teachers from working collaboratively, despite their need to use collaborative classroom grouping and learning structures after graduation. Within the M.Teach program, there have been attempts to deal with the reality of classroom and school contexts and the impact of student teachers' experiences of schooling within a collaborative framework.

MASTER OF TEACHING PHILOSOPHY

The M.Teach degree uses an interdisciplinary inquiry-based approach arising from the presentation of a range of different kinds of cases over two years of study. The use of cases is developmental. It is linked to different phases of the program and the student teachers' experiences and development as teachers, and moves from initial case analysis to case authoring. Many of the cases employed have been written by experienced teachers. The cases provide the main framework for the course, rather than just one segment as has been the practice in other teacher education programs piloting this kind of approach (e.g., Morine-Dershimer 1996).

A major assumption of the program made explicit in its organization and practices is that even in the two year degree it is not possible to provide everything a beginning teacher needs to know to begin his or her journey. This assumption is reflected in a reduction from previous face-to-face teaching time and a concomitant emphasis upon student-directed learning, individually, including web-based interactions, and in small groups. The course cannot cover every aspect of what it means to be a teacher, nor does it try to do so.

In addition, the use of a case-based framework implies that every student teacher's experience in the course will be unique. In each phase of the program student teachers are encouraged to adopt a socially critical and reflective approach to the profession: to see their own actions and schooling embedded in a wider historical, political, and economic set of contexts (Smith 1997). Questions of equity and the effects of various pedagogies are examined with respect to the interrelated phenomena of class, gender, race, and ethnicity. Student teachers are introduced to a variety of modes of teaching and learning, both within sessions at university and through the direct observation of school and non-school contexts. They build on these experiences to develop their own teaching styles and rationales for teaching practice within a context of the exploration of their own experiences of schooling, using a variety of individual and collective strategies. The use of a wide range of information and instructional technology including e-mail, the Internet, and online learning are also features of the program.

Assessment is ungraded and criterion-based with peer assessment being an important component. Student teachers are expected to keep a journal of their learning and professional development during the two years, and the course provides explicit strategies for student teachers to develop the necessary metacognitive skills. This forms part of their portfolio. Such forms of assessment model those they will be required to use in developing curriculum and teaching in Australian schools.

THE STRUCTURE OF THE M.TEACH

The degree is built around two major "studies." In "Study 1" student teachers are grouped in multidiscipline groups with candidates for both primary and secondary schools working together. Each Study 1 group works with two members of staff. The Study 1 themes are Students, Teachers, Knowledge and the Curriculum, Schools, and Communities. "Study 2" focuses on the particular curriculum area(s) the student teacher will teach, or in the case of elementary candidates, the six Key Learning Areas mandated for children from years K to Year Six (New South Wales Ministry of Education 1989).

The use of cases has been conceptualized in different ways at different stages of the course. In Phase I, which runs for the first seven weeks of the program, questions are organized around four "triggers" designed to introduce issues related to the themes: Communicating, Knowing, Curriculum, and the Sociopolitical Contexts of Education. Student teachers, individually and in each Study 1 group, frame their questions after engagement with a variety of stimuli (e.g., staff presentations, videos, collaborative activities, and print material). They investigate these questions during their school visits, and through independent or small group research. Assessment centers around an individual mediated reflection, based on journal entries linking learning in Phase I with reflections on students' own experiences of schooling, within a context of peer feedback.

During Phase 1 there is a strong emphasis on the use of activities to promote team building and effective group processes. Cooperative learning is an important underlying philosophy of the M.Teach and much of the modeling and basis for this occurs during Phase 1 (Hill and Eckert 1995).

In Phase II, student teachers are introduced to more detailed case material written by classroom teachers. These reflect the teachers' own concerns and issues within their school contexts. Contributors teach in a range of Sydney and rural schools across the K-12 spectrum. They include executive staff and beginning teachers. Student teachers, both individually and in small groups, spend time analyzing these cases, researching relevant policy documents and related articles and resources, and formulating a response or plan of action. The results of this research and analysis are shared with other students in the relevant Study 1 group. It is also possible to share these responses with other Study 1 groups using electronic chat lines.

After student teachers complete their first practicum, they are involved in authoring their own cases for use by other seminar groups during Phase 4 at the beginning of the second year of the program. Again, although each case authoring is individual, there are a variety of group processes to support individual work. Peer assessment forms a critical part of the process.

In Study 2, which begins in Phase II, students work in courses in their curriculum areas. In many of these, a case-based approach, often using online technology, has also been used to explore the pedagogy in a particular discipline area.

The work in Study 1 and Study 2 continues in the first semester of Year 2. In Study 1 the main focus is a small group project researching and reporting on some aspect of the relationship between school and community. Groups share their projects with other students in the whole program through poster format. At the same time, Study 2 continues with subject-specific curriculum work.

After the second practicum in May of the second year of the course, successful candidates are deemed to have completed their initial teaching qualification (Bachelor of Teaching). This accredits them to teach in schools in Australia as well as internationally. Although some eight to ten student teachers leave the course at this point, the vast majority undertake a ten week internship in a school of their choice, as Associate Teachers (Smith and Ewing 1999). To date, although the majority of internships occur in Sydney-based schools, a number of internships have been completed in rural contexts, interstate, and in countries overseas. During the ten week internship, associate teachers teach about two-thirds of a full load and also undertake an action research project, again negotiated with the individual school. Following the internship there is a post-internship conference in which associate teachers present their action research in poster form and attend workshops and seminars designed to help them reflect on their initial induction into the profession and look forward to a lifelong learning journey. Students who are completing their internship overseas join their peers at the conference electronically, sharing their own action research, commenting on the keynotes and poster summaries, and raising issues from their perspectives and contexts.

THE PEDAGOGY: PARTNERSHIPS BETWEEN FACULTY MEMBERS

Members have been teamed in Study 1 groups. Where possible, staff work with someone from a totally different background. An educational psychologist with secondary teaching experience, for example, may work with a former primary teacher who is an English curriculum specialist. More traditional "expert knower"–"neophyte teacher" seminar relationships are not used. Staff members are encouraged to see themselves as co-learners alongside their student group members. In the following excerpt, one of the seminar group leaders commented at the end of the first year of the course:

> No longer is the seminar group leader the sole warehouse of knowledge; no longer is it her responsibility, and hers alone, to ex-

plain and transmit knowledge to her students. Potentially the teaching involves a student-centred approach which is based on a philosophy of teaching and learning that puts the learner centre-stage with a long-term view of producing "life-long" learners who are visibly independent, autonomous and take responsibility for their own learning. (Hunter 1996, 1)

Teacher education staff involved in the M.Teach who were used to more traditional pedagogy were thus challenged to reflect on their own approaches to teaching and learning, and, in many cases, changed their practices.

These changes were not easy for some and an ongoing professional development program for staff, begun two years prior to the implementation of the M.Teach, and intensifying in the six months prior to its introduction, was an important part of community building. Ideas about the nature of cases were discussed, resources were shared and increasingly people began to take risks with one another about the way they were feeling and about how they thought teaching at the secondary level should be undertaken. People began to be more aware of colleagues' research interests; and connections and friendships were established in a climate where mutual respect was growing. O'Loughlin (1996), one of the inaugural course members, described this as "genuine dialogue along with a great deal of soul searching about the nature of inquiry" (2). She asserted that we finally achieved an interdisciplinary course as distinct from a multidisciplinary one because there was "a unifying approach . . . the various people involved have allowed their thoughts and their ideas to be influenced by one another" (2). This was especially important given that the education faculty at the University of Sydney had amalgamated with the Sydney Institute of Education several years earlier, and staff were still adjusting to different viewpoints about teacher education.

One of the challenges, as the course expanded and more staff members became involved in teaching the course, has been to continue this dialogue and professional learning. Increased enrollment has also been accompanied by resource and staff cuts and pressure to return to mass lectures and fewer seminars, within a national political ideology of increasing economic rationalism (Lovat and Smith 1995). The team teaching approach is also under threat for budgetary reasons as we write.

The involvement and support of teachers and school communities, along with teacher-employing bodies and teacher unions, was a central factor in the development of the degree. Thus, notions of partnership, co-learning, and "community of learners" have become more than mere rhetoric. An advisory committee includes representatives from each employing union, and parent organization as well as principals and classroom teachers, current students and staff, staff from other faculties and institutions, and graduates of the program. Although this fairly large group is only able to meet infrequently, it is hoped that all involved feel that a real community of learning and inquiry has been developed and that their input is valued. One of the course components in which the advisory committee has had an important role is in the framework for the development of field experiences.

PARTNERSHIPS WITH THE PROFESSION: THE PRACTICUM AND INTERNSHIP

The practicum has always been a central, if not controversial, element of any teacher education program in Australia. It has been shown many times both in evaluations of Sydney programs and in other research, that student teachers consider the practicum to be the most important component of their preservice education. It is where they consider they are able to experience the realities of schooling and teaching (Turney, Eltis, Towler, and Wright 1985) and where they are able to develop their professional knowledge base through the application of knowing-in-action (Schön 1983, 1987). For teacher educators, the practicum is also seen as central to all other components of a teacher education program but difficult to implement effectively, expensive of time and resources, and often in conflict with the other university demands of teacher educators (Turney and Wright 1990).

In an evaluation of the Bachelor of Education degree at Sydney (Smith and Pannell 1995) the following general criticisms of the practicum experience were made. Students complained their cooperating teachers, those teachers who supervised them in schools, did not provide the degree of support that they, the students, were expecting. In New South Wales we in the university have no control over the teachers who are available to work with student teachers. This control is vested with the teacher union and the school. Thus, it may be that a student teacher is placed with a teacher who, for various reasons, is not committed to the supervision role. In addition, the student teachers commented that university staff did not have time to carry out the pre- or post-lesson observation discussion effectively. This perception is reinforced by the comments of the university staff who said this was because they had to supervise students in too many schools that were too geographically separated. These problems, identified by both student teachers and teacher educators, were addressed explicitly in planning the practicum for the M.Teach degree. A central aspect of this was the development of partnerships with particular schools.

There are many different forms of partnership that have been developed between universities and schools in a range of countries. The United States has long been famous for its various university Laboratory Schools, and Canada for the University of Toronto Schools. The partnership schools of Oxford and Cambridge universities in the UK are also well known. In Australia, and particularly at the University of Sydney, there is a strong tradition of partnership and programs in school-based teacher education (e.g., Smith, Williams, and Watson 1978).

Recent Australian research demonstrates that the most effective workplace learning for student teachers occurs when it is carefully designed and structured to achieve specific purposes (National Board of Employment, Education, and Training 1995). The in-school experience component is likely to be most effective when there is a close working relationship between universities and schools/centers (e.g., Linnell 1996). Such a working relationship should be characterized by both parties being committed to realizing the objectives, perspectives, and processes established in a particular teacher education program. The effectiveness of the practicum is enhanced further if there is collaborative planning, developing, implementing, assessing, and evaluating by student teachers, teachers, and university staff. These principles were used as a basis for developing the partnerships with schools. In hindsight, it can be said that some were able to be implemented more quickly and effectively than others.

There are three main elements of in-school experience for students in the M.Teach degree. In Year 1 there is the school visit program and the first practicum. In Year 2 there is the second practicum and the internship.

School Visit Program. Another important comment made by student teachers is that they are keen to have contact with schools from the beginning of their course (Turney et al. 1985). Thus, in the first eight weeks of the M.Teach during March and April, each Study 1 group visits six learning sites. Three of these are school sites including a state and independent school and a primary and secondary school. Three visits are deliberately organized to non-school sites (e.g., museums, zoos, botanical gardens, scientific sites) where educational programs for school students are conducted. The locations and visits are negotiated with staff in each site, and the seminar leader and student teachers decide which sites they will visit from some thirty available.

These visits are designed to support the collaborative case-based inquiry being undertaken by the Study 1 groups in Phase 1. In organizing the visits, the philosophy and pedagogy of the M.Teach are explained to site staff and they are requested to set up activities so that student teachers can engage with the philosophic and pedagogic approaches to learning and teaching that undergird the work in each site. Visits occur on Mondays prior to seminar meetings on Tuesdays. Thus, observations made during the visits can be discussed the next day. There is both a formative and summative evaluation of the program, and focus discussions occur with staff from each of the sites regarding the success and improvement of the program. In addition, Study 2 staff also organize school visits around particular questions in their discipline area.

Practicum. There are two practica. The first, in August-September of Year 1 (four days + four weeks) and the second in May of Year 2 (four weeks). Again, teachers with an understanding of the philosophy and purposes of the M.Teach program were involved in discussion prior to the organization of these. A key principle in selecting schools for the practicum is to maximize the number of student teachers in the minimum number of schools. This not only optimizes the possibility of student teachers working cooperatively and as "critical friends" (Smith 1997) but also minimizes the number of schools in which any staff member has to work and thus reduces travel time. In addition, where possible the same university staff member supervises in the same schools for a number of years. This provides the opportunity to build strong, close, and effective relationships between participating schools and the university.

Where possible, schools involved are briefed by M.Teach lecturing staff to ensure the program's approach is understood. University staff visit each student three times in each practicum and consult with the cooperating teacher in preparation of the final report. The practicum is outcomes-based with the criteria being developed from recent government and professional guidelines about desirable attributes for beginning teachers (New South Wales Ministry for Education 1995). A practicum curriculum (Turney, Eltis, Tower, and Wright 1985) has also been developed to structure student observations of their school as a workplace over the six weeks.

The focus of the first practicum is on the teacher in the classroom. Thus, although student teachers are expected to get to know the school, the majority of their time is spent in classroom teaching. As already indicated, on return to the university, student teachers develop their own case story based on their experience during the practicum. In analyzing the case stories of two 1998 seminar groups (thirty-two students), a wide range of themes emerged. Topics addressed by more than one student are listed below to provide an insight into the issues that were important to these beginning teachers:

- Working with students with special needs (5);
- Working with students with difficult home backgrounds (5);
- Developing meaningful learning experiences for diverse student groups (5);
- Managing the class (4);
- Relating to the cooperating teacher (4);
- Meeting mixed ability needs in one class (3).

These concerns are typical of beginning teachers and have often been reported in the literature (Hatton and Harman 1997). The kind of reflective writing that has developed through this case authoring indicates an understanding of the complexities of the roles of teachers and demands both within and outside the classroom. Anne, for example, talks about her first practicum as

intense, layered learning when there were moments of feeling control or triumph and I gasped quickly then for air, for I would soon be flailing again madly but quietly in the dreamlike waters, both displaced and consumed by my situation.

Michelle discusses her concern for the student as a whole person thus:

I'm not saying that we should baby the children we have in our care but to acknowledge the need to create a deeper understanding of their whole selves not just the bits that sit in a chair for 40 minutes and write essays and answer a few questions.

Despite our attempts to place students in positive contexts, some students have not experienced a collegial relationship with their cooperating teachers. Inge wrote that her cooperating teacher constantly undermined her authority in the classroom, making her feel small and insecure and eroding any little confidence she may have had.

The second practicum in Year 2 focuses not only on the classroom but also on the teacher in the school. In this practicum, although classroom teaching is still important, more of the student teacher's time is spent in activities that are whole school focused. Evaluation of student performance is again outcomes-based using a framework that develops from that used in Practicum 1. Again, it is ungraded with the final report negotiated between the cooperating teacher, university supervisor, and student teacher. As with Practicum 1, there is an opportunity for review and evaluation of all aspects of the practicum and supporting documentation with those teachers who have worked with student teachers in the partnership schools.

Successful completion of this second practicum means the student teacher has satisfied all requirements for being appointed as a teacher in New South Wales. As already indicated, a small number of student teachers exit from the program at this point with a Bachelor of Teaching degree. Those who wish to graduate with the M.Teach, however, must complete the internship.

Internship. As with partnerships, there are many different forms of internships both in teacher education (Hatton and Harman 1997) and professional education more generally. In 1996 in New South Wales, for example, there were 970 teacher interns in programs in eight universities. In the case of the M.Teach the internship is seen as a culminating experience to teacher education, with an emphasis on an induction into the profession of teaching and schools as workplaces: a bridge between university teacher education and employment. The internship not only provides the opportunity for putting learned skills and knowledge into practice but extends this to include understanding how a school and its culture operates, and the roles and responsibilities of a teacher in this professional workplace culture. The emphasis of the internship is not only the teacher in the classroom in the school, but also the teacher in the school and the school in its community.

The internship lasts for ten weeks, the entire school Term 3. As such it provides an extended opportunity for reflection on practice and a deeper understanding of what informs the practice (Hatton and Smith 1995; Lovat and Smith 1995; Smith 1999). As far as possible, emphasis is again on having associate teachers placed together to enhance cooperative work. The internship process begins at the end of the second practicum with student teachers applying to schools in which they would like to undertake their internship. This process is seen very much as a professional development experience. On the basis of their application, supported with their resumé and portfolio, they are interviewed by the school. The interview enables school personnel to make judgments about both the associate teacher and the nature of the proposed internship program.

Although the exact nature of the internship differs for individual associate teachers, broadly, one-half to two-thirds of their time is spent in classroom teaching where they have total responsibility under the guidance of their mentor for one class. This includes all the normal tasks of teaching, attendance, discipline, pastoral care, reporting at parent-teacher night, and any other welfare matters. These roles will acquaint the associate teacher very quickly with whole-school issues, with the need to work in teams with other teachers in other classes or faculties, and with dealing with parents and the community. In addition, each intern completes an action research project that is negotiated with the school. Although the main emphasis of this project is on the investigation by the intern of his or her own practice, it is also possible to undertake a project that has some benefit for the school. Finally, interns work with school committees and in other school-based activities that will assist them to gain a deeper knowledge of the culture of the school as a workplace.

Since associate teachers are fully qualified teachers it is possible to release the mentors from school duties for the purposes of their own professional development or for some form of development work to assist the school. As part of this the university provides a professional development program (Smith and Ewing 1999). One course offered specifically addresses the nature of mentoring. Mentors may gain credit for this course in their M.Ed. degree if desired.

Mentoring. The internship program necessitates a different form of relationship between teacher and beginning teacher than that expected during the practica. The role of the cooperating teacher in the internship, is that of mentor. Again, there are many different notions of a mentor. In the Sydney program the mentor is an experienced colleague who, as a co-learning and critical friend, assists the neophyte teacher to: understand her/his own practice and what informs it; enter the cultures and profession of teaching; and understand the school as a workplace. Ideally mentors make their own practices and understandings available for investigation and this partnership inquiry facilitates the professional development of both the mentor and the associate teacher.

Earlier, teacher dissatisfaction with their own preservice experiences was mentioned. It has therefore been even more important to monitor students', teachers', and employers' reactions to this new degree. The next section of the chapter briefly examines student evaluations of the M.Teach to date.

STUDENT RESPONSE TO THE M.TEACH

As the degree is only in the middle of its fourth year, evaluations are not final in any sense. At the same time, in the light of the program's philosophy and structure, evaluation has been ongoing, and student teachers have been involved in regular discussions about the nature of the course and their reactions to various aspects. One student member from each Study 1 group attends a regular meeting with the Study 1 co-ordinator to provide feedback. Students have also formed an M.Teach association and have their own home page. In response to students' feedback, a number of significant changes to the organization, structure, and delivery of the degree have been made.

Both cohorts who have completed their M.Teach degree have been asked to voluntarily complete an extensive exit evaluation of their course at the postinternship conference. In addition, in 1998, graduates of the M.Teach in their first year of teaching were asked to complete a questionnaire that requested them to think about the effectiveness of their degree in retrospect. Table 1 shows the number of returns for each of the questionnaires.

Table 1: Evaluation responses

Cohort	1997 exit eval	1998 exit eval	End Yr 1 teaching
No. in course	140	153	NA
No. returned	53	72	53
% No. returned	37%	47%	

The response patterns in Table 1 cannot necessarily be claimed to be representative of the total cohort. Further, there is the possibility that the respondents were a biased sample, being either those who wanted to positively support the program or those with criticisms to vent. In addition, twelve open-ended interviews were conducted with first year graduates who had been teaching either full time or in casual positions since leaving the M.Teach. Interviewees chosen were from those who had volunteered to be interviewed and whose open-ended responses provided a range of interesting comments that merited further probing.

Most (more than 80 percent) student teachers responded positively toward the case-based and inquiry nature of the program and stated that it was useful in preparing them both for classroom teaching and for the profession. Responses were stronger, however, for Study 1 than Study 2, suggesting that the intensive professional development with Study 1 seminar group leaders had been more successful in developing the partnership concept. Student teachers, generally, also commented very positively on the opportunity to be part of a Study 1 group that remained together for the two years and the collaborative manner in which these groups operated. The opportunities to share experiences and work cooperatively were strongly appreciated, although a small minority of respondents expressed a dislike of having to work cooperatively. This latter comment raises important questions about catering for individual learning styles within teacher education programs based on a particular ideology and approach to learning, especially if this ideology is strongly reflected in the criteria for assessment and success.

Many respondents to the evaluation cited the practicum and internship components as the most useful of the degree. Student teachers found the articulation of outcomes and expectations for both practica clear (92 percent). More than 90 percent were satisfied with their experiences during both Practicum 1 and Practicum 2. Comments such as "fantastic," "both my pracs were amazing," "the practicum was the best thing in the course" were not uncommon. Difficulties were largely related to factors outside the M.Teach itself. For example, some of the geographic locations of partnership schools caused travel problems for a small number of students. In addition, relationships between cooperating teachers and students or university staff were not always optimal. There were a number of students who experienced less positive experiences with either their cooperating teacher (15 percent) or their university supervisor (13 percent) in one of the practicum experiences. The section asking students to make suggestions for improvements reflected this, with comments such as "need to screen cooperating teachers" and "not as much support from the cooperating teacher as expected." Teacher union policy means the university has little choice in its selection of cooperating teachers, so, addressing these perennial concerns is not easy.

In addition, all students have been asked to participate in focus discussions and to provide written comments at the end of each phase of the degree. Space constraints prevent a lengthy discussion of these comments, but several excerpts from student writing have been included below with the permission of their authors:

> My perceptions concerning the role of the teacher are constantly developing. With each new situation that I see, and article that I read, something is added to my mental library. The role of teachers has changed from the past, when it was accepted that teachers would be at the front of the room giving instruction. The techno-

logical and social demands placed on adolescents mean that we must prepare them for an uncertain and ever changing future. Only by considering the students as the most important people that we deal with, by involving them in the decision making, by providing them with a relevant education and by doing all that we can to make school equitable, enjoyable and effective, can we say that we have truly fulfilled the role of a teacher. (Mary-Jane)

How could I have been so wrong in my understanding of what it means to be a teacher?
So far this year the two things that have become strikingly obvious to me are the multi-skills that are required of teachers working in Australian education systems and the growing importance and recognition of the "non-assessable" areas that help devise students' learning experiences. . . . My clean cut answers fade into oblivion to be replaced with an increasing myriad of questions. It has driven me to frustration in an attempt to discover what is *learning and education* and when I become a teacher, will I have gained the ability to show others how to achieve it? I am driven to be a teacher through an intense desire to share my love of learning, especially in the areas I love most, and yet as a teacher I am yoked into accepting that which society considers politically correct, a curriculum that chooses my texts, and a government that puts a price on the value of education by offering microscopic amounts of funding. (Tamminee)

OTHER RESPONSES TO THE M.TEACH

In 1998, Gavin Little, an M.Teach Honours student, completed four case studies of beginning teachers. Two of these teachers had completed their M.Teach in 1997 and two had graduated from another institution. Through interviews, he developed narratives of their experiences both of their first year of teaching and their preservice preparation. The narratives of the M.Teach graduates reflected a very positive response to the case-based approach to learning about teaching, although there were some concerns about teaching strategies used in their particular curriculum area. Both graduates were very aware of how their own past experiences had impacted strongly on their experience of their teacher education program. Their narratives provided evidence that both were strongly committed to the notion of lifelong learning within their chosen profession and the concept of partnership with students, colleagues, and parents was wholeheartedly endorsed. This was in stark contrast to the two narratives of the non M.Teach graduates.

Employing bodies have also been very positive about the M.Teach graduates interviewed for employment in the government system. In both 1997 and 1998, 40 percent were chosen for immediate graduate employment. This is at least 10 percent more than the average number targeted from any other university in New South Wales. Teacher members of a number of panels interviewing graduates for positions in New South Wales schools have told the directors in informal contexts how impressive the M.Teach graduates have been. They commented particularly on their enthusiasm, their knowledge of teaching, their ability to articulate their philosophy, their ideals, and their excitement about teaching in the context of a dispirited profession. To date, M.Teach graduates have been highly successful in gaining employment in both private school systems and government schools, often in the schools in which they completed their internship.

CLOSING THOUGHTS

The Master of Teaching has attempted to acknowledge students' prior learning and experiences. It has deliberately prepared teachers to recognize the complexities and challenges of teaching as a profession both in the 1990s and for the twenty-first century. It has encouraged deliberate and critical reflection about teaching and learning issues that demand a new vision, given the rapid change in education and its social contexts.

All aspects of the M.Teach are as bold and challenging for staff as for the student teachers. The program is based upon a desire not only to improve the past by addressing recognized problems in teacher education, but more importantly, to find a way of successfully bringing university and school together in a partnership, ultimately providing a more effective preparation for entry into the profession. In addition, the program explicitly creates opportunities for lifelong learning and professional development for teachers in schools associated with the university. These attempts are recognized and supported by partnerships with the teacher unions and employers, as well as with parent organizations and professional associations. Teacher education, like any professional preservice, depends for its quality and success on the active contribution of all stakeholders in the enterprise of schooling and the willingness of members of these groups to negotiate what, at times, are difficult and sensitive partnerships. Attempts to make expectations of all participants clear, and to more closely articulate university-based learning with workplace experiences continue.

To date, graduates who have participated in follow-up research record largely positive experiences, particularly in the case-based Study 1 as well as during practicum and internship components of the program. Clearly, more work needs to be done in specific curriculum areas to achieve the same inquiry-based philosophy. We are encouraged by these early evaluations, but time will be important in affirming whether we are able to achieve lasting reform in teacher education and have a continuing impact upon practices in schools and classrooms. Longitudinal evaluations of a sample of M.Teach graduates now in their first or second year of teaching are continuing. It seems appropriate to conclude with a poem written by Meg, one of our inaugural M.Teach student teachers as part of her mediated reflections, at the conclusion of the first phase of the program:

I AM AN EXPLORER

and you who would help me explore
    . . . place a kaleidoscope in my hands
    that I may see the world in perspective.
    "Look through this . . ." you say.
    (Will it help me find my way?)
and you who would help me explore
    . . . arrange fragments of experience on my lens
    that they may shift my focus and colour my view
    "They are beautiful . . ." you say.
    (Will I see them or not?)
and you who would help me explore
    . . . select your maps and place them in front of me
    that I may plot my course
    These will guide you . . ." you say.
    (Do you know where I am going?)
remember
I AM THE EXPLORER
and perhaps more valuable than all the tools you may equip me with
for my journeys . . .
    is your belief that I am
    a great explorer
    and your acceptance that my journey
    is unique.

10 Project Partnerships

An Account of Partnership-Based Teacher Education at Victoria University

Brenda Cherednichenko, Jan Gay, Neil Hooley, Tony Kruger, Rose Mulraney, and Maureen Ryan

The School of Education at Victoria University of Technology offers programs in education, youth studies, and computer-mediated art. The university is community focused and located on fifteen campuses in Melbourne's western region, a large metropolitan area where issues of equity, social justice, cultural diversity, and disadvantage dominate. More than 50,000 students and 3,000 teaching staff from ninety nationalities make up the greatest ethnic mix of any Australian university. A defining development in the university's practice is the unique Personalized Access and Study policy, which provides multiple pathways for study, entry points, and accredited exit points in the vast range of courses at undergraduate level. The Personalized Access and Study policy emphasizes work-integrated learning and supports the development of partnership-based teacher education in the School of Education.

Partnership between the university and local schools is the principle of course organization and curriculum of the Bachelor of Education at Victoria University. The course, a four year undergraduate program, which prepares graduates to teach in both primary and secondary schools, was introduced in 1991. The course conceived of a possible ongoing development through partnerships in teacher education. Since then the partnership between the School of Education and local schools has expanded from conception to practice through the development of "Project Partnerships." Through it, the Bachelor of Education has constructed a collaborative foundation for learning and teaching with partner schools, and youth and community organizations. Project Partnerships begins with the learning needs of school students and young people in a range of educational environments. From a commitment to inquiry-based learning, Project Partnerships establishes teacher education as grounded in practice-theory pedagogy, based on principles of equity and social justice. Currently, six hundred preservice teachers from two campuses are learning alongside teachers and mentors in more than 120 schools and other learning environments each week through Project Partnerships. They are documenting their practice in many forms, with particular emphasis on case writing and the development of teaching and learning portfolios.

In this chapter we present an account of partnerships in the School of Education at Victoria University. We describe how the School of Education conceives of partnerships as a practical relationship with schools and other learning centers. In addition, we briefly explain how case writing enables student teachers to document their practice through partnerships as the basis for their learning and understanding. Finally, we summarize how the School of Education's commitment to partnership-based practice has enabled it to work with an Indigenous Australian community to develop an innovative higher education program that has the graduation of Indigenous Australian teachers as one of its key goals.

THE CONTEXT OF PARTNERSHIP-BASED TEACHER EDUCATION IN AUSTRALIA

Emerging pressure from governments and the profession to enhance student teacher experience of teaching and learning through increased school-based practice has been powerful in challenging the domination of the university in teacher preparation. The Chalk Circle Dialogue on Teacher Education (Department of Employment, Education, and Training 1995) identified the development of education industry partnerships as a critical strategy in addressing these challenges for teacher education. Partnerships in education, which extend the view of the school as a learning organization, provide the framework for inquiry about educational practice, research, and the development of a discourse that encourages the connection of practice to theory.

The commitment to partnership-based teacher education within the School of Education is endorsed by policy support for increased emphasis on authentic teaching practice for beginning teachers. Hargreaves has explained the question clearly.

> One of the central purposes of educational practice and research is the improvement of learning. But behind the mastery of learning stands the mystery of teaching. Understanding teaching, unmasking the mysteries of its practice has presented a persistent and formidable challenge to those who have sought to improve the quality of teaching and learning over the years. (Hargreaves 1994, 141)

The establishment of teacher education partnerships as the essential structure for developing centers for pedagogy, or schools as centers for learning, has also been proposed by Goodlad (1994), who described the three essential elements of teacher education as general liberal education, praxis, and praxeology (the study of practice). Within a partnership model all three are critical to all the layers of learning. The development of the partnership relationship needs to reflect these elements from the beginning, including declared mutual self-interest and benefit.

In reviewing current issues in teacher education in Australia, Gore (1995) prepared a conceptual and practical framework for evaluating partnerships in teacher education. She supported partnership, recognizing potential difficulties that may occur as educators go about building closer links between members of the profession. When the school becomes the center of learning—a learning organization—the focus is not on the integration of distinctive and often contrasting cultures of teaching and teacher education. Rather, the strength of the connections to learning that brings teachers and teacher educators together, creates a new ethos based on inquiry. It is the promise of improved classroom practice and learning outcomes, coupled with negotiated arrangements for learning and authentic assessment of critical experience, that motivates the groups to work together.

Partnerships as conceived at Victoria University differ from prominent international models, although international trends must be understood. In the United Kingdom, partnerships are mandated through curriculum and funding arrangements controlled by the Teacher Training Authority. The experience of partnerships in the UK is variable and continues, contentiously, to develop as much through ongoing policy change as through the building up of local relationships (Hoyle and John 1998; Wilkins 1996; Williams 1995). In North America, the development of Professional Development Schools portrays a more positive experience in teacher education, with partnerships that are essentially university driven, but which respect, recognize, and encourage the professional contribution of teachers as partners (Darling-Hammond 1994; Moore 1996).

In Europe, there are some accounts of innovative but isolated approaches to partnerships in teacher education. The establishment of teacher networks has been seen as successful where teachers and university- or college-based teacher educators work together in mentoring relationships to improve teacher education at the preservice and inservice levels (Autio and Ropo 1998; Finke and Lipphardt 1998; Grankvist 1996; Osterberg 1996). These provide models of good practice, but usually involve small numbers of teachers, student teachers, and partner schools. Like the work of Goodlad's (1988) partnership networks in the United States, most rely on goodwill by many educators, and have been difficult to resource adequately, precluding their generalization across larger programs.

PARTNERSHIP-BASED TEACHER EDUCATION IN PRACTICE

Project Partnerships at Victoria University began with a small group of student teachers and partner schools, and now attempts to generalize the benefits of school-university partnerships for six hundred student teachers in the Bachelor of Education. The School of Education negotiates a "project" focus with each participating school. Enhancing the learning of school students is the starting point for each partnership, in which between four and eight student teachers work with school colleagues over the course of the academic year. The development of an ongoing extended relationship with teachers and school students is the outcome of the student teachers' school-based practice. During the four years of this preservice degree, student teachers spend approximately 150 days in school. In Year 1 of the course, student teachers spend twenty days in curriculum and program support, and thirty-five days in each of Years 2 and 3 in curriculum investigation and teaching in primary and secondary schools and/or community settings. In their final year, student teachers work alongside teachers in an action research curriculum development project for fifty days, including seven continuous weeks of teaching practice.

In reconstructing teacher education as partnership-based, Project Partnerships provides the opportunity to link practice, assessment, and competence as student teachers, inquire about teaching and learning. The partnership emerges from collaborative engagement by school teachers, student teachers and teacher educators with the learning needs of school students. From this perspective, learning in university programs begins with practice that stimulates theoretical inquiry, critique, and understanding. Using action research approaches, student teachers develop support and curriculum with teachers, teach alongside teachers, and investigate the enhancement of student learning.

This model of teacher education, based on action research, embodies the essential principle of practice-theory, where practice drives investigation and development of theories of teaching and learning. The notion of placing theory first, or theory as a basis of practice, tends to devalue the primacy of students' learning as the intended consequence of teachers' work. In arguing to reverse this process, for learning to be based on practice-theory, Project Partnerships commit to a democratic relationship with schools, teachers, and their students. The thoughts and actions of all partners are valued and necessary in the generation of theory and do not need to be refracted through theory to gain meaning.

Through the university's partnerships with schools, beginning teachers are exposed to authentic teaching and learning. As they work in schools, student teachers can connect their own practices and those of their colleagues to a theoretical base, further developing theoretical explanations for such practice. One of the characteristics of successful schools is that teachers talk about teaching. Hopkins, Ainscow, and West (1994) suggest that teachers are then encouraged to move beyond talk to study the literature to focus inquiry and discussion on improving practice. Project Partnerships provides the opportunity for student teachers to work and reflect with teachers. New practice emerges from collaborative reflective discourse based on the artifacts of teaching and learning, such as student work samples and student teacher cases of practice. The development of professional discourse, which enables this type of theorizing by beginning teachers, is enhanced through extensive and meaningful teaching practice alongside mentor teachers. Continuing opportunities to reflect on and examine practice in an action research approach provides the basis for student teachers to develop and critique theoretical understandings and thus initiate change.

Preservice teacher education is conceptually the beginning of a professional partnership in the development of new teachers. Project Partnerships recognizes equal but different roles for practicing teachers in schools and other education settings and for the university teacher educator. Both bring different perspectives and experiences of practice and together offer the opportunity for collaborative reform for improvement in the profession. Project Partnerships intends that each partnership be constructed on essential criteria that embody the principles of equity and inquiry:

- The purpose of the partnership is to achieve learning opportunities and outcomes for school students;
- The partnership is negotiated between the partners;
- Learning is fostered when it is student centered, builds on previous knowledge, encourages risk taking, and is responsive to the learners' background and needs.

All participants have both teaching and learning roles. Project Partnerships provides the opportunity for mentor teachers, student teachers, and teacher educators to enhance communication, understanding, and respect for young people and the issues present in their lives. Project Partnerships, articulated through practice-theory, recognizes that school students too have fields of knowledge that contribute to the learning environment.

Project Partnerships focuses on young people's learning and may be located in schools, at university, on a camp, in a youth activity, at a community center, or potentially on the Internet. The following examples of Project Partnerships illustrates some of the possible ways in which student teachers can work with school teachers to address the learning needs of school students as the focus for their own education.

Sample Primary School Project Partnership

A team of six Year 2 and four Year 1 student teachers who are undertaking general studies in Physical Education and Information Technology work in all classes. The Year 2 student teachers spend thirty-five days at the school in junior and upper grades. They assist with the development of the camps program in each year level and lead physical education activities with class teachers. The student teachers based in the junior classes are immersed in Early Years Literacy and work with the other student teachers to begin to develop some applications of early years literacy to the upper grades. Literacy and numeracy curriculum inquiry is the focus of the university program for these student teachers. In their classrooms, they are also involved in the normal teaching and learning program.

The Year 1 student teachers spend twenty days at the school in grades 3 and 4 supporting the introduction of information technology across these grade levels. They gradually take responsibility for leading some of the class learning program and have better information technology skills than some of the teachers. They also work alongside the teacher supporting the curriculum in other areas.

Sample Secondary School Project Partnership

Four student teachers from Year 3 of the Bachelor of Education K-12 work with the Assistant Principal as mentor to establish a Student Representative Council (SRC) across two campuses of the school. The student teachers have general studies in English, social science, business studies, and accounting and information technology. They spend thirty-five days at the school. Student teachers also inquire about science and studies of society and environment curriculum in Year 3.

The student teachers work with teachers and students in years 8 and 9 across a range of subjects, teaching in their areas of speciality and learning about curriculum in others. They meet with school leaders, teachers, and students, to develop a process for electing an SRC. The SRC is elected and the student teachers conduct training sessions in meeting procedures, government, and management, keeping records and a range of other practices that inform the conduct of the SRC and build from the strengths of the student teachers. They mentor the SRC members through their early development and assist in organizing and conducting a camp for the group in the final term. They also continue to teach and learn in classrooms.

Projects such as these, which deliberately structure student teachers' experiences around questions concerning young people's learning, challenge traditional practices of teacher education. In developing new ways of working in the preparation of teachers that involve practice-based learning, reflection on practice, and problem solving, a new pedagogy is emerging in the university. These new practices are both personalized and localized; that is, they are shaped by the learning needs and pedagogical skill of the partners, and the local context in which they are situated. As such, each partnership is unique in its focus and learning outcomes. The practice of teacher educators is changing as university teaching, learning, and reflective and collaborative inquiry about practice very often occur in small groups at the partnership site.

Case Writing

The School of Education at Victoria University, through its commitment to partnerships and practice-theory pedagogy, has adopted case writing as a means of making an authentic representation of practice and as a research tool. Documenting practice, and sharing it publicly in collaborative reflection on personal practice, requires engagement with educational and societal contexts marked by continual change and increasing demands. The wide range of applications of case and commentary writing at Victoria University has its significance in the way it makes teachers' knowledge respected, accessible, and enhancing of educational discourse.

This approach to understanding is derived from the work of Connell, Ashenden, Dowsett, and Kessler (1982) who take as a starting point a contentious definition of practice when they write about the teacher-student relationship as:

> This, like all other relationships, exists only in practices and (those) practices are always being constructed anew. The particular form of those practices, their circumstances, changes and assumptions, are matters for investigation, not assumption. (100)

Placing teachers' and students' practices at center stage raises three questions in relation to the utilization of case writing in prompting reflection and discourse:

- Can a discursive representation of personal teaching practice, such as case writing within agreed interpretive structures, enhance the generation of ongoing professional development?
- Does a collection of case writing and other evidence of practice contained for example, within a teaching portfolio, provide an insight into the nature and quality of the curriculum, teaching, learning, organization, and practices of a school, as followed by an individual teacher?
- Can a portfolio collection of the discursive representations of

teaching practice enable a comparison of the student learning outcomes from different classrooms or different schools and consequently serve as a basis for improvement between schools and programs?

It is not a simple matter however, to investigate these questions because of the nature and culture of teachers' work. According to Yeatman and Sachs (1995), for example, the distinctive feature of the practice of teaching is its oral mode of communication and thus the practical knowledge of teachers is highly contextualized, often private and undisclosed. Case writing then requires teachers to take on an explicit and continuing process of making their practical knowledge of teaching discursively available.

The exact nature of case writing and the type of discussion it prompts, therefore, has significance. It can be distinguished from journal writing in that it is expressly written for public display around specific moments of teaching and learning, rather than for private reflection on issues the writer may feel are too "risky" for publication. It contributes to principled democratic relationships between teachers anticipated by Dewey (1916). Additionally, it promotes a professional language of terms, concepts, and understandings on which collaborative educational analysis, interpretation, and theorizing can be based.

Informal, naturalistic case writing that begins with and describes teaching practice and involves reflective comment on experience, establishes the conditions that enable personal theorizing to occur. Although cases mainly describe practice, they are also occasions for the suggesting of personal explanations, no matter how brief and tentative. The author writes from a theoretical framework that has been fashioned by classroom experience, reading, professional development, and a lifetime of economic, cultural, and educational experience. On the other hand, the reader or commentary writer contributes new experiences to the case, generating amended explanations, new tentative understandings, and perhaps most importantly, new avenues for further action and investigation in the classroom.

Case writing may bring special benefits to those who write, prompting student teachers to reflect on their practices and to become more analytical about their work in classrooms and schools. The inclusion of case methods into the Bachelor of Education at Victoria University seeks to engage student teachers in more intellectually stimulating classroom problems, so that they are more likely to bridge the gap between theory and practice and to "think like a teacher" (Shulman 1992).

It is hoped that the process of reflective case writing supports the broader scope of participation in political and cultural life through the enhancement of the quality of democratic educational discourse, such as gender relations in classrooms or the impact of government policy on curriculum development. Within a partnership framework, case and commentary writing provide a means of reflecting on teaching and learning and of theorizing change and improvement. Student teachers' writing about practice enables them to represent their world of teaching, encourages them to attend to the details of practice and the consequences of their actions and to initiate a discourse for the critical examination of this practice with others.

At Victoria University, the case writing of student teachers has been examined in response to the question: How do student teachers understand practice? The framework developed by Cherednichenko, Hooley, Kruger, and Mulraney (1995) suggests three broad characteristics of benchmark cases written by student teachers: practice described, practice interpreted and practice theorized. The following examples from student teacher case writing demonstrate these elements.

> **Practice Described.** I went into the grade six class with an open mind. During the first two days I observed the dynamics of the class in which James was a focal point. The teacher constantly disciplined James for his disruptive behavior. I would estimate that the total amount of teaching time that Mrs. D. had to sacrifice to James was about a third. . . . On the third day Mrs. D's frustration began to show and she eventually got angry.

The student teacher is describing a rich setting in which to develop this case. It is simply and directly stated and suggests the important role the mentor teacher plays in this second year student teacher's understanding of practice.

> **Practice Interpreted.** The students took longer than I had expected to decide which piece of work they wanted to use. They compared their stories with those of their classmates and the object of the exercise became lost in the excitement of reading each other's work. I took a mental note that next time I would choose the piece of work. We did not quite finish within the allocated time and many did not finish at all but all the students did attempt to improve their story writing. The weaker students struggled to find nouns in their stories . . .

The student teacher critically reports the learning experience for her students, recognizing individual learning styles and outcomes. She applies a framework for interpretation by being aware of the need to consider both student learning outcomes and her own pedagogy when constructing new learning experiences. She makes explicit connections between the social context, the practice of teaching, and student learning.

> **Practice Theorized.** At lunch time I asked the teacher about David's behavior. She explained that he had a medical condition which prevented him from participating in the same way as the other children. . . . When this student is misbehaving in class I now understand WHY. I have learnt and I now understand that there must be a reason behind a child's behavior. This should be found out first before I give out any punishment as this is not fair to the child.

In this excerpt, a Year 2 student teacher reflects on her practice. Drawing on the expertise of the mentor teacher, she is able to construct new principles for action. She begins to explicitly construct theoretical understandings, and to develop principles for improving practice.

Case writing in the Bachelor of Education is supplemented by other approaches to the documentation and understanding of practice including:

- Teaching and learning records, including curriculum plans, lesson plans and evaluations, and samples of school students' work, and
- Portfolios that collect examples of student teachers' records of practice and progress through the course.

The prominence afforded to the description, interpretation, and theorizing of practice in the Bachelor of Education is not simply an exercise in narrative writing or analysis. Through the documentation of and reflection on practice, student teachers become aware of the possibility of consciously and intentionally changing practice. Case writing forms a significant component of the work of student teachers in the Bachelor of Education and provides an important window on practice through which the student teacher, mentor teacher, and university colleague are able to reflect on practice.

THE NYERNA STUDIES PARTNERSHIP IN
COMMUNITY-BASED TEACHER EDUCATION

Nyerna: "to sit, to listen, to hear, to remember,"
          a local Wembawemba word.

Changing practice is not only an expectation for student teachers. It is
an inevitable condition for the School of Education and its staff as they
generate deeper understandings about the "curriculum of practice-
theory" in education. One recent development is the preparation of an
innovative program that constructs partnerships and considers practice
in the lives and interests of Australia's Indigenous community.

In mid-1997, Victoria University of Technology entered into a
partnership arrangement with the Indigenous people of the Echuca-
Moama region of southeastern Australia to plan and implement a Bachelor of Education and Bachelor of Arts program. Over time, it is
intended that a university center under the control of Indigenous people will be established.

Teaching of the new course Bachelor of Education (Nyerna
Studies)/Bachelor of Arts (Nyerna Studies) began in Semester 1, 1998,
structured around studies in the four areas of Education, Indigenous
Culture and Knowledge, Sport and Recreation, and Youth and Community. The course is open to Indigenous and non-Indigenous people, and
approximately forty students are currently enrolled.

The key feature of the program is its attempt to locate teaching
and learning in the culture of the local community for the benefit of the
community, and to take as its starting point the knowledge and understandings of the students and their families. In other words, the program aims to organize learning around a set of principles consistent
with Indigenous life, thereby reversing the traditional flow and origins
of knowledge found in most postsecondary programs. The process of
learning that links the university and community is that of participatory inquiry where an integrated approach to knowledge is the framework for shaping knowing from systematic experience. A flexible and
informal teaching arrangement that focuses on "critical incidents" allows for small group discussions and emphasis on practice to be the organizational norm.

Australia's Indigenous people have long been treated badly by the
formal education system, with culture, history, language, and identity
being generally denied (Reynolds 1999b) and not, as Scourgall (1997)
has recommended, with "authority for the construction of meanings
resting with the community" (58). Although colonialism and disposses-

sion have meant that many connections with the land have been made difficult, the Nyerna Studies program is in the fortunate position of being physically located close to one of Australia's major river systems and a large area of red gum forest. This means there are opportunities present for learning environmentally from the rivers, lakes, trees, and animals that abound, and for ensuring that all students are encouraged to inquire and reflect about their place in the natural landscape. Creating the conditions for reflection on, in, and for practice is designed to stimulate learning and connect educational and social commitments.

Connected to the environmental question is the strong significance of community and culture. All students are able to draw upon their own knowledge and culture when considering a major idea such as science, mathematics, art, or law: where do these ideas and practices come from, how are they viewed by different groups, how is each tempered by economic, political, and moral considerations? The importance of elders (Abednego 1999) needs to be recognized in this regard for the role they play in traditional lore and community participation. When ideas and practices are scrutinized from different cultural perspectives, contrary viewpoints are treated with respect, without one trying to dominate the other. Such a process does not exclude analysis and interpretation as in the Western scientific tradition, but enables a "two way" approach to be respected and explored.

In general terms, Nyerna Studies seeks to become a part of the ongoing narrative of the local community in the quest for reconciliation. Life as encountered at the university is not separated from life at home. The issues of importance to the local community form the basis for constructing questions and investigations for study and research. The experiences gained are mutual, challenging, and not superficial or abstracted from daily living. Narrative living and production need to be fully collaborative and very much within the control of the local community. This contrasts with the traditional role of the university researcher in writing accounts that, as Foley (1998) notes, "create a common denominator people of social archetypes and roles" (110). These techniques support the action research model of Project Partnerships and the Bachelor of Education, and provide new challenges in fostering community participation in the program.

The establishment of open, respectful, and democratic partnerships with local communities, needs to go beyond the educational and connect with the impulses of social change and justice that are to be found everywhere. This is not possible or at least is exceedingly difficult when confined by university structure and procedure. With their intimate connections with the land, Indigenous peoples should quite rightly expect to stand alongside historians (Reynolds 1999a) and educators in living, creating, and documenting histories, narratives, and struggles for a more enlightened future. Moves for local reconciliation and self-determination as embodied in the operation of Nyerna Studies could contribute to this historic trend.

The course is unique in its curriculum, its structure, and in the provision of multiple exit points at the successful completion of each year level, and subsequent exit. Nyerna Studies represents an unprecedented and powerful response to university policy, and more significantly to educational and vocational needs and abilities of Indigenous Australians. It responds to the strong commitment Victoria University has made to developing community responsive education through the Personal Access and Study initiative.

PARTNERSHIP-BASED TEACHER EDUCATION: A NEW PEDAGOGY

The School of Education at Victoria University is applying its partnership approach to other programs. Already students in the Bachelor of Arts (Youth Studies) and the Graduate Diploma in Education (Secondary) are committed to practice-based education through partnerships. Increasingly, partnerships with other learning and community organizations are being established. Fundamental to the development of Project Partnerships is the quality of the basis of the partnership, that is, meeting the learning needs of young people, normally school students. This will be the outcome of closer collegial relationships with teachers, the school, and its community. Partnerships of this type have the potential to bring people together in local community organizations for action around key issues in their lives, for social justice and the common good.

However much Project Partnerships has fostered a conceptual and practical advance in teacher education, problems remain. In the current educational, political, and economic climate in Australia, the most pressing issue for delivering effective partnership-based teacher education is the development of appropriate resource structures. An increased role for teachers in the preparation of beginning teachers requires a review of funding for teacher education recognizing the additional contribution of teachers above current workload and workplace agreements. Without valuing, respecting, and appropriately recompensing teachers' work, the opportunity to reconstruct teacher education is severely hindered.

The focus for the future in the School of Education is the construction of partnership-based teacher education founded on agreed understandings about the nature of partnership, young people's learning, and graduating competent professionals. With this goal, the ability to initiate, negotiate, develop, and sustain partnerships that are focused on the learning of school students and that deliver social and educational equity is imperative. This demands the constant review and renegotiation of roles for all partners. Substantial rethinking of the role of teachers, community leaders, and teacher educators continues to be highlighted, leading to important change as Project Partnerships grows. Student teacher learning is also strengthened, especially through mentoring with teachers that enables student teachers to participate in authentic teaching practice and collaborative and critical reflections on that practice. The School of Education is committed to partnership-based education, is engaged in research that examines partnerships, and is pursuing further development and associated research to inform practice.

11 Creating a Community of Teacher Educators

Miriam Ben-Peretz and Moshe Silberstein

> There is no recipe for community building—no correlates, no workshop agenda, no training package. Community cannot be borrowed or bought.
> —Sergiovanni

The notion of the importance of teachers working in communities is gaining ground in the literature on teaching and teacher education (McLaughlin 1994; Rosenholtz 1989b; Talbert and McLaughlin 1994). Replacing the myth or reality of "the lonely teacher" is a growing belief in restructuring teachers' work so that teachers will be able to work together, learn from each other, and continue their professional development through sustained interaction and sharing of experience. There are attempts to create such communities of teachers in the context of schools as described by Talbert and McLaughlin (1994). It is reasonable to assume that the disposition toward involvement in ongoing and viable communities of teachers has to become part of pre- and in-service education programs.

The creation of a community of teacher educators is conceived herewith as an important step toward forming teacher communities by student teachers during their studies and in their future professional practice. By learning to work and study together student teachers will be better prepared for the kinds of interactions that foster the development of collaborative engagement in education. Experience sharing, joint problem solving, and interpersonal support of members of their community could enrich the professional knowledge base of teacher educators themselves.

According to Sergiovanni (1994), successful community building depends on each institution creating for itself its own practice of community. In this chapter we present a portrait of one community that developed within the framework of a professional specialization course for pedagogy instructors in teacher education colleges in Israel. Pedagogy instructors in Israel are expected to accompany student teachers and act as mentors in their field work, to assist them in their attempts to integrate their theoretical and practical knowledge. A special two-year program was planned for pedagogy instructors to develop and consolidate the professional concepts, abilities, and tools conducive to their role in the process of teacher education.

CONCEPTUAL FRAMEWORK

The concept of community adopted in our study is based on the distinction between *Gemeinschaft* (community) and *Gesellschaft* (society) suggested by Tonnies ([1887] 1957) and elaborated by Sergiovanni (1994).

In Tonnies's view Gemeinschaft exists in three forms: Gemeinschaft by kinship, by place—through sharing a common habitat—and Gemeinschaft of mind. According to Tonnies, "Gemeinschaft of mind expresses the community of mental life" (42). It emerges as a result of sharing a common goal and a common set of values. Tonnies states that "whenever human beings are related through their wills in an organic manner and affirm each other we find one or another of the three types of Gemeinschaft" (42).

Gesellschaft, on the other hand, is characterized, according to Tonnies, by more impersonal relationships and more contrived connections among people and between them and their institutions. "In Gesellschaft every person strives for that which affirms the action of others only and insofar as and as long as they can further his interests" (Tonnies [1887] 1957, 47). The outcomes of such situations might be loneliness and isolation (Seeman 1959).

Gemeinschaft and Gesellschaft never exist in the real world in pure form. They represent polar opposites on a continuum. Some organizations lean more to one pole, the Gemeinschaft, such as the extended family, and some are dominated by Gesellschaft values, such as the court system. Sergiovanni (1994) argues for building a Gemeinschaft within Gesellschaft-like organizations, saying: "It is time that the metaphor for school was changed from formal organizations to community" (14).

Parsons (1951) used Tonnies's concepts to describe types of social relations, patterns of variables that represent choices between alternative value orientations. Such variables are: affective/affective neutrality; collective orientation/self-orientation; particularism/universalism; ascription/achievement; diffuseness/specificity. These variables are viewed on a continuum and can be used to ascertain the extent to which social relationships in a specific context present a Gemeinschaft and lean more toward the affective, collective oriented, particular, determined by ascription, and diffuse (holistic) poles or are conversely, more Gesellschaft-like, leaning toward the opposite pole. These variables, as well as additional ones suggested by Sergiovanni (1994), such as substantive versus instrumental, and altruism versus egocentrism, and one we have added: collective identity versus personal identity, form the conceptual framework of our inquiry.

Relations in educational institutions can be affective, or affectively neutral. Will standard rules or regulations be imposed (universalism), or will people be treated individually (particularism)? Will relationships be inclusive and holistic (diffuseness), or will role relationships determine specific topics for attention (specificity)? Will a person be judged according to achievement, or will everyone be accepted because of his or her belonging to the group (ascription)? Do people keep at a distance from each other (self-orientation), or do they view themselves as part of a group (collective orientation)?

In Gesellschaft, means and ends are separated, communicating an instrumental view of society. Conversely, in Gemeinschaft the distinction is blurred, means too are important for their own sake, and are viewed as having substantive value. For instance, members of a community associate with one another not just because this helps the community achieve its goals, but because doing so is valuable in itself.

According to Rousseau (1991), when people in a community show selfless concern for one another stemming from a sense of devotion (altruism) they represent an "authentic" community. People who share an activity or project seeking their own fulfillment as their end, might be considered as representing egocentrism. They live in a "counterfeit" community.

We have added yet another dimension for analyzing the nature of communities, namely, collective versus personal identity. Do people in a community develop a sense of collective identity, or do they continue to consider themselves as individuals who happen to share a program or project?

The conceptual framework described above served as the basis for the instrument used in our study.

THE NATURE OF THE INSERVICE PROGRAM

The professional specialization program for teacher educators, which serves as the focus of our study, is planned and implemented at the MOFET Institute in Israel. MOFET is a special institute devoted to research, curriculum, and program development for teacher educators in colleges of teacher education. The program helps participants acquire the knowledge and skills necessary for pedagogy instructors. The principles of experiential learning, combining theory and practice, are applied. Learning is based on participants' personal teaching experience, as well as on their experience as pedagogy instructors in colleges of education. Team frameworks, personal case studies, case literature, and the principles of reflective guidance are utilized. Completion of the professional specialization program meets the first requirement for a diploma as Professional Pedagogy Instructor.

Target Population

Pedagogy instructors in all areas of teacher education.

Acceptance requirements

- A recognized Ph.D. or M.A. degree
- A teaching certificate
- At least five years' teaching experience at any level of the educational system
- Experience as a pedagogy instructor
- An interview with the acceptance committee.

Among the topics studied in the program

- Educational ideologies and their influence on programs for teacher education

- The pedagogy instructor in the learning community: learning, teaching, and instruction processes in light of the psycho-educational literature of the last two decades
- Curriculum issues, problems, and possibilities: cultivating autonomy in curricular planning, development, and implementation
- Evaluation as an integral part of the learning, teaching, and instruction processes; alternative methods of evaluation in teacher education
- Professional tools for the development of the pedagogy instructor
- Reading and writing scientific papers; integrating research in the process of instruction
- The characteristics of adult learners; implications for teacher education
- Models and styles of instruction: ways of working with students and mentors
- Analyzing case studies and case literature, learning from the experience of others
- Alternative programs for teacher education: collaboration between college and school for teachers' professional development—a symbiotic model
- Developing flexible learning environments in teacher education by means of advanced technologies

Participants are required to submit two personal projects at a seminar level—one involving topics in the field of general pedagogy and the other dealing with a specific discipline. In addition, they are expected to keep journals, prepare portfolios, and use a variety of documentation methods. Each participant is assigned a supervisory tutor.

The tutors work with the participants both in small groups and individually, strengthening aspects of a developing community. There are manifold opportunities for interactions among the participants, as well as between them and program staff. Moreover, as participants spend one full day each week together, sharing study time, collaborating on projects, and having meals together, there are many occasions for social cohesion, or "gibush," to emerge among members of the group. Social cohesion has great value in the lives of Israeli teachers. It can be understood in the framework of Katriel and Nesher's (1986) and Katriel's (1991) study of Israeli schools. They found that one of the major concerns of teachers was the creation of a cohesive atmosphere in their classes, a sense of community. The same orientation shaped the program for pedagogy instructors at MOFET.

Twenty-nine pedagogy instructors from different colleges participated in this program and devoted one full day each week to their studies. Participants were asked to provide feedback after each study day.
At the end of the year, they also responded to a summing up questionnaire that focused on their sense of satisfaction with the course and its
various components.

OUR STUDY

We devised a special instrument based on Sergiovanni's (1994) framework. Eight possible characteristics of the program were presented as a
continuum, and the two extreme ends of the continuum were described
briefly. These dimensions were: affective versus affective neutrality; collective orientation versus self-orientation; particularism versus universalism; ascription versus achievement; diffuseness versus specificity;
substantive versus instrumental; altruism versus egocentrism; collective identity versus personal identity. In the particularism versus universalism set of variables, for instance, the continuum was represented
by two descriptors at the extreme poles; "decisions and activities stem
from the particular context of each case" (particularism) or conversely,
were "based on the implementation of general standards, rules and regulations" (universalism).

The participants were asked to state their view of the characteristics of the program by placing a mark on a scale from 1 to 10 for each
characteristic that best matched their perception of the course relationships. 1 signified the most extreme expression of relations reflecting a
"society" (Gesellschaft) mode, and 10 signified the most extreme expression of relation reflecting a "community" (Gemeinschaft) mode.
Several open-ended questions were included in the instrument. These
were based on interviews with the participants.

One of the participants stated in the interview that the group had
been transformed into a "community of learners" with very intensive
interactions among its members. Respondents were asked to note
whether they agreed with this statement and if so to provide an example. They were also asked to discuss the main features of communities
of learners. Another open question concerned their preferences for the
composition of study groups in the program, whether these should be
formed according to shared professional context, such as pedagogy instructors for kindergarten teachers, or should include participants from
diverse contexts. Finally, respondents were asked to rank their choice of
persons to turn to for professional advice from a list of six alternatives:

principal at the college; department head at the college; colleague at the same institution; lecturer in the program; program tutor; participant in the program.

In addition to our special instrument for determining participants' perceptions of the nature of the program, we used the end of the year summing up questionnaire that focused on the general level of satisfaction and included suggestions for changes and improvements.

PARTICIPANTS' PERCEPTIONS

For each dimension on the "community" versus "society" continuum there was a scale of the ten possible responses, from 1 on the extreme end of the society pole to 10 on the extreme end of the community pole. We assigned a positive (+) value to the community pole.

The responses for each dimension were given two marks: 1) the number of respondents choosing each pole; 2) the intensity of choices for the mean weight of all responses for each pole. Table 1 presents the perceptions, the distribution of choices of fourteen participants of the program who responded to the instrument according to the eight dimensions included in it.

The most extreme choice on the "society" pole, no. 1, was assigned the weight of 10, parallel to the most extreme choice on the "community" pole, also 10. Following the scale on the "society" pole, choice no.

Table 1: Distribution of Participants' Choices

Society						Community					
											rank
1	2	3	4	5		6	7	8	9	10	dimension
2		1	1	3	affective neutrality		1	1	2	2	affective
					self-orientation			6	3	5	collective orientation
2	2	5			universalism	2		1	1	1	particularism
	1	1			achievement	1	1	3	2	5	ascription
1					specificity		2	2	2	7	diffuseness
3	1		1		instrumental			2	1	6	substantive
	1			2	ego-centered	2	4	1	2	2	altruism
1		3	1		personal identity	2	1	1	4	1	collective identity

2 equals the weight of 9, no. 3 equals 8, no. 4 equals 7, and no. 5 equals 6. Addition of all weights at each pole and dividing the result by the number of people choosing this pole gives the intensity of choice shown in Table 2.

Generally speaking, the tendency of the respondents was toward the community pole, with one notable exception. More respondents chose the society pole for the particularism/universalism dimension. Apparently they viewed the program as functioning in large measure according to general rules and standards in relation to all participants. The respondents seem to be divided in their perception of the affective nature of the program. More chose affective neutrality as characteristic of the program climate, though their responses clustered close to the middle of the scale, rather than at the extreme end of the "society" pole. All respondents chose the "community" pole for collective versus self-orientation, reflecting a shared sense of the basic collective stance of the program. The majority of respondents perceive the relations in the program to be based on ascription, that is, membership in the group is the determining factor. This perception is supported by the responses to the diffuseness versus specificity dimension. All but one of the respondents chose the community-oriented pole of diffuseness, namely, relations are holistic and inclusive, and not dependent on specific roles of participants. This finding shows that the program is experienced as representing a community stance. It is important to note here that organizations are never pure representations of Gemeinschaft or Gesellschaft, and that a certain balance is necessary for organizations to function.

Table 2: Participants' Perceptions of the Nature of the Program

Dimension			Dimension		
Community	N	Mean	Society	N	Mean
affective	6	8.8	affective neutrality	8	7.7
collective orientation	14	8.9	self-orientation	0	0
particularism	5	7.8	universalism	9	8.7
ascription	12	8.8	achievement	2	8.5
diffuseness	13	9.1	specificity	1	10
substantive	9	9.3	instrumental	5	9.2
altruism	11	7.8	ego-centered	3	7
collective identity	9	8.1	personal identity	5	8.2

N=Number of participants choosing each pole for each dimension

In order to take into consideration both the number of respondents choosing each pole and the intensity of their choices, we calculated the adjusted mean for each pole by multiplying the actual number of respondents choosing the pole with the mean representing the intensity of their choices and dividing by the total number of respondents to the questionnaire, as for example the adjusted mean of the affective dimension on the community pole in (6 x 8.8) : 14 = 3.8. The adjusted mean represents an overall weight of responses at each pole. By adding the adjusted mean of both poles on each dimension we obtain a value that represents the general tendency of all respondents. As we assigned negative (-) values to the "society" pole, the general tendency value is negative whenever the tendency is toward the "society" pole, and positive whenever the tendency is toward the "community" pole. The adjusted means of both poles and the general tendency of participants' perception of the program is presented in Table 3.

As we have already seen, the general tendency leans toward the society pole in two dimensions: affective/affective neutrality and particularism/universalism. Still the intensity of these tendencies is noticeably lower than the positive, community-oriented, tendency for some of the other dimensions: collective orientation/self-orientation, ascription/achievement, and diffuseness/specificity. These differences in the intensity of perceived qualities of the program are important. They indicate that participants are sensitive to, and aware of, the variations in the impact of these qualities. They also highlight those qualities of rela-

Table 3: General Tendencies of Participants' Perceptions of the Program

	Community		*Society*	*General tendency*
		Weighted values at both poles		
affective	3.8	affective neutrality	4.4	-0.6
collective orientation	8.9	self-orientation	0	8.9
particularism	2.8	universalism	5.6	-2.8
ascription	7.5	achievement	1.25	6.3
diffuseness	8.5	specificity	0.7	7.8
substantive	6	instrumental	3.3	2.7
altruism	6.1	ego-centered	1.5	4.6
collective identity	5.2	personal identity	2.9	2.3

tions in the program that are dominant, whether at the community pole, such as "collective orientation," or at the society pole, such as "universalism."

COMMUNITY INDEX OF AN ORGANIZATION

Finally, we tried to calculate the *community index* of the organization, in our case the inservice program for pedagogy instructors at colleges of teacher education, according to the perceptions of the members of that organization.

We calculated the mean of all values for the general tendency for each dimension, adding the positive values and subtracting the negative values, and dividing into eight. In our study, the community index for the program is 3.5 on a scale from 1 to 5, with 1 lowest to 5 highest value for a community set of relationships. This means that overall the relationships in the program are experienced by the participants as reflecting a community more than a society.

Asking for professional advice

One of the features of professional communities of teachers, or teacher educators, is the transformation of teaching from an individual to a collective practice. "When practice is collective, successful teachers offer help to those that are having difficulties. Teachers with special insights share them with others" (Sergiovanni 1993, 147). In the light of this view we asked participants in the program to rank order the persons to whom they would turn for professional advice. We believe that within the framework of a community, participants would be ready to ask their peers and tutors, or lecturers for any needed advice. Table 4 and Figure 1 present the calculated weight of each alternative.

The weight for each alternative was calculated as follows: First choice was assigned six points and last choice one point. The most popular response was the tutor in the program (61 points); the second choice was colleagues in their home institution with 59 points. Participants in the program were ranked as fourth choice (37 points). These results might be interpreted as reflecting the community that developed throughout a year of studying together. This community includes both participants in the course and tutors who are conceived as trusted members of the group one may turn to for professional advice. In Sergiovanni's (1994) words: "[C]ommunity members connect with each other as a result of felt interdependencies, mutual obligations, and other ties" (5).

Table 4: Whom Would You Ask for Professional Advice?

	first choice										last choice		Combined
ranking	1		2		3		4		5		6		CW
alternatives	Nu	CW	Nu	CW	Nu	CW	Nu	CW	Nu	CW	Nu	CW	
participant in the course	1	6	2	10	3	12	2	6	1	2	1	1	37
tutor	6	36	3	15	1	4	2	6					61
lecturer					3	12	4	12	3	6			30
colleague	4	24	4	20	3	12	1	3					59
department head	2	12	3	15	1	4	1	3	5	10			41
principal									1	2	6	6	8

Nu = Number of choices of each alternative and its ranking
CW = Calculated weight of each alternative-first choice = 6 points, last choice = 1 point

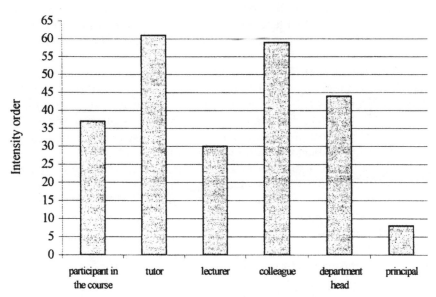

Figure 1 – Whom Would You Ask for Professional Advice?

The readiness to turn to tutors is greater than to one's peers. It might be that in the context of an inservice program, tutors are perceived as appropriate sources of advice. In the context of daily work in teacher education colleges it seems to be easier and less threatening to turn to one's colleagues for advice.

A COMMUNITY OF LEARNERS: PARTICIPANTS' STATEMENTS AND CONCRETE EXPERIENCES

The first open question in our instrument asked the respondents whether they believe that a community of learners had developed within the framework of the program. Thirteen out of fourteen responded positively. Among the examples provided were the following statements:

> I was personally involved in a number of cases in which members of the group voiced their feelings of apprehension and asked for support and encouragement, as well as for materials and ideas. The response was highly positive with assistance provided in all areas. People listened with empathy to their colleagues and were ready to share their ideas and materials.

> In our meetings with the tutors we discussed issues arising in our work with student teachers. Many things were clarified and I benefited from the examples provided by members of the group.

Though almost all respondents sensed a community of learners had been established, not all were equally convinced that this community was meaningful and enduring. For instance, one respondent stated, "I did not feel that the interaction among members of the group was intensive, though we had positive and constructive interactions. Yes, we definitely became a 'community of learners.' "

The affective elements of the community were emphasized by some respondents: "I felt our relationships are very warm, a kind of embrace"; "Beyond the cognitive openness among members of the group we sensed affective ties."

Relationships are perceived as leaning toward altruism, in the sense described by Sergiovanni (1993), with people ready to contribute to others without benefit for themselves—"People wish to support and help others."

A sense of collective identity prevails—expressed in the development of an "esprit de corps": "One enjoys knowledge combined with warm relationships only in our group"; "New friendships emerged."

According to program participants, the most important features of a community of learners are: mutual support; constructive feedback; acceptance; mutual respect; openness and readiness to see the viewpoint of others; interest in the personal aspects related to work; emphasis on personal narrative. All these features reflect a community, Gemeinschaft, mode of relationships, based on unconditional acceptance and mutual support.

It is interesting to note that participants were equally divided in their preferences for homogenous versus heterogeneous composition of groups. Those who advocated homogenous grouping claimed, for instance: "a common background is more effective"; "discussing common problems contributes to the relevance for all participants"; "We can address specific problems we are familiar with."

The arguments for heterogeneous grouping were: "Exposure to problems and issues concerning people in other contexts was very interesting and constructive"; "I find heterogeneous grouping more rewarding and enriching." It seems that according to the experiences of participants in our program, communities might emerge in both homogeneous and heterogeneous forms of grouping.

ESTABLISHING AND SUSTAINING COMMUNITY

The most important finding of our study concerns the fact that relatively limited opportunities for professional contact among teacher educators suffice to create the basic bonding for establishing a community. The necessary conditions are: a common purpose and collaborative learning experiences sustained over time, with special attention given to providing opportunities for transforming a group of people who enter a program as individuals into a Gemeinschaft-oriented community. These opportunities are provided by the close interactions with tutors who promote sharing of experiences and set the stage for mutual acceptance and selfless support to emerge.

Another important feature of the program concerns the time allocated to it—one full day each week throughout a year. It seems that the sense of security and well-being, an essential component of communities, needs time to develop. Last, but not least, in our study, participants shared a common goal—professional growth in their role as pedagogy instructors.

A strong desire for sustaining a community seems to characterize the participants in our program. Most, twenty-one of twenty-nine, expressed a high level of satisfaction at the end of the first year of studies and all but one enrolled in the second year.

Still, several comments were made by the participants expressing expectations and needs for community building. For instance, one participant asked for more involvement in program planning, in line with a more particularistic orientation. Another voiced her wish for allocating group work according to subject matter, or target populations differentiation, which would provide opportunities for more intensive sharing of experiences. This expectation is in line with an approach that views "the ties that bond and bind the most are those that emerge from a compact of mutual shared obligations and commitments, a common purpose. These are the ingredients needed to create a community of the mind" (Sergiovanni 1994, 28).

From a theoretical viewpoint, this study expands the notion of community to include teacher educators in the context of inservice learning of participants who come from different educational institutions. The Gemeinschaft-Gesellschaft distinction enriches our understanding of the nature of communities of educators. We suggest that the instrument we developed and used in the frame of our study could be helpful as well in other contexts.

From a practical viewpoint the study might serve in the planning of professional development courses for teacher educators. It seems advisable that distinctions concerning features of social relationships in groups, especially groups of people who work together, are reflected upon in the context of professional development programs. The distinctions between Gemeinschaft and Gesellschaft could provide a highly productive and constructive framework for such reflection.

Part IV

CLOSING THE CONVERSATION

Part Four contains a single chapter written by the editors. The primary purpose of this chapter is to make the connections among common themes running through the various chapters. This leads to a discussion of being in relationship, teacher education and change, and teacher educator reflective practice. The chapter concludes with a few thoughts on our experience as editors.

12 *Gathering the Threads*

Helen Christiansen and S. Ramadevi

As we read the different stories of community building in teacher education, we noticed a number of threads weaving their way through the fabric of the chapters. These are narratives of practice (cf., Clandinin and Connelly; Connelly and Clandinin) that explore the ways in which teacher educators live in the world. These narratives have a strong sense of relation and caring, and commitment to teacher educator reflective practice. Informed by feminist thinking and postmodernism, they link the personal and the professional, and they are multivocal.

In this last chapter, we bring what we saw as common themes to the foreground, and conclude with a few comments on our experience as editors. Before we do that, however, we must issue a word of caution to readers. There is always a danger of reductionism at the "metalevel" of narrative (Connelly and Clandinin 1998). The stories in this book have rich "plotlines" (cf., Clandinin and Connelly; Connelly and Clandinin), and are filled with "thick description" (Geertz 1973). Each story, therefore, needs to be read on its own terms.

TEACHER EDUCATORS LIVING IN THE WORLD: BEING IN RELATIONSHIP

As teacher educators, our reaching out for community seems naturally to involve reaching out to the students we teach, and to the colleagues with whom we work. These two groups form a significant part of our day and our world. When teacher educators and their students and colleagues share their stories, the process becomes one of self-empowerment. Stories cannot be shared, however, unless the storytellers feel cared for, and so the gradual emergence of a caring community is part of the process. A sense of empowerment and community relationships is something that develops over time and it is also over a period of time that the value of this for professional development is realized. One of us shares an excerpt from her professional journal.

> I cannot work without others. I cannot perform successfully without others. The extent of my professional growth or retardation is in relation to how successfully I have been able to work together with students and colleagues on institutional programs, and have been able to nurture the culture and growth of the community.

Beattie as well understands her teaching within the "context of relationship and community." When she began her career at the university, seeking relationships with others enabled her to deal with the tensions inherent in trying to meet the demands of her students (teaching) and those of the academy (publishing). Smits and Friesen write about this double life of teacher educators as trying at one and the same time to live "the discourse of the university" (largely theoretical) and "the life of schools and teachers" (largely practical). Like Smits and Friesen, Flockhart and Woloshyn taught different sections of the same course. They had originally met as student and professor. Teaching together allows them to build upon that earlier relationship, deepening and strengthening their rapport, coming to a point of complete personal and professional trust. Samson and her colleagues link narrative and community because for them both are "relational by nature."

As teacher educators we participate in multiple communities of practice. In each of these communities we may find ourselves playing different roles depending upon whether we are part of the "inner" or "outer circle," or floating on the periphery. As long as we are able to respect the goals of the community, our position with regard to any given community may be irrelevant. Furthermore, being in community cannot be an end in itself. Sometimes a community is formed with a specific goal in mind. When this goal is achieved, the individuals or interest groups who formed the community go their separate ways. Whether or not we are part of a given community or communities at any point in time may also be irrelevant. What is important for teacher education, however, is sharing in the sense of community that various members of the institution or faculty have cared enough to build. Successful community building requires a favorable climate.

One of the ongoing tensions of being in community is linked in part to the notion of understanding the other. It is paradoxical, however, to note that in saying we understand we come to the limits of our own empathy, thereby actually limiting our potential for understanding. In other words, "I" can understand "you" only on my own terms. Saying "I understand" could place the one who says it in a situation of "false consciousness" (e.g., Lather 1991)—a state of limbo that prevents him or her from going any farther. Finally, it would seem that communities are not necessarily "tidy" and progressive entities. On the other hand, "chaos is often the seed bed of creativity" (Nias 1995, 309).

TEACHER EDUCATION AND CHANGE

We cannot make change happen to others. This does not mean we only work to change ourselves. The reality may lie somewhere in between. Without individual changes, collective change cannot happen. Without change around as a principle in others, an individual cannot afford to change without being considered a misfit. Change occurs at the interface between the individual and the collective, and this is what makes the process both fascinating and complicated.

For Ling, Burman, and Cooper, change is inherent in postmodernism. The key to change for Smits and Friesen lies in a search for a "deeper understanding" of collaborative practice in teacher education. Mullen and Diamond turn to arts-based inquiry as they seek to develop new ways of conducting research and building community in teacher education. Nevin, Hood, and McNeil argue that technological influences need to be accommodated by teacher educators. Finally, as a result of their experience at the Centre for Teacher Development, Florence Samson and her colleagues have come to view change as a reciprocal process involving the individual and a community nurtured by narrative inquiry.

TEACHER EDUCATOR REFLECTIVE PRACTICE

In his introduction to *The Reflective Turn* (1991) Donald Schön, whose name was long associated with the term *reflective practitioner* (1983, 1987), suggests that researchers who want to reflect on practice need to explore the answers to a set of questions. The first of these is useful for our present purpose: "What is it appropriate to reflect *on?*" (1991, 9; author's emphasis). The contributors to this book have offered many answers to Schön's question. Indeed, teacher educator reflective practice is an underlying theme throughout.

The editors reflected on their practice as academics within their respective institutions, questioning as they did so the "sacred stories" (Connelly and Clandinin 1998; Crites 1971) of teaching and research in the academy. Beattie reflected on her practice as a beginning professor and a colleague. Two pairs of contributors, Flockhart and Woloshyn, Smits and Friesen, reflected on their practice of community as they taught different sections of the same course. Mullen and Diamond reflected on the communities in which they had participated as arts-based inquirers. Samson, Brewer, Chan, Dunne, and Fenton reflected on the experience of becoming narrative inquirers. Nevin and her colleagues reflected on the meaning of community building online. In Australia, Ewing and Smith, and Cherednichenko, Gay, Hooley, Kruger, Mulraney, and Ryan reflected on partnerships developed between their institutions and local schools, and in the case of Cherednichenko and her colleagues, between their institution and an aboriginal community, as part of a reorganization of the teacher education curriculum. Finally, Ben-Peretz and Silberstein reflected on the meaning of community in teacher education and reported on a study of what they called the "necessary conditions" to establish community.

CLOSING THOUGHTS: COMMUNITY BUILDING AND THE
POSTMODERN

As we worked through the process of editing and contributing to a
book on community building in teacher education, we struggled to
build a community of two from very different vantage points. Rama
lives and works in a country trying to modernize, facing as it does so
horrendous obstacles of every kind, from the most basic—lack of water
at every level, lack of sufficient food for more than half of the population—to the more sophisticated—frequent power failures making the
technological advances we take for granted in the West useless at times.
Furthermore, Rama comes from a country of deeply rooted traditions
where what is old is venerated, and thinking and talking to one another
are valued. Helen lives and works in a country where everything new is
celebrated, and action is believed to drive the engine of progress—in a
country that has begun to question both the reality and the price of
progress as it becomes increasingly aware of the growing numbers of its
citizens on social assistance or living in the streets.

In working together on this book we have experienced aspects of
what Hargreaves (1994) calls the "paradox of globalization." Access to
technology meant we were able to work through e-mail and attach-
ments. The paradox came from the way in which we used that technology. Here there were cultural differences. For one of us, e-mail messages
need to be dealt with immediately. For the other, e-mail, when it is received (i.e., no power failures along the way), can be dealt with in its
own time. There is no sense of urgency. For one of us, anything that is in
print or can be retrieved electronically is almost immediately available.
For the other, access to such resources is often limited. This means it is
not always easy to check references and do the kinds of things that are
part of the practice of Western academics. Our experience suggests that
teacher educators need to learn how to work across cultures if we are to
benefit from the richness of one another's thinking and experience.

During the past three years, as editors we moved in and out of
each other's space, both physically and electronically. The richest exchanges occurred when we were actually together involved in long discussions about the book project. The following is an excerpt from one
such discussion:

> **R:** I went through all those things you sent me and what I was re-
> ally wondering about is why we thought we could do a book to-
> gether.

H: I think there was a feeling that something could be concrete, sort of getting things down on paper. My feeling was that I don't do enough of that kind of thing.

R: Something like that happened to me also. People say this about the Indian academic. They talk a lot. Nothing is recorded and nothing is done about dissemination. Before the summer institute other people had been coming from Australia and other parts of the world. When they came here they were referred to me. People said, "She's also involved in a curriculum project. Go and talk to her."

And they came to me, and always ended up saying, "Where have you published this? You say the project has been on for three years. Why don't you tell us about this? It sounds exciting." And things like that. And I thought, "Well, here's a chance." (August 1997)

The above conversation took place in Rama's office at CIEFL, when Helen was there on a visit, a year before Rama herself visited Canada. Rama would not live to see the book project come to fruition. She died in the summer of 2001 after a lengthy illness. Our community of two has come to an end. Although Rama did not live to see the product of our collaboration, her spirit is very much present in these pages.

Epilogue

The stories told by contributors to this book suggest there are a lot of similarities from one teacher education faculty to another. They tell of the attempts of teacher educators as individuals and as faculty members to form communities of many different kinds and with many different purposes. The stories speak of reaching out beyond the university to teacher colleagues in schools, and to the broader community—the public whose interests teachers and teacher educators ultimately serve. Moreover, the ways in which faculties of education and individual teacher educators deal with change have been part of many of the stories.

Over the three-year life of the "book project" the contributors and editors who shared their stories became another kind of community.

And now readers have temporarily joined the "book community," moving in and out of the multiple communities represented in its pages. Regardless of how individuals came to the book, each focused for a time on what the expression "reeducating the educator" means or could mean in a rapidly changing world.

References

Abednego, J. 1999 March. Recognising traditional lores. In *Walking to-gether*. Council for Aboriginal Reconciliation 24: 11–16.

Adams, H. 1993. *Focusing on the campus milieu: A guide for enhancing the graduate school climate*. Notre Dame: National Consortium for Graduate Degrees for Minorities in Engineering and Mathematics, Inc.

Aiken, J., and D. Mildon. 1991. The dynamics of personal knowledge and teacher education. *Curriculum Inquiry* 21(2): 141–162.

Apple, M., and J. Beane. (Eds.) 1999. *Democratic schools: Lessons from the chalkface*. Buckingham, UK: Open University Press.

Arendt, H. 1958. *The human condition*. Chicago: University of Chicago Press.

Atwood, M. 1996. *Alias Grace*. Toronto: Doubleday.

Autio, T., and E. Ropo. 1998 April. Leading, curriculum and cultural change: A school-university partnership network in Finland. Paper presented at the American Educational Research Association Annual Meeting, San Diego, California.

Bakhtin, M. M. 1981. *The dialogic imagination*. Austin: University of Texas Press.

Barnard, R., D. Cosgrave, and J. Welsh. 1998. *Chips and pop: Decoding the nexus generation*. Toronto: Malcolm Lester Books.

Barone, T. E. 1995. The purposes of arts-based educational research. *International Journal of Educational Research* 23(2): 169–180.

Barone, T. E., and E. Eisner. 1997. Arts-based educational research. In R. M. Jaeger (Ed.), *Complementary methods for research in education*, 73–103. Washington, DC: American Educational Research Association.

Bateson, M. C. 1989. *Composing a life*. New York : Atlantic Monthly Press.

Beattie, M. 1989–1996. *Unpublished teaching journal*.

———. 1995. *Constructing professional knowledge in teaching: A narrative of change and development*. New York: Teachers College Press, and Toronto: OISE Press.

———. 1996. The faculty development group initiative. In D. Booth and S. Stiegelbauer (Eds.), *Teaching teachers*, 167–176. Hamilton: Caliburn Enterprises Inc.

———. 1997. Collaboration in the construction of professional knowledge: Finding answers in our own reality. In H. Christiansen, L. Goulet, C. Krentz, and M. Maeers (Eds.), *Recreating relationships: Collaboration and educational reform*, 133–152. Albany: State University of New York Press.

———. 2001. *The art of learning to teach: Preservice teacher narratives*. Columbus, OH: Merrill/Prentice Hall.

Belenky, M., B. Clinchy, N. Goldberger, and J. Tarule. 1986. *Women's ways of knowing*. New York: Basic Books Inc.

Blake, W. 1966. *Blake: Complete writings*, ed. G. Keynes. London: Oxford University Press.

Bogdan, R., and S. Biklen. 1992. *Qualitative research for education*. (2nd ed.). Boston: Allyn and Bacon.

Boice, R. 1991. New faculty as colleagues. *International Journal of Qualitative Studies in Education* 4: 29–44.

Borgmann, A. 1992. *Crossing the postmodern divide*. Chicago: The University of Chicago Press.

Bower, A. M. 1991. Formalized mentoring relationships: Do they work? Paper presented at the Academy for Leadership in Teacher Education of the Association of Teacher Educators, Anaheim, CA.

Bresler, L. 1995. A symposium on arts, knowledge, and education. *Educational Theory* 45(1): 1–84.

Briton, D. 1995. The decentred subject: Pedagogical implications. *Journal of Curriculum Theorizing* 11(4): 57–73.

Britzman, D. P. 1991. *Practice makes practice: A critical study of learning to teach.* Albany: State University of New York Press.

Brookfield, S. 1992, April. The skillful teacher. Paper presented at Brock University, St. Catharines, Ontario.

Buber, M. 1957. *Pointing the way: Collected essays.* New Jersey: Humanities Press International, Inc.

Bullough, R. V., Jr. 1991. Exploring personal teaching metaphors in preservice teacher education. *Journal of Teacher Education* 42(1): 43–51.

Bullough, R., and A. Gitlin. 1995. *Becoming a student of teaching.* New York and London: Garland Publishing.

Butt, R., D. Raymond, G. McCue, and L. Yamagushi. 1992. Collaborative autobiography and the teacher's voice. In I. F. Goodson (Ed.), *Studying teachers' lives,* 51–98. New York: Teachers College Press.

Calderhead, J. 1991, April. The nature and growth of knowledge in student teaching. Paper presented at the Annual Meeting of the American Educational Research Association, Chicago.

Carr, D. 1986. *Time, history, and narrative.* Indianapolis: Indiana University Press.

Carson, T. 1997. Reflection and its resistances: Teacher education as a living practice. In T. Carson and D. Sumara (Eds.), *Action research as a living practice,* 77–92. New York: Peter Lang.

Carson, T., and D. Briton. 1997, June. Pedagogical interventions: Locating spaces for teacher education. Paper presented to the Canadian Society for Studies in Education. St. John's, Newfoundland.

Chafin, J. 1999. *Rural inclusion project: 4 web based courses.* Lawrence, KS: University of Kansas [Online]. Retrieved 6/7/99 from the World Wide Web: *http://www.sped.ukans.edu/ spedprojects/rural_inc/*

Charney, R. S. 1994. *Teaching children to care: Management in the responsive classroom.* (6th ed.) Greenfield, MA: Northeast Foundation for Children.

Cherednichenko, B., N. Hooley, T. Kruger, and R. Mulraney. 1995. Benchmarking, competencies and teacher education. Symposium paper. Conference proceedings of the Australian Association for Research in Education Conference, Hobart.

Cherland, M., and D. Friesen. 1999. *Discovering who we are: Responses to "Giving voice to the vision."* Regina, SK: Faculty of Education, University of Regina.

Chisholm, I. M. 1997. Multicultural learning preferences: Implications for technology education. In J. Willis, J. Price, S. McNeil, B. Robin, and D. Willis (Eds.), *Technology and teacher education: Proceedings of SITE 97—Eighth International Conference of the Society for Information Technology and Teacher Education*, 85–97, Orlando, Florida.

Chong, M. 1991–1992. *Unpublished Journal.*

———. 1992. *Unpublished Personal Narrative.*

Christiansen, H., L. Goulet, C. Krentz, and M. Maeers (Eds.) 1997. *Recreating relationships: Collaboration and educational reform.* Albany: State University of New York Press.

Christie, A. 1977/1996. *Agatha Christie: An autobiography.* New York: Berkley Books.

Clandinin, D. J. 1989. Developing rhythm in teaching: The narrative study of a beginning teachers' personal practical knowledge of classrooms. *Curriculum Inquiry* 19(2): 121–141.

Clandinin, D. J., and F. M. Connelly. 1992. Narrative and story in practice and research. In D. Schön (Ed.), *The reflective turn: Case studies in and on educational practice*, 258–282. New York: Teachers College Press.

———. 1995. Safe places on the professional knowledge landscape: Knowledge communities. In D.J. Clandinin and F. M. Connelly (Eds.), *Teachers' professional knowledge landscapes*, 137–142. New York: Teachers College Press.

———. 1995. *Teachers' professional knowledge landscapes.* New York: Teachers College Press.

———. (1999). *Narrative inquiry: Experience and story in qualitative research.* San Francisco: Jossey-Bass.

Clark, S. M., and M. Corcoran. 1986. Perspectives on the professional socialization of women faculty. *Journal of Higher Education* 57: 20–43.

Clifford, J. 1984. Introduction: Partial truths. In J. Clifford and G. E. Marcus (Eds.), *Writing culture: The poetics and politics of ethnography*, 1–26. Berkeley: University of California Press.

Cole A., and J. G. Knowles. 1993. Teacher development partnership research: A focus on methods and issues. *American Educational Research Journal* 30: 473–495.

Cole A., and N. Watson. 1991. *Support for beginning teachers: Ontario perspectives.* Final report submitted to Teacher Education Council, Ontario.

Commonwealth of Australia. 1994. *Whereas the people: Civics and citizenship education.* Report of the Civics Expert Group, AGPS, Canberra.

Conle, C. 1996, June. Moments of interpretation in teaching and learning. Paper presented at the Canadian Society for the Study of Education, Brock University, St. Catharines, Ontario.

Connell, R. W., D. J. Ashenden, S. Kessler, and Dowsett. G. W. 1982. *Making the difference: Schools, families, and social division.* Sydney: George Allen and Unwin.

Connelly, F. M. 1987, June. Becoming a teacher: A narrative approach to the education of teachers. An Invited Address. Unpublished document.

Connelly, F. M., and D. J. Clandinin, 1988. *Teachers as curriculum planners: Narratives of experience.* New York: Teachers College Press.

———. 1990. Stories of experience and narrative inquiry. *Educational Researcher* 19(4): 2–14.

———. 1994. Telling teaching stories. *Teacher Education Quarterly* 21(1): 145–158.

———. 1998. *Shaping a professional identity: Stories of educational practice.* New York: Teachers College Press.

Connelly, F. M., D. J. Clandinin, and M. F. He. 1997. Teachers personal practical knowledge on the professional knowledge landscape. *Teaching and Teacher Education* 13(7): 665–674.

Constas, M. A. 1998. The changing nature of educational research and a critique of postmodernism. *Educational Researcher* 27(2): 26–33.

Cranton, P. 1989. *Planning instruction for adult learners.* Toronto: Wall and Thompson.

Crawford, S. 1998. Organizer participation in an online computer mediated conference. [Online] *CMC Magazine.* Retrieved 6/15/98 from the World Wide Web: *http://www.december.com/cmc/mag/1998/jun/craw.html*

Crites, S. 1971. The narrative quality of experience. *Journal of American Academy of Religion* 39(3): 291–311.

Darling-Hammond, L. 1994. *Professional development schools: Schools for developing a profession.* New York: Teachers College Press.

Deer, C., and D. Williams. 1995. Professional development schools: Do they have anything to offer to teacher education in Australia? ERIC Document Reproduction Service No. ED 399218.

Department of Employment, Education, and Training. 1991. *Recently recruited teachers.* Canberra: Australian Government Printing Service.

Department of Employment, Education, and Training. 1995. *Education industry partnerships for quality teaching.* Report of the Chalk Circle on Teacher Education, Sydney, June 25–26.

Deutsch, M. 1949. A theory of cooperation and competition. *Human Relations* 2:129–152.

Dewey, J. 1916. *Democracy in education.* New York: Macmillan.

———. 1927. *The public and its problems.* Denver: Alan Swallow.

———. 1934. *Art as experience.* New York: Capricorn Books.

———. 1938. *Experience and education.* New York: Collier Books.

Diamond, C. T. P., C. A. Mullen, and M. Beattie. 1996. Arts-based educational research: Making music. In M. Kompf, W. R. Bond, D. Dworet, and R. T. Boak (Eds.), *Changing research and practice: Teachers' professionalism, identities, and knowledge.* London: Falmer Press.

Diamond, C. T. P., and C. A. Mullen. 1997. Alternative perspectives on mentoring in higher education: Duography as collaborative relationship and inquiry. *Journal of Applied Social Behavior* 3 (2): 49–64.

Diamond, C. T. P., and C. A. Mullen, (Eds.), 1999. *The postmodern educator: Arts-based inquiries and teacher development.* (Counterpoints Series) New York: Peter Lang.

Diamond, C. T. P., and C. A. Mullen, 2000. Rescripting the script and rewriting the paper: Taking research to the "Edge of the Exploratory." *International Journal of Education & the Arts* 1 (4): 1–23. [Online]. Available: http://ijea.asu.edu/v1n4

———. in press. Postmodernist pedagogy: A living/ decaying example of the "gothic" in teacher development. In *Passion and pedagogy: Relation, creation, and transformation in teaching,* D. Sherman and E. Mirochnik (Eds.). New York: Peter Lang.

Dillard, A. 1982. *Living by fiction.* New York: Harper and Row.

Dipple, E. 1988. *The unresolvable plot: Reading contemporary fiction.* London: Routledge.

Dreher, G. F., and R. A. Ash. (1990). A comparative study of mentoring among men and women in managerial, professional and technical positions. *Journal of Applied Psychology* 76: 539–546.

Dunne, J. 1997. *Back to the rough ground: Practical judgement and the lure of technique.* Notre Dame: University of Notre Dame Press.

Education Faculty, University of Sydney. 1999. *Master of teaching handbook.* Sydney: University of Sydney.

Eisner, E.W. 1985. *The educational imagination.* (2nd ed.) New York: Macmillan.

———. 1988. Foreword. In F. M. Connelly and D. J. Clandinin, *Teachers as curriculum planners: Narratives of experience,* ix–xi. New York: Teachers College Press.

———. 1997. The promise and perils of alternative forms of data representation. *Educational Researcher* 26(6): 4–10.

Elbaz, F. 1983. *Teacher thinking: A study of practical knowledge.* London: Croon Helm.

———. 1991. Research on teachers' knowledge: The evolution of a discourse. *Journal of Curriculum Studies* 23: 1–19.

Elliott, A., and V. Woloshyn. 1997. Female professors' perceptions of collaboration: Mapping out the collaborative process through rough terrain. *Alberta Journal of Educational Research* 47: 23–36.

Erdman, B. 1997. My favorite quote about technology: Pogo: We are confronted by insurmountable opportunities. *Teaching Spirit: Newsletter of the Center for Teaching and Learning at Western Kentucky University.* Retrieved 4/25/99 from the World Wide Web: *http://www.wku.edu/Dept/Support/AcadAffairs/CTL/newsltrs/7newltr .htm*

Erikson, E. 1963. *Childhood and society.* (2nd ed.) New York: W.W. Norton.

Felman, S. 1987. *Jacques Lacan and the adventure of insight: Psychoanalysis in contemporary culture.* Cambridge: Harvard University Press.

Fenstermacher, G. 1994. The knower and the known: The nature of knowledge in research on teacher thinking. *Review of Research in Education* 20: 3–36.

Finke, K., and V. Lipphardt. 1998. The Potsdam Model of teacher training: The student's viewpoint. *European Education* 30(2): 79–90.

Finley, S., and J. G. Knowles. 1995. Researcher as artist: Artist as researcher. *Qualitative Inquiry* 1(1): 110–142.

Foley, D. 1998. On writing reflexive realist narratives. In G. Shackloch and J. Smyth (Eds.), *Being reflexive in critical educational and social research,* 110–129. London: Falmer Press.

Ford, M. 1994. Collaboration within and beyond the campus community. A paper presented at the Annual Meeting of the National Reading Conference, San Diego.

Freire, P. 1970. *Pedagogy of the oppressed.* New York: Continuum.

Friedman, M. 1983. *The confirmation of otherness: In family, community, and society.* New York: The Pilgrim Press.

Friesen, D. 1994. The action research game: Recreating pedagogical relationships in the teaching internship. *Educational Action Research* 2(2): 243–258.

———. 1995. Expanding global horizons: Student stories from an international teacher education project. *Action in Teacher Education* 17(2): 40–46.

———. 1996. Towards educative community: Pushing the borders of student teaching. *Journal of Professional Studies* 3(2): 15–24.

Fullan, M. 1991. *The new meaning of educational change* (2nd ed.) (with

Suzanne Stiegelbauer). Toronto and New York: OISE and Teachers College Press.

———. 1993. *Change forces: Probing the depths of educational reform.* London and Philadelphia: Falmer Press.

———. 1999. *Change forces: The sequel.* London and Philadelphia: Falmer Press.

Furman, G. C. 1998. Postmodernism and community in schools: Unravelling the paradox. *Educational Administration Quarterly* 34(3): 298–328.

Gadamer, H-G. 1975. *Truth and method.* New York: Crossroad.

———. 1981. *Reason in the age of science.* Cambridge: The MIT Press.

———. 1996. *The enigma of health.* Stanford: Stanford University Press.

———. 1997. Reflections on my philosophical journey. In L. E. Hahn (Ed.), *The philosophy of Hans-Georg Gadamer,* 1–63. Chicago and LaSalle: Open Court.

Gaffney, N. 1995. *A conversation about mentoring: Trends and models.* Washington, DC: Council of Graduate Schools,

Gardner, H. 1983. *Frames of mind: The theory of multiple intelligences.* New York: Basic Books.

Geertz, C. 1973. *The interpretation of cultures.* New York: Basic Books.

Gilligan, C. 1982. *In a different voice.* Cambridge: Harvard University Press.

Gilligan, C., J. Ward, and J. M. Taylor. (Eds.). 1988. *Mapping the moral domain.* Cambridge: Harvard University Press.

Goodlad, J. 1988. School-university concerns, partnerships for educational renewal, rationale and concepts. In K. Sirotnik and J. Goodlad (Eds.), *School–university partnerships in action: Concepts, cases, and concerns,* 3–31. New York: Teachers College Press.

Goodlad, J. 1994. *Education renewal: Better teachers, better schools.* San Francisco: Jossey-Boss.

Goodson, I. F. (Ed.) 1992. *Studying teachers' lives.* New York: Teachers College Press.

Gore, J. 1995. *Emerging issues in teacher education.* Murdoch University, Perth: Innovative Links Project.

Govinda, R., and M. B. Buch. 1990. Indian research in teacher education: A review. In R. Tisher and M. Wideen (Eds.), *Research in teacher education: International perspectives,* 141–161. Basingstoke, Hampshire: Falmer Press.

Grabe, M., and C. Grabe. 1998. *Integrating technology for meaningful learning* (2nd ed.) Boston: Houghton Mifflin Company.

Grankvist, R. 1996. Practical experience in teacher education: The

Norwegian case from a mid-Norwegian perspective. *European Journal of Teacher Education* 19(3): 337–347.

Gray, W. A. 1989. Advice on planning mentoring programs for at-risk youth. *Mentoring International* 3: 17–22.

Greene, M. 1990. *Landscapes of learning.* New York: Teachers College Press.

Hafner, K., and M. Lyon. 1996. *Where wizards stay up late: The origins of the Internet.* New York: Simon and Schuster.

Hammond, S. A., and C. Royal. (Eds.) 1998. *Lessons from the field: Applying appreciative inquiry.* Plano, TX: Practical Press.

Haney, W. V. 1992. *Communication and interpersonal relations, text and cases.* (6th ed.) Boston: Richard D. Irwin. Inc.

Hargreaves, A. 1994. *Changing teachers, changing times.* New York: Teachers College Press.

———. 1996. Revisiting voice. *Education and Society* 13(1): 67–81.

Harnish, D., and L. A. Wilds. 1993. Faculty peer mentoring: A strategy for improving instruction. *Community College Journal* 64: 22–27.

Hatton, E., and S. Grundy. 1994, November. Teacher for the 21st century: The passions and perplexities of some graduating teachers. Paper presented at Australian Association for Research in Education Conference, Newcastle.

Hatton, N., and K. Harman. 1997. *Internships within teacher education programs in NSW: A further review of recent Australian and overseas studies.* Sydney: Faculty of Education, University of Sydney/ NSW Department of Education and Training.

Hatton, N. and D. Smith. 1995. Facilitating reflection: Issues and research. *Forum of Education* 50(1): 49–65.

Heaney, S. 1995. *Crediting poetry.* The Nobel Lecture 1995. County Meath, Ireland: The Gallery Press.

Hill, S., and P. Eckert. 1995. *Collegial tutoring program: Leading communities of learners.* Adelaide: University of South Australia Management and Research Centre.

Hollingsworth, S. 1992. Learning to teach through collaborative conversation. *American Educational Research Journal* 29: 373–404.

———. 1994. *Teacher research and urban literacy education: Lessons and conversations in a feminist key.* New York: Teachers College Press.

Holmes Group. 1986. *Tomorrow's teachers.* East Lansing, MI: Author.

Hopkins, D., M. Ainscow, and M. West. 1994. *School improvement in an era of change.* London: Cassell.

Hoyle, E. and P. John. 1998. Teacher education: The prime suspect. *Oxford Review of Education* 24(1): 110–129.

Huebner, D. 1987. The vocation of teaching. In F.S. Bolin and J.M. Falk (Eds.), *Teacher renewal: Professional issues, personal choices*, 17–29. New York: Teachers College Press.

Hunt, D. E. 1987. *Beginning with ourselves in theory, practice, and human affairs*. Cambridge, MA: Brookline Books.

———. 1992. *The renewal of personal energy*. Toronto: OISE Press.

Hunter, J. 1996. *What is innovative about the M.Teach course?* Unpublished paper. Education Faculty, University of Sydney.

Husu, J. 1997. The pedagogical context of the virtual classroom. In J. Willis, J. Price, S. McNeil, B. Robin, and D. Willis (Eds.), *Technology and teacher education: Proceedings of SITE 97—Eighth International Conference of the Society for Information Technology and Teacher Education*, 534–537, Orlando, Florida.

Ingersoll, R. 1996. Teachers' decision making power and school conflict. *Sociology of Education* 68(2): 159–176.

Jipson, J., and N. Paley. (Eds.) 1997. *Daredevil research: Re-creating analytic practice*. New York: Peter Lang.

Johnson, D. W., and R. Johnson. 1994. An overview of cooperative learning. In J. Thousand, R. Villa, and A. Nevin (Eds.), *Creativity and collaborative learning: A practical guide to empowering students and teachers*, 31–45. Baltimore: Paul H. Brookes.

Johnston, M. 1997. *Contradictions in collaboration*. New York: Teachers College Press.

Jones, A. R., and W. Tydeman. 1972. *Wordsworth: Lyrical ballads*. London: Macmillan.

Katriel, T. 1991. *Communal webs*. Albany: State University of New York Press.

Katriel T., and P. Nesher. 1986. Gibush: The rethoric of cohesion in Israeli school culture. *Comparative Education Review* 30(2): 216–232.

Kelly, M. 1995, February. Towards purposeful partnerships. Keynote address, Practicum Experiences in Professional Education Conference, Gold Coast, Queensland.

Kirby, S., and K. McKenna. 1989. *Experience research social change: Methods from the margins*. Toronto: Garmond Press.

Kirkpatrick, F. G. 1986. *Community: A trinity of models*. Washington, DC: Georgetown University Press.

Knowles, G., and C. Holt-Reynolds. 1991. Shaping pedagogies through personal histories in preservice teacher education. *Teachers College Record* 93(1): 87–113.

Knowles, G., and A. Cole. 1994. We're just like the beginning teachers we study: Letters and reflections on our first year as beginning professors. *Curriculum Inquiry* 24(1): 27–52.

Knowles, G., A. Cole, with C. Presswood. 1994. *Through preservice teachers' eyes*. New York: Macmillan.

Kram, K. 1985. *Mentoring at work*. Glenville, IL: Scotts and Foresman.

Krishnaswamy, N., and T. Spiraman. 1994. *English teaching in India*. Chennai, India: T.R. Publications.

Kruger, L. and J. Struzziero. 1997. Computer-mediated peer support of consultation: Case description and evaluation. *Journal of Educational and Psychological Consultation* 8(10): 75–90.

Krupp, J. A. 1987. Mentoring: A reason by which teachers become staff developers. *CIJ and Journal of Staff Development* 8(1): 12–15.

Lather, P. 1991. *Getting smart: Empowering approaches to research and pedagogy*. New York: Routledge.

———. 1997. Drawing the line at angels: Working the ruins of feminist ethnography. *Qualitative Studies in Education* 10(3): 285–304.

Lave, J., and E. Wenger. 1991. *Situated learning: Legitimate peripheral participation*. Cambridge: Cambridge University Press.

LeGuin, U. 1989. *Dancing at the edge of the world: Thoughts on words, women, and places*. New York: Harper and Row.

Leinhardt, G. 1988. Situated knowledge and expertise in teaching. In J. Calderhead (Ed.), *Teachers' professional learning*, 146–168. London: Falmer Press.

Levine, M., and R. Trachtman. (Eds.) 1997. *Making professional development schools work*. New York: Teachers College Press.

Levinson, D. 1977. *The seasons of a man's life*. New York: Ballantine.

Lewin, K. 1935. *A dynamic theory of personality*. New York: McGraw Hill.

Lewis, R. 1997. *The discipline dilemma*. (2nd ed.) Melbourne: The Australian Council for Educational Research.

Lieberman, A., and L. Miller. 1990. Teacher development in professional practice schools. *Teachers College Record* 92(1): 105–122.

Linnell, A. 1996. *A review of partnerships in teacher education*. Unpublished M.Ed. Long Essay, University of Sydney.

Long, J. S., and R. McGinnis. 1985. The effects of the mentor on the academic career. *Scientometrics* 7: 255–280.

Lovat, T., and D. Smith. 1995. *Curriculum: Action on reflection revisited*. Wentworth Falls, Sydney: Social Science Press.

Luna, G., and D. Cullen. 1995. *Empowering the faculty: Mentoring redirected and renewed*. Higher Education Report No. 3, Washington, DC.

Maack, M. N., and J. Passet. 1994. *Aspirations and mentoring in an academic environment: Women faculty in library and information science*. Westport, CT: Greenwood Press.

MacIntrye, A. 1981. *After virtue: A study in moral theory*. London: Duckworth.

Martinez, K. 1992. Teacher education: Wasteland or watershed? *Australian Education Researcher* 19(1): 59–68.

Mathew, R. 1997. CBSE-ELT Curriculum Implementation Study. Unpublished final report. Hyderabad, India: Central Institute of English and Foreign Languages.

McCarthy, M. 1959/1972. *The stones of Florence and Venice observed*. New York: Penguin.

McCollum, Kelly. 1997, February 21. A professor divides his class in two to test value of on-line instruction. *The Chronicle of Higher Education:* A23.

McLaughlin, M. W. 1994. Strategic sites for teachers' professional development. In P. R. Grimmet, and J. Neufeld (Eds.), *Teacher development and the struggle for authority*, 31–51. New York: Teachers College Press.

McLuhan, M. 1965. The medium is the message. In M. McLuhan, *Understanding media: The extension of man*, 7–21. New York: McGraw Hill.

McNeil, M. E. 1997. *Leadership programs in inclusive education: The certificate of advanced graduate studies, ASCD leadership institutes, and other partnerships*. Plymouth, NH: Plymouth State College.

Merriam, S. 1988. *Case study research in education: A qualitative approach*. San Francisco: Jossey-Bass.

Minnes Brandes, G., and G. Erickson. 1998. Developing and sustaining a community of inquiry among teachers and teacher-educators. *The Alberta Journal of Educational Research* XLIV(1): 38–52.

Moore, J. H. 1996. *Teacher education at Trinity University*. San Antonio: Trinity University.

Morine-Dershimer, G. 1996, April. Tracking salient comments in case discussions. Paper presented at the American Educational Research Association Annual Meeting, New York.

Mullen, C. A. 1999. Reaching inside out: Arts-based educational programming for incarcerated women. *Studies in Art Education* 40(2): 143–161.

Murray, M. 1991. *Beyond the myths and magic of mentoring*. San Francisco: Jossey-Bass.

Nagel, N., A. Driscoll, and G. Grimala. 1991. Criteria and selection of cooperating teachers involved in alternative education programs. Paper presented at the Annual Meeting of the Association of Teacher Educators, New Orleans.

National Board of Employment, Education, and Training. 1995. *Teacher education in English language and literacy*. Canberra: Author.

Nevin, A. 1997. *Exploring the Internet as an Instructional Delivery Model.* Report of Instructional Development Support Grant entitled Revising an ASU West Virtual University Asynchronous Learning Class (*Applying Best Special Education Practices*) Based on a Systematic Evaluation Process. Arizona State University West, College of Education [On-line], Phoenix, AZ: Author. Retrieved 6/7/99 from the World Wide Web: *http://www.west.asu.edu/icaxn/vu97advice.html*

Nevin, A., A. Hood, and M. McNeil. 1998, August. New directions in university professional education preparation programs: Using the internet as an instructional delivery model. Presentation at the 23rd Annual Conference of the Association for Teacher Education in Europe, Limerick, Ireland.

Nevin, A., A. Hood, and J. Thousand. 1998. *EDUC 501: Mainstream instruction for students with special learning needs.* California State University San Marcos [On-line], San Marcos, CA. Retrieved 5/22/98 from the World Wide Web: *http://www.csusm.edu/COE/faculty/thousand/501syl.html*

New South Wales Ministry of Education. 1989. *Excellence and equity.* Sydney: Government Printer.

———. 1995. *Desirable attributes for beginning teachers.* Sydney: Government Printer.

Nias, J. 1989. *Primary teachers talking: A study of teaching as work.* London: Routledge.

———. 1995. Postmodernity and teachers' work and culture: An essay review of *Changing teachers, changing times. Teaching and Teacher Education* 11(3): 307–312.

Noddings, N. 1984. *Caring: A feminine approach to ethics and moral education.* Berkeley: University of California Press.

———. 1996. On community. *Educational Theory* 46: 254–267.

Novak, J. 1992. *Advancing invitational thinking.* San Francisco: Caddo Gap Press.

Oakley, B. 1997. *Sloan Center for Asynchronous Learning Environments.* University of Illinois [On-line]. Champaign-Urbana, IL: Author: Retrieved 9/17/97 from the World Wide Web: *http://franklin.scale.uiuc.edu/index.html*

Oakes, J., and K. Quartz. 1995. Creating new educational communities. *Ninety-fourth yearbook of the National Society for the Study of Education.* Chicago: University of Chicago Press.

Oberg, A., and S. Underwood. 1989, February. Facilitating teacher self-development: Reflections on experience. Paper presented at the

International Conference on Teacher Development: Policies, Practices and Research. Toronto, Ontario Institute for Studies in Education.

O'Connell, C. 1998. *Judas child*. New York: Putnam.

O'Loughlin, M. 1996. *Cross disciplinary and hybridity: Study I as subordinate or superordinate to the disciplines or neither*. Unpublished paper. Sydney: Faculty of Education, University of Sydney.

Osterberg, T. 1996. Practical experience in teacher education: The Swedish case as seen from Uppsala. *European Journal of Teacher Education* 19(3): 347–349.

Owston, R. D. 1997. The World Wide Web: A technology to enhance teaching and learning. *Educational Researcher* 26: 27–33.

Parsons, T. 1951. *The social system*. New York: Free Press.

Pearl A., and A. Knight. 1998. *Democratic classrooms: Theory to guide practice*. New Jersey: Hampton Press.

Petrie, H. 1995. *Professionalization, partnership, and power: Building professional development schools*. Albany: State University of New York Press.

Pinar, W. F., W. M., Reynolds, P. Slattery, and P. M. Taubman. 1995. *Understanding curriculum: An introduction to the study of historical and contemporary curriculum discourses*. New York: Peter Lang.

Poe, E. A. 1841/1936. The murders in the Rue Morgue. In *Tales of mystery and imagination*, 56–99. New York: Cuneo Press.

Polanyi, M. 1958. *Personal knowledge*. Chicago: University of Chicago Press.

Queralt, M. 1982. The role of the mentor in the career development of university faculty. Paper presented at the annual conference of the National Association of Women Deans, Administrators and Counselors, Indianapolis, Indiana.

Radcliffe, A. 1797/1968. *The Italian*. Oxford: Oxford University Press.

Ragins, B. R. 1989. Barriers to mentoring: The female manager's dilemma. *Human Relations* 42: 1–22.

Rausch, D.K., B. P. Oritz, R. A. Douthitt, and I. I. Reed. 1989. The academic revolving door: Why do women get caught? *College and University Personnel Association Journal* 40: 1–16.

Readings, B., and B. Schaber. 1993. Introduction. In B. Readings and B. Schaber (Eds.), *Postmodernism across the ages*, 1–28. Syracuse, NY: Syracuse University Press.

Reynolds, H. 1999a. New frontiers: Australia. In P. Havemann (Ed.), *Indigenous peoples' rights in Australia, Canada, and New Zealand*. Sydney: Oxford University Press.

Reynolds, H. 1999b. *Why weren't we told? A personal search for the truth about our history.* Melbourne: Viking.

Rich, A. 1977. Conditions for work: The common world of women. In S. Ruddick and P. Daniels (Eds.), *Working it out,* xiv–xxiv. New York: Pantheon.

Richardson, L. 1994. Writing: A method of inquiry. In N. K. Denzin and Y. S. Lincoln (Eds.), *Handbook of qualitative research,* 516–529. Thousand Oaks, CA: Sage.

Ricoeur, P. 1992. *Oneself as another.* Chicago: University of Chicago Press.

———. 1995. Pastoral praxeology, hermeneutics, and identity. In P. Ricoeur, *Figuring the sacred: Religion, narrative, and imagination,* 303–314. Minneapolis: Fortress Press.

———. 1998. *Critique and conviction: Conversations with Francois Azouvi and Marc de Launay.* New York: Columbia University Press.

Riley, S., and D. Wrench. 1985. Mentoring among women lawyers. *Journal of Applied Social Psychology* 15: 374–386.

Risser, J. 1997. *Hermeneutics and the voice of the other: Re-reading Gadamer's philosophical hermeneutics.* Albany: State University of New York Press.

Roche, G. R. 1979. Much ado about mentors. *Harvard Business Review* 57: 14–28.

Rosenholtz, S. J. 1989a. Workplace conditions that affect teacher quality and commitment: Implications for teacher induction programs. *Elementary School Journal* 89: 421–439.

———. 1989b. *Teachers' workplace: The social organization of schools.* New York: Teachers College Press.

Rousseau, M. F. 1991. *Community: The tie that binds.* New York: University Press of America.

Ruddick, S. 1982. Maternal thinking. *Feminist Studies* 6. Reprinted in A. Cafagna, R. Peterson, and C. Staudenbaur (Eds.), *Child nurturance: Philosophy, children, and the family,* 70–96. New York: Plenum Press.

Schön, D. 1983. *The reflective practitioner: How professionals think in action.* New York: Basic Books.

———. 1987. *Educating the reflective practitioner: Toward a new design for teaching and learning in the professions.* San Francisco: Jossey-Bass.

———. 1991. *The reflective turn: Case studies in and on educational practice.* New York and London: Teachers College Press.

Schwab, J. 1983. The practical, 4: Something for curriculum professors to do. *Curriculum Inquiry* 13(3): 239–265.

Scott, G. 1999. *Change matters: Making a difference in education and training.* New South Wales: Allen and Unwin.

Scourgall, J. 1997. Giving voice: The conduct of evaluation research in Aboriginal contexts. *Evaluation Journal of Australia* 9(1/2): 54–63.

Seeman, M. 1959. On the meaning of alienation. *American Sociological Review* 24: 783–791.

Seidman, I. E. 1991. *Interviewing as qualitative research.* New York: Teachers College Press.

Sergiovanni, T. 1992. *Moral leadership: Getting to the heart of school improvement.* San Francisco: Jossey-Bass.

———. 1993. *Building community in schools.* San Francisco: Jossey-Bass.

Shelley, M. 1818/1994. *Frankenstein or the modern Prometheus.* Oxford: Oxford University Press.

Shields, C. M. 1999. Learning from students about representation, identity and community. *Educational Administration Quarterly* 35(4): 106–129.

Shields, C. M., and P. A. Seltzer. 1997. Complexities and paradoxes of community: Towards a more useful conceptualisation of community. *Educational Administration Quarterly* 33(4): 413–439.

Short, B., and M. Seeger. 1984, April. Mentoring and organizational communication: A review of the research. Paper presented at the Annual Meeting of the Central States Speech Association, Chicago.

Short, K. 1992. Living the process: Creating a learning community among educators. *Teaching Education* 4(2): 35–42.

Shulman, L. 1986. Those who understand: Knowledge growth in teaching. *Educational Researcher* 15(2): 4–14.

Shulman, L. 1992. *Case methods in teacher education.* New York: Teachers College Press.

Shutte, J. 1996. *On-line students fare better.* California State University Northridge: [On-line]: Retrieved from the World Wide Web *http://www.csun.edu/~hrlcc007/wcp/*

Simonsen, P. A. 1999, August. How do we communicate in "cyberclassrooms?" Presentation at the 24th Annual Conference of the Association for Teacher Education in Europe, Leipzig, Germany.

Slattery, P. 1994. *Curriculum development in the postmodern era.* New York: Garland.

Smith, D. 1987. *The everyday world as problematic: A feminist sociology.* Boston MA: Northeastern University Press.

———. 1997, September. Facilitating reflective practice in professional preservice education: Challenging some sacred cows. Paper delivered to the British Educational Research Association, York University.

———. 1999, February. The what, why, and how of reflective practice in teacher education. A keynote address presented to Faculty of Education staff at Auckland College of Education, New Zealand.

Smith, D., and R. Ewing. 1999, January. The internship: New possibilities for professional education. Paper presented at the Practicum Experiences in Professional Education Conference, Christchurch, New Zealand.

Smith, D., and S. Pannell. 1996. *An Evaluation of the Practicum.* Faculty of Education, Unpublished study, University of Sydney.

Smith, D., G. Williams, and G. Watson. 1978. *School-Based Teacher Education.* Occasional Paper No 2. Department of Education, University of Sydney.

Smits, H. 1997a. Hermeneutically-inspired action research: Living with the difficulties of understanding. *Journal of Curriculum Theorizing, Spring* 13(1): 15–22.

———. 1997b. Reflection and its (dis)content(s): Re-thinking the nature of reflective practice in teacher education. *Journal of Professional Studies* 4(2): 15–28.

Solzhenitsyn, A. 1973. *The gulag archipelago.* New York: Harper & Row.

Sorcinelli, M. D. 1992. New and junior faculty stress. In M. Sorcinelli and A. Austin (Eds.), *Developing new and junior faculty,* 27–38. San Francisco: Jossey-Bass.

Sorg, S., and B. Truman. 1997. Learning about teaching through the Internet: Lessons learned. In J. Willis, J. Price, S. McNeil, B. Robin, and D. Willis (Eds.), *Technology and teacher education: Proceedings of SITE 97—Eighth International Conference of the Society for Information Technology and Teacher Education,* 318–385. Orlando, Florida.

Stevenson, R. L. 1886. *Strange case of Dr. Jekyll and Mr. Hyde.* V. Nabokov, Introduction, 7–34. New York: Signet Books.

Strauss A., and J. Corbin. 1990. *Basics of qualitative research: Grounded theory procedures and techniques.* London: Sage.

Strike, Kenneth A. 1999. Can schools be communities? *Education Administration Quarterly* 35(1): 46–70.

Strobe, E., and J. M. Cooper. 1988. Mentor teachers: Coaches or referees? *Theory Into Practice* 27: 231–236.

Swartz, O. 1996, November. The value of the undergraduate teaching/tutoring experience for graduate school success: A personal narrative. Paper presented at the Annual Meeting of the Speech Communication Association. San Diego, California.

Talbert, J. E., and M. W. McLaughlin. 1994. Teacher professionalism in local school contexts. *American Journal of Education* 102: 123–153.

Taylor, C. 1995. Overcoming epistemology. In C. Taylor, *Philosophical arguments,* 1–19. Cambridge: Harvard University Press.

Tom, A. 1997. *Redesigning teacher education.* Albany: State University of New York Press.

Tonnies, F. 1957. *Gemeinschaft and gesellschaft (community and society),* C. P. Loomis (Ed. and Trans.). New York: Harper Collins (originally published in 1887).

Toulmin, S. 1990. *Cosmopolis. The hidden agenda of modernity.* Chicago: University of Chicago Press.

Turney, C., and R. Wright. 1990. *Where the buck stops: The teacher educators. A study of the characteristics, roles, and effects of teacher educators, with special reference to those who work in Australian tertiary institutions.* Sydney: Sydmac Press.

Turney, C., K. Eltis, J. Towler, and R. Wright. 1985. *A new basis for teacher education: The practicum curriculum.* Sydney: Sydmac Press.

Valadez, J., and R, Duran. 1991. *Mentoring in higher education.* North Carolina. ERIC Document Reproduction Service No. ED 331451.

van der Post, L. 1962. *Patterns of renewal.* Wallingford, PA: Pendle Hall Pamphlets.

van Manen, M. 1990. *Researching lived experience.* London, ON: Althouse Press.

———. 1991. *The tact of teaching: The meaning of pedagogical thoughtfulness.* London, ON: Althouse Press.

Varela, F. J., E. Thompson, and E. Rosch. 1993. *The embodied mind: Cognitive science and human experience.* Cambridge: The MIT Press.

Vattimo, G. 1992. *The transparent society.* Baltimore: The Johns Hopkins University Press.

Vidal, G. 1993. *United States: Essays 1952–1992.* New York: Random House.

Warring, D. 1991. The effects of a mentor-mentee program on the learning environment. Paper presented at the Annual Meeting of the American Educational Research Association, Chicago.

Welch, O. 1996. An examination of effective mentoring models in the academy. Paper presented at the Annual Meeting of the American Educational Research Association, New York.

Wells, M. 1992. *Unpublished Professional Journal.*

Wenger, E. 1997, February. Practice, learning, meaning, identity. *Training:* 38–39.

———. 1998. *Communities of practice: Learning, meaning, and identity.* New York: Cambridge University Press.

Wetzel, K., and Strudler, N. 1998. Lessons from exemplary teacher education programs. Presentation at the Annual Meeting of the Society for Information Technology & Teacher Education Conference, Washington, DC.

Wheatley, M. J., and M. Kellner-Rogers. 1998. The paradox and promise of community. In F. Hesselbein, M. Goldsmith, R. Beckhard, and R. F. Schubert, (Eds.), *The community of the future*, 9–18. Drucker Foundation. San Francisco: Jossey-Bass.

Wilbur, D. 1987. Does mentoring breed success? *Training and Development Journal* 41: 38–41.

Wilkins, M. 1996. *Initial teacher training: The dialogue of ideology and culture*. London: Falmer Press.

Williams, E. A. 1995. An English perspective on change in initial teacher education. *South Pacific Journal of Teacher Education* 23(1): 5–16.

Yeager, A. 1996, June. Addressing the tension in my teaching: A study of transformation. Paper presented at the Canadian Society for the Study of Education, Brock University, St. Catharines, Ontario.

Yeatman, A. and J. Sachs. 1995. *Making the links: A formative evaluation of the first year of the Innovative Links Project between universities and schools for teacher professional development*. Murdoch University, Perth: Innovative Links Project.

Zeichner, K., R. Tabachnick, and K. Densmore. 1987. Individual, institutional, and cultural influences on the development of teachers' craft knowledge. In J. Calderhead (Ed.), *Exploring teachers' thinking*, 21–60. London: Cassell.

About the Contributors

Mary Beattie is an associate professor at the Ontario Institute for Studies in Education at the University of Toronto, where she teaches in both the graduate and preservice programs. Her ongoing research focuses on teachers' knowledge, narrative inquiry, professional development, and educational change.

Miriam Ben-Peretz is Head of the Center for Jewish Education in Israel and the Diaspora at the University of Haifa, and is Visiting Professor at several universities internationally. She was former Dean of the School of Education at the University of Haifa, and President of Tel-Hai College. In 1997, she was awarded the Lifetime Achievement Award by the American Educational Research Association, for her contributions to curriculum studies.

Bev Brewer has been teaching in the Ontario Community College system since 1980. Her Ph.D. thesis work is a narrative inquiry into student and teacher identity and how those identities shape, and are shaped by the classroom experience on the shifting community college landscape. The concept of community weaves throughout her practice and her research.

Eva Burman currently is a lecturer in education and convener of the Primary Teacher Education program at LaTrobe University, Victoria, Australia. She is an experienced classroom teacher and has undertaken research in the area of classroom management and discipline for the past seventeen years.

E. Angela Chan was a doctoral student at the Ontario Institute for Studies in Education of the University of Toronto. She is a researcher in the area of nursing education and health care reform. She taught nursing for many years, and recognizes the critical role of community in the process of teaching and learning. The concept of community underpins her professional role as a nurse educator in a community college setting.

Brenda Cherednichenko is a lecturer in the School of Education, Victoria University of Technology (Australia). She teaches education studies, social theory, and Asia Pacific studies. Brenda's research projects include: school change and reform, industry-education partnerships, and the teaching of thinking and enquiry about Asia in the classroom.

Helen Christiansen is an associate professor in the Faculty of Education at the University of Regina (Canada), specializing in second language teacher education. In 1995, she presented a series of papers at the International Summer Institute on English Language Teaching (ELT), in Hyderabad, India. She has returned to India on four other occasions since then to work with ELT colleagues in Chennai, and Tiruchirappalli. Community building both locally and globally are very important to her.

Maxine Cooper is a senior lecturer in education at the University of Melbourne, Australia. She is an experienced classroom teacher and past president of the Australian Teacher Education Association. Maxine is presently working on a longitudinal study on gender in teacher education. Her other research interests include values in education and classroom power relations.

C. T. Patrick Diamond is a professor at the Centre for Teacher Development at the Ontario Institute for Studies in Education of the University of Toronto. His areas of specialization include arts-based narrative inquiry, qualitative research and personal construct theory, and teacher-researcher-educator development. Patrick has just completed an inquiry into the preservice and induction experiences of beginning teachers, and is currently writing a book on creating better teacher selves.

Maureen Dunne, from St. John's, Newfoundland, is a recent graduate from the Ontario Institute for Studies in Education of the University of Toronto. She has been an administrator, a consultant, and a teacher. She has worked at the elementary, secondary, and board of education levels, and is currently a principal of an elementary school in St. John's. She writes about the importance of putting both the heart and the head in education, and emphasizes the significance of community.

Robyn Ewing (formerly Cusworth) is a senior lecturer in the Education Faculty at the University of Sydney, where she lectures in curriculum, literacy, and drama to both undergraduate and graduate students. Robyn is an experienced primary teacher and teacher educator, and is frequently involved in professional development activities, and as a consultant to schools and school systems. She has a commitment to innovative teaching and learning at all levels of education, and is a recipient of the New South Wales Director General's Award for Excellent Service to Public Education.

Vicki Fenton is a doctoral candidate at the Ontario Institute for Studies in Education of the University of Toronto, completing her second year of residency. Before coming to OISE, she was an elementary classroom teacher for ten years. The notion of community is an important part of her experience as both a teacher and a learner.

Katie Flockhart is completing the final phase of a doctoral program in education. Recently, she assumed the role of a guest lecturer within the preservice teacher education program, as well as part-time instructor in the Master of Education program at Brock University (Canada). She has also had the opportunity to present several papers at higher education conferences. Katie is currently exploring ways in which mentoring may facilitate a smooth transition into teaching within higher education.

David Friesen is a professor of Educational Professional Studies in the Faculty of Education at the University of Regina (Canada). His teaching interests focus on the development of middle years and secondary teachers' pedagogical understandings and practices. David's research interests in teacher education include: using action research to understand and improve the teaching internship; exploring teacher voices to study the development of aboriginal teacher identity in aboriginal teacher education programs; and establishing collaborative action research projects with teachers of "at risk" students.

Jan Gay is a senior lecturer in the School of Education, Victoria University of Technology (Australia). Jan has been involved in giving workshops on case methods and case writing for student teachers in Western Melbourne schools. She has also conducted research and published on case writing with teachers and colleagues from the School of Education.

Sigrun Gudmundsdottir is a professor at the Norwegian University of Science and Technology, in Trondheim, Norway. She is an Associate Editor of *Teaching and Teacher Education*, and the author of many publications in the area of narrative knowing and pedagogical content knowledge.

Antonette Hood began her career as a Special Day Class Teacher and Resource Specialist in Massachusetts, where she taught children in primary and upper elementary grades, and in junior and senior high school settings. Her work has focused on children with a wide variety of disabilities, including autism, mental retardation, severe emotional disturbance, language and learning disabilities, and sensory and orthopaedic impairments. Toni is currently on the faculty of the College of Education, California State University, San Marcos.

Neil Hooley is a lecturer in the School of Education, Victoria University of Technology (Australia). He is interested in creating environments at all levels of education which promote enquiry learning, including the application of information technologies and democratic partnership arrangements between schools and the university. He is particularly interested in the social justice aspect of education and access to knowledge and procedures for disadvantaged groups. His other interests include participatory action research, artificial intelligence, and the history and philosophy of science.

Tony Kruger is an associate professor in the School of Education, Victoria University of Technology (Australia). He is the Convener of the School for Education Partnership and Community Portfolio Team. He teaches in undergraduate and graduate education courses, particularly in the areas of curriculum and educational policy. Tony is the convener of a government funded longitudinal study of school reform.

Lorraine Ling has taught in the primary, secondary, and postsecondary sectors. She is currently employed at La Trobe University, Victoria, Australia, as a teacher educator. Her research interests focus upon policy construction, change and restructuring of education systems, values in education, and the sociopolitical context of education.

Mary McNeil is a professor of education and Director of the Center for Educational Partnerships at Plymouth State College, University of New Hampshire. She publishes widely in the area of special education, and is an international consultant in Europe and Latin America. Her areas of specialization include partner learning, collaborative consultation, and systems change.

Carol A. Mullen is an assistant professor in the Leadership Development Department at the University of South Florida. She specializes in arts-based narrative development, collaborative forms of mentorship, and diversity development in university, prison, and school settings. Carol has conducted research in prisons, universities, and schools, and has published widely in scholarly journals. She received the 1998 Division K Teaching and Teacher Education Research Award from the American Educational Research Association.

Rose Mulraney is a senior lecturer in the School of Education, Victoria University of Technology (Australia). Rose works with her university colleagues and educators in schools in the western region of the Link Project; and a Quality Teaching project, both of which are researching quality teaching and learning, institutional changes; and the development of partnerships through case writing. Her doctoral work is an investigation of differentiated mathematics programs for students of high intellectual potential in Victorian state primary schools.

Ann I. Nevin is a professor in the College of Education at Arizona State University West, specializing in educational psychology. She has been involved in experimental education programs for the past thirty years, and has field tested cooperative and collaborative learning processes aimed at increasing the academic and social progress of students with exceptional needs. She has taught both graduate and undergraduate students since 1969, and most recently collaborated with other faculty and technical support staff to create, implement, evaluate, and redesign several undergraduate and graduate classes using the Internet as an instructional delivery model.

S. Ramadevi was a professor in the Materials Production Department at the Central Institute of English and Foreign Languages (CIEFL), Hyderabad, India. During her twenty-year career at CIEFL, Rama specialized in materials production and the designing of new courses for teachers taking the Postgraduate Diploma in the Teaching of English. More recently, Rama was involved in a research interest group in the area of collaborative action research and narrative inquiry.

Maureen Ryan is an associate professor and Head of the School of Education at Victoria University of Technology (Australia). Her research interests include families, youth at risk, inter-professional collaboration, and teachers' careers.

Florence Samson, from St. John's, Newfoundland, recently completed her Ph.D. at the Centre for Teacher Development at the Ontario

Institute for Studies in Education of the University of Toronto. After completing the two year residency at CTD, she returned to Newfoundland as vice-principal and teacher with the intention of writing her thesis. From time to time she would return to the CTD community to connect with her supervisor and old friends. The Centre played an important part in her successful journey to the doctorate.

Moshe Silberstein is an associate professor in the School of Education at Tel Aviv University. He is also Co-Chair of the School-Based Curriculum Research Unit. His main interests are in the area of teacher and teacher education research, and school-based curriculum development. He has published several books and many articles, most of them in Hebrew.

Hans Smits is an assistant professor in the Faculty of Education at the University of Calgary. His teaching and research interests include social studies and multicultural education, qualitative inquiry and action research, and the application of hermeneutics to education.

David Smith has been engaged in teacher education since the 1970s after some years teaching in both primary and secondary rural and city schools. His main interests lie with teaching and research related to curriculum, particularly curriculum evaluation, change and futures, new ways of learning, and leadership issues. David has acted as a facilitator with teachers in a wide range of schools and school systems, and with other people in government agencies both in Australia and overseas in processes of personal and organizational change and development.

Vera E. Woloshyn is an associate professor in the Faculty of Education at Brock University (Canada). Her research interests include the investigation of effective learning strategies and study techniques. Vera is a member of the Centre on Collaborative Research at Brock University. Her work with Katie is a natural extension of her research interests in collaboration and explicit strategy instruction. She has edited several books and published numerous papers pertaining to her research and role as faculty member at Brock University.

Index

"A–Ha! Moments", 144
Action research, 74, 75, 80, 82, 84, 156, 173
  and students, 84, 86
  and teacher educators, 74
  as "living practice", 83
  engagement in, 83
  journey, 85
Action research project, 77
Active citizenship, 65
Adult education
  pedagogical knowledge, 45
Adult learners, 45
Alias Grace, 111
Ambiguous space, 72
Among Teachers Journal, 92
Anonymity factor, 140
"Applause", 141, 142, 143
Approach
  case based, 155
ARPANET, 137
"*Art*", 116

Arts
  and prison workshop, 123
Arts-based inquiries
  and collaborative community, 114
Arts-based inquiry, 107, 114, 123
  and postmodern, 107
  and teacher development, 116, 124
  researchers, 109
  texts, 114
Assessment, 154, 155
Associate teachers, 156
Australia, 56, 151, 153, 156, 158
  and Indigenous people, 180
Melbourne, 58, 59
Australian
  educational context, 56
  national identity, 57

Bachelor of Arts
  Nyerna Studies, 180

Bachelor of Education
    evaluation, 158
    Nyerna Studies, 180
Bachelor of Teaching
    Australia, 156
"Balanced", 48
Beginning teachers
    concerns of, 161
Belenky, M.F., 26–27
Belonging
    and sense of community, 65
Benchmark cases, 178
Biographical sketch, 141
Borgmann, A., 81, 82, 86
Bricolage, 123
British Council, The, 8
Bulletin Board, 139
    system, 132

CAGS
    community, 131
    Home page, 131
    participants, 130
    program, 131
Case authoring, 155, 161
Case–based
    approach, 155
    framework, 154
    methodology, 152
Case stories
    topics, 161
Case writing, 176, 177, 179
    and other approaches, 179
    naturalistic, 177
    reflective, 178
    utilization of, 176
Central Board of Secondary
    Education (CBSE), 8
Central Institute of English and
    Foreign Languages, (CIEFL), 4, 7, 8,
    14, 11, 12
Centre for Teacher Development
    (CTD), 92, 95, 96, 97, 98, 101, 103,
    104, 105
    and community, 101

Certificate of Advanced Studies
    (CAGS), 130, n 149
Challenges, 157
Chalk Circle Dialogue on Teacher
    Education, 171
Charney, R.S., 63–64
Christie, A., 119
CIEFL programs
    and resistance to change, 13
Civics
    and teacher education, 57
Civics Expert Group, 56
Clandinin, D. J., 6, 93, 94, 97
Class community
    sense of, 142
"Clear credential", 131, n 149
Cognitive controversy, 134
Collaboration
    among educators, 70
    as lived experience, 85
Collaborative action research project,
    73
Collaborative
    classroom, 31
    communities, 112
    community, 20
Collaborative practices
    stitched together, 117
Collaborative projects
    requirements of, 48
Collaborative roles
    "new", 135
Collective identity
    sense of, 196
"Commonplace", 75
"Commonplace book", 75
Communication
    and community, 96
Communication skills
    cooperative learning groups, 134
Communities
    of affinity, 97
    of inquiry, 7
    of practice, 6
    in education, 6

posttraditional era, 67
Communities of inquiry, 7
  authentic, 27
  creation of, 27
  of practice, 6, 203
  of teachers, 185
Communities of learners
  in cyberspace, 146
Community, 17, 95
  and change, 9
  and culture, 181
  and narrative inquiry, 91
  and narrative methodology, 103
  and reconstruction of meaning,
    197
  and the Centre for Teacher
    Development, 101
  as computer game, 68, 69
  as concept, 56
  as container for micropolitical ac-
    tivities, 57
  as negotiation of narratives, 95
  "authentic', 187
  based on shared purpose, 66
  "counterfeit", 187
  culture of, 105
  "giving back" to, 35
  local and global, 55, 56
  new metaphors for, 67
  of arts-based researchers, 109
  of inquiry, 20
  of teacher educators, 186, 198
  of teacher selves, 120
"Community" versus "society" continuum, 191
Community building, 51, 157, 186
  and favorable climate, 203
Community establishing
  necessary conditions, 197
Community index, 194
  creation of, 20
Community of learners, 63, 131, 158,
  190, 196
  creation of, 129
  emergence of, 137

Computer games
  characteristics of, 68
Computer mediated peer support
  group, 131
Concerns
  of beginning teachers, 161
Connelly, F. M., 6, 92, 93, 94, 96, 97, 98,
  102, 104
Consciousness
  bifurcation of, 100
Construction
  multiple teacher identity, 122
Cooperating teachers, 158
Cooperative learning, 155
Cooperative learning groups, 134
Course
  practitioner-oriented, 132
Crawford, S., 136
Cullen, D., 48

Data analysis
  negotiation and reciprocity, 42
Dewey, J., 93, 95
  and notion of growth, 18
Dialectics
  of theory and practice, 101
Disciplinary approach
  interactionist, 64
  interventionist, 64
  noninterventionist, 64
Discipline
  and curriculum, 64
  educational function of, 64
  managerial function of, 64
Discipline policy
  and democracy, 66
Drucker, P., 15
Dunne, J., 84

Education
  and teacher education, 67
  of children with special needs, 132
Educational action research
  as a "living practice", 74
Educational communities, 20

Educational community
and posttraditional era, 64
Educational Professional Studies
(EPS), 73, 74, 87
Effective collaborative ventures
goals, 49
Effective workplace learning
and student teachers, 159
Elders
importance of, 181
Electronic
list serve, 130
mail (e-mail), 130
Electronic communication
concerns, 137
Electronic media
adjustments to, 136
Electronic reflective journal, 130
Eisner, E., 26
"Emoticons", 134
Enclosure
sense of, 56
English Language Teaching (ELT), 8,
12, 13
and academics, 12
and theory, 13, 14
English Language Teaching
Community (ELTC)
Bangalore, 8
Erdman, B., 147
Evaluation
outcomes-based framework, 164
Exemplary teaching
critical component of, 46
Face-to-face (F2F), 132
compared to online classes,
137–140
"Jigsaw" technique, 139

Faculty development
process, 18
Faculty Development Group, The, 35,
36
Faculty of Education
community, 14
"False consciousness", 203

Family discussion room(s), 133
"Family team", 132
Feedback, 20
constructive, 28
Female faculty
compared to male counterparts, 41
Focal reality, 81, 82
experiences of students, 82
Foundations of curriculum course, 98
Frankenstein, 107, 109, 110, 111
"Freshers", 13
"Full class shuffle", 61
Fullan, M., 9, 37
Furman, G.C., 60, 61, 63

Gadamer, H. G., 77, 82–83
Gattegno, C., 10, n 16
Gemeinschaft, 186, 187, 190, 192, 197
Gesellschaft, 186, 187, 190, 192
Gemeinschaft-Gesellschaft distinc-
tion, 198
"Getting to know you", 141, 142
Global community
sense of, 58
Goal structures
competitive, 127
cooperative, 128
Grabe, M. and C., 146
Graduate Leadership Preparation
Program, 130
Greene, M., 18
Group presentations online
reaction to, 142
Growth
as the reconstruction of experience,
18

Haney, W.V., 139–140
Hargreaves A., 70, 171
Held knowledge, 19
Hermeneutic experience
as "repetition", 83
Hermeneutics, 72, 78, 79
"Holistic and Narrative Pedagogy",
20
Holmes Group, 7

Homer, 39
Human action
    as text, 75
Hunter, J., 156–157
Hybridized forms, 114
Hyde, 108, 117, 119, 124
"Hydizations", 112
Hyperactivity, 86

Imposter syndrome, 43
Incarcerated women, 123
In-school experience, 159
Instructors
    undergraduate, 46
    successful, 46
Interaction patterns, 135
Interconnectedness
    of climate, community, and change,
        14
    personal and professional, 19
Interdependence
    negative, 127
    positive, 128
Internet, 133
and "best practice", 148
    as instructional delivery model, 131
    impact of, 128
Internet-based collaboration tools,
    132
Internet instructional activities
    designing of, 129
Internship, 156, 162
    and associate teachers, 163
Interpersonal relationships
    within the classroom, 61
Interrelatedness
    all aspects of the person, 21
Interviews
    phenomenological, 42

Jekyll, 117, 124
"Jigsaw" technique, 139
Joint Centre for Teacher Development
    (JCTD), 92, 94

Kellner-Rogers, M., 66
Kirkpatrick, F.G., 68

Knowledge
    and student experience, 19

Lave, J., 6
Learning communities
    in classrooms, 35
Learning community, 7
    and cyberspace class, 144
    for collaborative meaning making,
        21
    as "community of otherness",
        96
Learning style, 129
Learning theory
    and technology-based instruction,
        128
Life narrative, 101
Likemindedness, 95, 97
Luna, G., 48

M. Teach
    degree, 153
    exit evaluation, 164–166
    graduates, 166–167
Makeshift quilt, 123
Mask series, 115
Mentor(s), 39, 40, 42, 48, 50, 51, 163
    and female faculty, 41
Mentoring , 39, 40, 163
    as critical component of a healthy
        life cycle, 48
    effective, 49
Mentoring programs, 40
    as "cycles of goodness", 47
    at the postsecondary level, 40
    in business and industry, 40
    in education, 40
Mentorship, 39, 40
    and reciprocity, 49
    collaborative, 41, 48, 50
Messages
    categories of, 133
Methodology
    case-based, 152
Miscommunication, 139
Modern Prometheus, The, 121

Modernism
  as "hyperactivity", 81
Modernists, 108
MOFET Institute, Israel, 188, 189
Multiple communities
  belonging to, 55

Narrative(s), 166
  and community, 91, 96
  as method of inquiry, 91
  as phenomenon, 91
  as research methodology, 91
  study of, 100
Narrative community, 94, 102
"Narrative identity", 79
Narrative inquirers, 93
Narrative inquiry, 93, 96, 97, 100, 101
  and community, 91
  and Dewey, 93
  and personal practical knowledge,
    93
  and teacher thinking, 93
  and the multiple "I", 105
  as a method of research, 94
  within the academic/school milieu,
    101
Narrative living and production, 181
Narrative research, 101
  as process, 91
Narrative space, 105
Negotiation of exit, 105
Networks
  of teachers, 172
New faculty
  and role models, 41
New teaching approaches
  development of, 45
Nexus, 4
"Nexus generation", 4, n 15
Nontraditional sites, 109
Normative practice, 84
Nyerna Studies, 181

Odyssey, 39
Off Campus Residential Experience
  (OCRE), 73, 75, 87

One Nation Party, 56
Online class
  and communication, 138
  and participants, 138
  environment, 141
  tutorials, 134
Ontario Institute for Studies in
  Education (OISE),
  91, 92, 98, 100, 104
Organizational theory, 57
"Others" 63
"Otherness", 63

Paradox
  of globalization, 205
  of learning new competencies, 23
Paradoxes
  of community, 59
Partnership(s), 152, 170
  different forms of, 159
  and local communities, 181
  school-university, 172
Patch–quilt studies, 109
Pedagogical knowledge
  and adult education, 45
Pedagogy instructors
  Israel, 186, 188
Personal
  and professional, 100
  disclosures, 135
  knowledge, 120
Personalized Access and Study
  Policy, 169
Piggyback, 139
Plymouth State College, 130
Portfolios, 130
Postmodern
  context, 118
  critique, and "reality", 81
  educational inquiry
  and teacher development, 114
Postmodern community
  of inquiring educators, 108
Postmodern Educator, The, 109, 117, 118
Postmodern perspective
  and experience, 81

Postmodernism, 110, 113
  and Frankenstein, 112
  and teacher education, 112
Postmodernist approaches, 113
Posttraditional
  society, as a community of others,
    67
  classroom community, 58
Posttraditional community, 56, 58
  and disciplinary processes, 66
  Posttraditional educational com-
    munity, 59
Posttraditional era, 56
  communities, 67
  society, 56
  dilemma, 67
Posttraditionalism
  and change, 69
  teachers and teacher education, 69
Practical judgment, 84
Practice
  as "theory-in-action", 100
  described, 178
  interpreted, 178
  partnership – based, 170
  theorized, 178, 179
Practice–theory pedagogy, 176
"Practice makes practice", 78
Practicum, 158, 160
Practitioner
  reflective, 19
Practitioner-oriented course, 132
Preservice teacher education
  professional partnership, 174
  Professional communities
  of teachers, or teacher educators,
    194
Professional development, 17, 157
  as a work-in-progress, 17
  as process, 94
  community, 7
  in the context of an individual's
    whole life, 20
  ongoing, for staff, 17
Professional Development Schools,
  172

Professional education
  and development, 28
Professional identity, 25
Professional journal, 17, 22
Professional learning, 18
Professional specialization program
  for teacher educators, 188
Professor – as facilitator, 130
Project Partnerships
  essential criteria, 174
  primary school, 174–175
  secondary school, 175–176
Prospective teachers
  values, 21
Protégé(s), 39, 40, 48, 50, 51
  ideal, 44

Received knowing, 28
"Recipes for success", 31
Reciprocal relationships
  with students, 28
Reciprocity
  as balance, 49
Reconstruction
  of meaning, 97
Recovery
  of meaning, 97
  of stories, 93
Reflection
  mediated, 155
Reflective practitioner, 204
Reflective practitioners
  educating, 20
Relationship, 17
  positive, 46
  reciprocal, 34
  supportive, 28
"Resourcefulness", 133
Ricoeur, P., 75, 78, 79
Roles
  "coordinator", 136
  electronic synthesizer, 133
"Rough ground" of practice, 76

Schön, D., 21, 23, 76, 204
School

as a form of community, 96
as a learning organization, 171
School visit program, 159–160
Schwab, J., 75
Scott, G., 69
Seltzer, P.A., 62
Shelley, M. 109
Shields, C.M., 62, 67
Social cohesion, 189
Storia, 116
Stories of experience, 94
Story, 97
Strike, K., 63

Teacher
    Indigenous Australian, 170
    self/selves, 119, 120
Teacher education
    action research, 173
    and hermeneutic engagement, 81
    and practice, 80
    and staff members, 156–158
    as a set of ambiguities, 80
    in Australia, 153, 171
    essential elements, 171
    graduate model of, 152
    Indian, 7
    of prospective secondary school
        teachers, 18
    preservice, 174
    transformation of, 147
Teacher educators
    ambiguous role of, 76
    and the new reality, 148
    in ambiguous spaces, 72
    dismissive attitude of students,
    limitations of expertise, 86
Teacher education practice
    as collaboration, 83
    identifiable elements of, 83

Teaching
    art of, 27
    good, 27
Team projects, 132
"Technical problem solution genera-
    tor", 135
Technological innovations, 128
Technology-based instruction
    and learning theory, 128
Threaded conversations, 142–144
Tree of paradise, 111

Unique communication relationships,
    137
University
    of Central Florida, 129
    of Kansas, 129
    of New Hampshire, 130
    of Sydney, 152, 153, 157, 159
    of Regina, 14
    Faculty of Education, 10
    of Toronto
    Faculty of Education (FEUT), 92
University Grants Commission
    (UGC), 4

Van der Post, L., 34–35
Victoria University, 172, 177, 178
    School of Education, 170, 171, 172,
        176, 182,
183
Victoria University of Technology, 180
    School of Education, 169
Virtual
    classroom, 128
    meetings, 135
Voice(s), 18

Wenger, E., 5, 6
Wheatley, M.J., 66
World Wide Web, 128, 129